Freud's Other Theory of Psychoanalysis

Freud's Other Theory of Psychoanalysis

The Replacement for the Indelible Theory of Catharsis

Ahmed Fayek, PhD

JASON ARONSON
Lanham • Boulder • New York • Toronto • Plymouth, UK

Published by Jason Aronson
A wholly owned subsidiary of The Rowman & Littlefield Publishing Group, Inc.
4501 Forbes Boulevard, Suite 200, Lanham, Maryland 20706
www.rowman.com

10 Thornbury Road, Plymouth PL6 7PP, United Kingdom

British Library Cataloguing in Publication Information Available

Library of Congress Cataloging-in-Publication Data

Fayek, Ahmed.
Freud's other theory of psychoanalysis : the replacement for the indelible theory of catharsis / Ahmed Fayek.
p. cm.
Includes bibliographical references and index.
ISBN 978-0-7657-0957-8 (hbk : alk. paper) -- ISBN 978-0-7657-0958-5 (ebk.)
1. Freud, Sigmund, 1856-1939. 2. Psychoanalysis. 3. Catharsis. I. Title.
BF173.F85F394 2012
150.19'52--dc23
2012033776

™ The paper used in this publication meets the minimum requirements of American National Standard for Information Sciences Permanence of Paper for Printed Library Materials, ANSI/NISO Z39.48-1992.

Printed in the United States of America

Contents

Introduction

Just after Freud's death, and maybe a little before that, there were signs of impending crises in psychoanalysis looming on the horizon. In the late 1940s and early 1950s, a crack developed in British society between the Freudians and the Kleinians. Despite the controversies, the society remained unified by creating three groups to accommodate the conflicting members. In the 1950s, the analytic movement in France had its own turmoil, resulting in two major splits. The first was by Lacan, Lagache, and a few other academic analysts who left the classical institute and society (Nacht and the traditionalists) to form their own group. A second split followed because of combined personal and technical disparities between Lacan and Lagache's followers. However, in spite of that second split the two accredited societies remained adherents to the classical theory and agreeable to polite coexistence, while the Lacan group took a clearly separate route; he referred to it as the "Freudian School." The U.S. scene seemed stable for a while, under the dominance of ego psychology. Ego psychology endeavored to vitalize the structural modality in metapsychology to make a better theory of psychoanalysis. In the late 1960s psychoanalysis in the United States entered a phase of mild disorganization caused by the emergence of self-psychology and the seeping in of Klein's object relations concepts. In the 1970s self-psychology attracted young ego psychologists, especially when the old ones were baffled by discovering limitations in the structural viewpoint. At the same time the censorship on Klein and the Kleinians was progressively weakened and the object relations trend gained ground.

While Freud was still alive psychoanalysis was accepted as he identified it. Adversaries to his theory renounced their linkage to it and left. However, the changes done to psychoanalysis in the United States, in addition to what was happening in Europe, took psychoanalysis to a point of almost total extinction. At the beginning those splits and disputes seemed more to be personal issues than matters of substance, but time has shown something else.

The arguments started with minor differences in interpreting Freud's intended meanings of some of his theoretical formulations. The disagreements seemed at first of minor importance and that analysis could live with them. However, the gaps between the differing positions regarding some of those topics kept widening, revealing some underlying flaws in the theory. The cracks were more in the theory of psychoanalysis itself, although they started to show in the body of the institution of psychoanalysis too. Still, there were no attempts to abandon psychoanalysis or declare it deficient, and the Freudian brand remained the designation of the major theory of the psyche.

It was peculiar that the critics of the theory were unwavering in keeping it despite its flaws. The peculiarity of the situation evolved in the 1960s to a desperate effort to improve the theory so it could be maintained. The critics of the theory went through the vocabulary of the theory, editing, interpreting, and offering substitutes in an eager effort to be more precise, offering better connotations or giving them new denotations. As an example, Lacan had a new explanation of the unconscious as "the discourse of the Other" and defined it as being "structured like a language" (Lanca, 1977b). The Kleinian concept—the Oedipus stance—expanded it, modified the role of the father, and changed the event that activates that stance. In fairness, those efforts sometimes made significant improvements and at other times were detrimental to the prospects of a general theory.

Notwithstanding the outcome of those efforts, they look now as efforts to reach a core of the theory by way of manipulating its vocabulary. The core of a theory is like the grammar of a language; it cannot be deduced from its vocabulary. Consequently, instead of getting to the core of the theory, psychoanalysis became a confusing field of definitions, interpretations, reformulations, meanings, and sometimes straightforwardly wrong conceptions. Strachey's *Standard Edition* is by all measures the most accurate source of the Freudian text. However, interfering with the vocabulary of the theory created major problems that were instrumental in creating equally major and unwarranted criticisms of the theory. Strachey translated *Trieb* to *instinct*, which, as he admitted, is an imprecise translation. Thus, after five decades of that translation (which eventually changed to *drive*) psychoanalysis was named a drive theory (which it is not) and as a result was disparaged. Another outcome of the preoccupation with the vocabulary of the theory was creating fundamental misunderstandings about metapsychology, misunderstandings that were used later to discredit the theory as a whole. For instance, Strachey put together Freud's revisions of some of his basic concepts and called them "papers on metapsychology." The papers were not in any way related to Freud's three modalities of topography, dynamics, and economy.

The result, once again, was added confusion created from misusing the vocabulary of the theory.

The aspects of the theory of psychoanalysis that derived criticism and called for modification were Freud's elaboration and sophistication of the cathartic theory, the theory that analysts are familiar with. The reason I underscore this notion is that the aspects of the theory that were found flawed and subjected to modification were all in the main premise of the *objectionable–repressible* modality of psychoanalysis (i.e., the mainstay of the theory of catharsis [the repressed and its contents, defense mechanisms and their functions, making the unconscious conscious, etc.]). Although Freud made fundamental revisions to those concepts between 1914 and 1920, they neither lessened the influence of the theory of catharsis nor changed the views concerning the discovered flaws. Freud remained captive of the catharsis theory until the end. This point is significant because it raises two important questions: If the catharsis theory, even in its best elaboration, remained flawed, then what is the theory of psychoanalysis that is not as flawed? If there is another theory of psychoanalysis that sustained, how do we get to it?

The theory of psychoanalysis is, and has always been, an elusive theory, even to Freud. *Freud shifted to free association not knowing what he would be listening to or what to do with what the patients would be talking about.* It was difficult for Freud to get rid of a theory that seemed comprehensive enough regarding its clinical formulations while he was embarking on a new method of investigation, having no idea where it would lead. His new approach to treatment was a "project in the making," and he used the catharsis theory to systematize his discoveries. It is not easy to find an angle to incorporate all the intuitions and insights that we encounter in the Freudian text, and to put them in one comprehensive definition that would constitute another theory of psychoanalysis to replace the catharsis theory.

However, Freud's inspired intuitions and significant insights, which were totally based on listening and thinking about what he listened to, ostensibly constituted a theory of psychoanalysis that he did not articulate enough to replace the defunct cathartic theory. The body of his work—over fifty years—contains that theory. To elicit it from his text we need to go through his discoveries in a detailed way to reveal the way each intuition and insight has ameliorated the next and, linked with the rest, built a theoretical system that encompasses most, if not all, the divergent formulations he made on the side. Moreover, we have to note the mistakes and blunders he sometimes made and how he recovered from those slips. This last point is important because what we need to achieve is not a theory of functions but a theory of structure; we need to uncover the main proposition around which his discoveries organize.

The literature is replete with attempts at finding a replacement for the obsolete catharsis theory. Those attempts could be divided in many ways, but

I will limit them to just two. One trend was critical of the flawed conceptions that had the imprint of the catharsis theory and ended by refuting the Freudian doctrine as a whole in different degrees, for example, the new schools of psychoanalysis that refused the intrapsychic in favor of the interpersonal yet could not get rid of the embedded notion that we deal with objectionable/acceptable psychical urges and tendencies that influence relationships. The other trend had a grasp of a core of a "true" theory of psychoanalysis that constitutes the main body of the text, although not clearly articulated. This trend elaborated the issues that related to that core, exemplified in exploration of certain infantile phenomena (sense of being) or basic structural concerns (the negative), and configuring their psychical connotations and thus enriching the theory. Nevertheless, very little is done to come up with a comprehensive Freudian theory of psychoanalysis that could replace the catharsis theory and that clearly originates from his text, without any additions or exclusions.

An endeavor such as mine is expected to face strong objections for two reasons: Although it is conceivable to derive the attributes of that theory from the text with proper documentation of that process, there will always be the shadow of personal bias in making those choices or in interpreting their implicit meaning. This type of objection could be curbed to an extent by showing the internal consistency of the elicited theory. The second objection will be to the theory of psychoanalysis "proper" being founded on major and fundamental revisions Freud made to the catharsis theory but neglected, continuing to use the old ones. It is easy to deny the legitimacy of attempting to configure a replacement theory based on Freud's own abandonment of those revisions.

A friend asked me whether I thought Freud would have approved of my attempt to bring out of his text a theory of psychoanalysis that could replace the one he considered his life's work. My answer was definitely no, because he was Freud. According to some recorded events in his biography he, as a leader of a movement and because of his pride, did not admit to mistakes or approve corrections. I expect the same reaction from some of my analytic colleagues for similar reasons. However, now that we have his complete text well indexed and the historical background of the man and his work, we could refer to most concepts and formulations in their personal and historical context (Makari, 2009), and educe the *other* doctrine of psychoanalysis to replace the catharsis theory despite those objections. We are in a much better position than Freud was to come up with a definitive theory of psychoanalysis based on the greater part of his writings. We are in an even better position to trace back that theory to its origins in his early formation as a thinker and researcher. Moreover, we can address, without trepidation, Freud's theoretical blunders and his recovery from them without feeling guilty or justified in rejecting psychoanalysis.

Chapter One

What Is Psychoanalytical in Psychoanalysis?

The literature of psychoanalysis in the past two decades—particularly in the classical camp—shows three clear features. There is an absence of a clear theoretical line that should run through both clinical and theoretical writings. This absence is almost characteristic of that literature, because there are indications it should have been dealt with. The central focus in modern psychoanalysis has shifted from the dynamics of the intrapsychic to object relations. Subsequently, the distinction in practice between transference material and relational material blurred with time. Added to those two features is more tolerance to deviating from the three imperatives of abstinence, neutrality, and anonymity in clinical practice and in theoretical formulations. Those imperatives are considered now in terms of degree and not as a matter of principle.

Those three features raise the question of what remained of psychoanalysis to still link modern classical analysis with the old classical one.

The literature shows clinical reporting is not organically linked to theoretical formulations. This gap was not clear at the beginning in psychoanalysis because analysts followed the core principle of the theory, which was the expansion, improvement, and amendment of the theory of catharsis. The core principle of that theory was that psychoneurosis is a product of repressing objectionable urges, fantasies, desires, and so on, and the framework of practice was to help the repressed surface in the analytic material, to be interpreted, constructed, and reconstructed. The cohesion between the theoretical core and the framework of practicing loosened up over the years when analysts rejected and shed off metapsychology, which was followed by mistranslating and misunderstanding the concept of *Trieb* to mean *drive*. The result was replacing the intrapsychic with notions of interpersonal psychologies.

However, the gap is not in fact between theory and practice, because what was refuted in the classical theory and created the gap was untenable after Freud shifted completely to listening to patients while they were awake instead of hypnotized and not participating in the process of analysis. In spite of his efforts to improve his theory of catharsis to integrate the burgeoning discoveries coming from free association, the theory became unsuitable either as a reference to practice or as a framework for configuring another psychoanalysis that was replacing the old one. The gap in the new classical psychoanalysis is between the catharsis theory of the hypnotic period, which is still the background of present-day psychoanalysis, and another theory that has to be elicited from Freud's text to account for the main volume of discoveries and formulations he gathered from using free association. In other words, *the practically demised theory of catharsis (which subliminally still dominates) has to be replaced with another theory of psychoanalysis that is implicit in the Freudian text and needs configuring and articulating.* That theory is not another interpersonal theory like the ones crowding the field. It is another Freudian theory that could account for the main discoveries of psychoanalysis as they emerged and still emerge from using free association.

There is a subtle difference in modern classical analysis between a practice based on interpreting patients' material and one based on correcting issues related to interpersonal relationships. The lack of distinction between transference and just relating to the analyst changed the meaning of repetition compulsion and its place in treatment. In the old classical theory, transference is a *function* of repetition compulsion (i.e., the unresolved past relationship with the parents is compulsively repeated in analysis). In the modern version, the relationship with the analyst reveals distortions that could be corrected and thus indirectly corrects the originally repressed parental relationship. In other words, the old practice endeavored to correct the old relationship as the originator of the compulsion to repeat (the cause or the intrapsychic structure) to stop it from repeating in other relationships including the one with the analyst. The modern version of analysis endeavors to treat the repeated (the result of the originator) as the subject matter of interpretation so that its origin could eventually be corrected too.

If we use a metaphor, we could say that modern classical psychoanalysis has its mind in the past while its heart is in a new time. Modern classical psychoanalysis has repudiated the intrapsychic to a great degree. The core of Freud's initial theory was that repression of certain psychical contents forms a main internal structure. Although that configuration expanded and became more sophisticated with time, it maintained its centrality, and the intrapsychic was modified but not dismissed. This meant that symptoms and other phenomena are products and expressions of that main internal core. Thus interpersonal relations (though they were not named as such then) were considered functions or reflections of the intrapsychic and could not replace it.

Modern classical analysis, on the other hand, made a change in that alignment. It did not totally accept the modalities of the object relations but let the interpersonal relationships creep quietly in to take the place of the intrapsychic and become an originator of functions. Modern classical psychoanalysis put itself in a precarious position by allowing that to happen. The relationship between the intrapsychic and the interpersonal is not complementary to permit one to complement the other. The intrapsychic is a structure that has functions. By shifting the centrality of the theory of psychoanalysis to interpersonal relationships, psychoanalysis has become analysis of the reflections, products, functions, or manifestations of the intrapsychic, and not of the intrapsychic itself. Moreover, when this change happened but the main proposition of the repression of the objectionable contents remained lurking in the background, the picture became fuzzier. What we have now is a deprecated theory of the intrapsychic that is replaced with a theory of interpersonal relations, yet the framework of the repudiated theory remains as it was. This is not plausible because we cannot make the cause (the repressed) take the place of the effect (flawed interpersonal relations) without getting into illogical theorizations.

Instead of recounting the literature where those ideas could be verified I will summarize a discussion group of a full analysis of a case to show the difficulties that situation creates. Although the discussion was demonstrating most of the points raised above it still somehow remained psychoanalytical, something that when underlined points to the existence of another Freudian theory of psychoanalysis and a proper solution to the crisis that analysis is in now.

In a recent meeting of a psychoanalytic organization[1] there was a discussion group on termination in which a full analytic case was presented. The patient came to analysis because of difficulty in establishing and maintaining relationships. She indicated that she was unable to do that even with her parents, who she said were not ready to have children when she was born. She gave a background for her statement in which the parents' limited time for the family was confused with ineffective parenting. The analyst reported in reasonable detail the difficulties the patient had in establishing a relationship with her at the beginning. The material of that introductory phase stimulated discussions of issues relating to transference but quickly moved to what the analyst might have missed and was supposed to have been revealed, in addition to speculative ideas about how that introductory phase could have been different if certain things had been done. The discussion was basically about identifying the *repressed* in her material, and the speculations were about the content of the repressed. This is one of the shortcomings of the expanded catharsis theory, which puts the emphasis (from its onset) on the repressed and not on repression itself. When we talk about the content of a psychical phenomenon there would be no criteria for right and wrong suggestions because "by definition" the right answer is repressed. Freud, captive of that notion until 1915, revised the concept of repression (see chapter 6) and discovered the systemic difference between the preconscious and the *Ucs.*

Nevertheless, what was significant in the discussion was the difference between the older, more experienced analysts and the younger ones, who showed an obvious lack of knowledge of the Freudian text and naturally more interest in relational ideas. The speculative olds leaned more toward repression as creator of intrapsychic conflicts, while the younger analysts were speculating about the patient's repressed relational aspirations. *The shadow of the catharsis theory hovered over the discussion*, be it in different shades.

At this point, I would like to underline that there was no diagnosis done regarding the referring cause for analysis. Having difficulty in relating is no diagnosis, and the analyst entered an analytic process without knowing what this difficulty was emanating from. This point is important because it shows that object relations has no theory of psychopathology, and without such a theory transference material becomes open to any and all sorts of speculations, as I mentioned above. Moreover, diagnosis (not a *DSM* or a *Psychodynamic Diagnostic Manual* diagnoses, but based on structuring aspects of the psyche, such as sexuality, significance of dreaming to the patient, insightfulness, receptivity to interpretations, etc.) would give the analyst more than the reason for referral with which to work. Nevertheless, the discussion was psychoanalytical despite the absence of a diagnosis, the replacement of the intrapsychic with the interpersonal, and the clear presence of the catharsis theory in at least the formation of the queries. For now, I could say that the general and strong tendency in the discussion was *to read something else* into what the patient said or what the analyst was saying, and sometimes what the discussants themselves were exchanging. The discussion was psychoanalytical enough and did not drift to issues not pertaining to the patient, as happens with other nonpsychoanalytic theories. The attitude of reading something else into what is said is the attitude analysts learn in their training, even if it could be short in its dedication to the Freudian text, because training in analysis is not education but formation.

The material reached the phase of working through, and the analytic work engaged more in the workings of repetition compulsion, where events, situations, and reactions are developed repeatedly in different forms and structures. During the reporting on that phase it became clear that the analyst had responded to pressures from the patient and some countertransference conflict by some self-disclosure. When asked, the analyst indicated that her self-disclosure was limited and done more to enhance the transference (transference cannot be enhanced but could only be restricted or interfered with). This part of the presentation evoked a great deal of arguing (polite mostly) but surprisingly distracted the discussants from very important changes in the material the patient was giving. The material was no longer interpretable because what was factual and what was imaginary were fused. In other words, the patient was more able to correctly guess the analyst's responses based on what self-disclosure revealed of the analyst's makeup. There was clearly less concern about self-disclosure and the contamination and distortion of the transference. The little attention given to the change in the material and the tendency to accept self-disclosure in principle resulted in implicit acceptance of changing the analytic situation from a scene of therapy to a scene of "corrective emotional experience," "a good container," "a safe environment," and so on. Although most of the ideas that were exchanged came from the works of eminent psychoanalysts and were relevant, there was little attention given to the difficulty of interpreting the material, most probably because there were more concerns over the degree of and limitations that should be put on self-disclosure than on self-disclosure itself. I found it rather interesting that no one considered asking about Freud's reason for stipulating the three imperatives that restrict self-disclosure.

Notwithstanding those grave oversights there was undeniably something psychoanalytical about the discussion: analysis is not just any interaction with the patient but a process that has, or should have, structure and a purpose related to change. The most significant part of the discussion at that stage was the emergence of the intrapsychic in the material despite the intentional effort to avoid it. Every effort to get the significance of phases of resistance and regression, even improvement and progression, led the discussants to talk about the "inner" anger, rage, narcissistic hurt, unresolved Oedipal attachment, and so on. Better transference material, even if contaminated by self-disclosure, could not be understood in relational terms but has to be considered in its intrapsychic construct.

The termination phase put in focus all the flaws that were made by ignoring the intrapsychic and making the interpersonal the main criterion for cure. Termination became a criterion of mutual success, which was expressed in a continual exchange of good feelings of pride, happiness, gratitude, and thanks. Because the phase of termination coincided with a major change in the patient's life, judging termination by manifestation of improved interpersonal conditions concealed some significant features in the termination of an analysis. The patient left the analysis with an unresolved identification problem with the good analyst.

This is a significant point in defining the psychoanalytic aspect of psychoanalysis. In the catharsis theory identification is an event between the subject and an object, mostly a pathological event. The subject identifies himself by the object in that event. It is pathological in that sense (even if the subject identifies with a healthy object) because it alienated the subject from his true self. In Freud's other theory, identification is a formative experience in which the subject assimilates—not copies—attributes in the object and rejects others to constitute an authentic self. The significant difference between the two kinds of identification is that one is a function of a certain type of relationship and the other is an input in the intrapsychic structure. Termination is possible only if the analyst does not identify himself (discloses himself) and lets the patient assimilate what suites him from the vague analytic relationship (i.e., transference).

The discussion about that phase was also atypical: it showed an aspect of psychoanalysis that I seldom if ever see mentioned in the literature. There were long exchanges of formulations of what could have brought about the termination of this case. The exchanges were characterized by an abundance of terminologies that reflected the absence of an agreed upon theory or, at least, a unifying point of view. Psychoanalysis is cluttered with variant, imprecise, individually coined terminologies and merely repetitions of key words or phrases used by famous analysts in other contexts. Using another metaphor, psychoanalysis is a language rich in vocabulary but poor in grammar. Nonetheless, the confusion of terms did not seem to result in confusion or misunderstanding, as if psychoanalysts know all that vocabulary and do not need a grammar to form mental phrases with them. What is dangerous about that attitude in psychoanalysis is ignoring the rules of differentiation and distinction in our theoretical formation.

The discussion group of this case exemplified in one event the divergent views we encounter in reading the literature. It revealed the absence of the unifying theoretical thread that used to exist and prevail in psychoanalysis in the first six decades of its history. At the same time it showed the continued search in modern psychoanalysis for a theoretical direction. This point entails clarification: The familiar theory of psychoanalysis of the first six decades was later considered either flawed or insufficient. There must have been something insidiously wrong with it to be critiqued and to invoke the need for its replacement. The attempts at correcting the original (classical) theory proved equally insufficient and in many cases contradicted the classical theory in ways that threatened the very existence of psychoanalysis. In fact, psychoanalysis, as it was, was not satisfying the need for a different theory of all the new and wide-ranging discoveries of the psyche. However, it was also so resilient as to be dismissed, even partially. Therefore, is there something about psychoanalysis that has not been recognized yet to keep it going in spite of its defects?

The discussion group exposed two significant facts about classical psychoanalysis. The old theory, even with its expansion, elaboration, and improvement, was no longer sufficient to integrate the increased experiences of analysts within the limited conception of repression and defense mechanism. I am saying that, because any way we look at psychoanalysis with which we are familiar, we see it as "variations on the theme of repression." Although Freud revised that concept substantially, he did not use his revision in a clear way that could have changed the theoretical framework of the catharsis theory. Analysts know now more than early analysts have known. Yet, they do not have the comfort of a suitable theory that could make them talk about what they know. The catharsis theory, even in its best expansion, is not enough to accommodate that knowledge.[2]

Three features could be identified as psychoanalytical in the discussion group: There is something entwined within what the patient overtly says (or the writer writes, or the painter paints, etc.), which makes it possible to identify how the entwinement happens. The second feature was the search for inner or intrapsychic structure that comprises that entwinement, which becomes the object of analysis. The third feature is that the two preceding features *produce* a vocabulary that is not expressing a defined theoretical body (such as repression and defenses in the catharsis theory) but beckons a different grammar or rules that do not constitute a theory but rather a theoretical framework that frees psychoanalysis from the old compulsion to become a nomothetic science.

There are three basic and foundational features that an analyst trained in a recognized institute of training *assimilates* and *integrates* in his way of thinking. When we add a good didactic analysis to the psychoanalyst's training his mind is formed in a distinct way that distinguishes him from the quasi-trained, contemporary psychoanalysts. Even though analysts might differ in their personal potentials their training will still distinguish them from the best nonpsychoanalysts. However, where do we find the theoretical framework for the power of that formation in Freud's text?[3]

Four years after finally adopting free association Freud wrote four major works within five years (Freud 1900a, 1901b, 1905c, 1905d). They were most important, but peculiar in a way. After about two decades of dedicating his whole effort to the treatment of psychoneuroses, those works explored normal phenomena such as dreams and sexuality in children. Investigating the normal phenomena revealed that psychical phenomena are products of an entwinement of two processes: a primary process that seems to have different workings from the one we are familiar with, another process that guides in our daily way of thinking. Although he grasped the essentials of the primary process in his three first books, it needed more time and more than Freud to unlock its secrets. He introduced to psychoanalysis a "fundamental": what we listen to, say more than what the speaker meant to say, and if we unwind the entwinement we will discover, in all probability, the real source of the neurosis. *Our job is not to discover something the patient is hiding from himself but to interpret what the patient says in order to discern the entwinement.* This shift came to Freud from normal, banal phenomena. It also came from the conscious person, something the hypnotized patient was unable to provide. This discovery has nothing to relate it to the theory of catharsis. Yet Freud tried hard to find a place for it in that theory by suggesting that the entwinement of the two processes is a function of repression. However, to say that, he had to assume that what the primary process entwines with the secondary process is of an objectionable nature and needs to be repressed. He had to wait until 1923 to say the entwinement happens merely because the primary process is aconscious (not conscious) and has to find a secondary thought to link with to have access to consciousness. He did something similar with infantile sexuality, something that was not derived from any hypnotic material or even recovered repressed memories. After "an intuition that does not fall in one's lot twice in a lifetime" (Jones, 1957), he changed the etiology of the neurosis from the frustration of sex, to regression, to a phase in the newly discovered childhood sexuality. He treated sexuality as a developmental process that could be subjected to repression and fixation. In other words, the etiology of the psychoneurosis remained sexual, but now it was childhood sexuality. Freud was at an early stage of discovering another theory of psychoanalysis but did not have what it took to abandon the catharsis theory.

The main thrust in the catharsis theory was to reach theoretical formulations that could be used as final statements about psychopathological conditions (i.e., to look like a nomothetic science). An example is the notion that repressed sexuality explains symptoms and symptom formation. Those formations were based on the idea of finding the cause (content) of the symptoms. Nevertheless, the new awareness of the working of the primary process and its cardinal role in symptom formation disagreed with the simplistic cause/effect theoretical formulation. In the simplest way, the entwined meaning in the symptom is only disguised and not repressed because there is no simple repression that could cause the psychoneurosis. There must be something preceding repression to instigate it. Concisely, the catharsis theory could not accommodate the other theory, but it had to be revised for the other theory to coexist.

It was only natural that forcing a theoretical modality on another modality would reveal the weakness of one of them. That is what happened in a gradual way to the catharsis theory, which showed its need for serious revisions if any part of it would remain in the other theory. I will just mention, for now, two weaknesses that required Freud's attention: the libido theory and the three interrelated concepts of *Trieb*,[4] repression, and *Ucs*. They were identified as the metapsychology papers, when they could barely be considered papers on the psychology of metapsychology.

Infantile sexuality contradicted the notion that sex is an entity, which constitutes a *content* of the repressed. It showed that sexual *Trieb* is a complex structure that evolves and generates various psychical conditions. This was enough to revise the causative place sex occupied in the cathartic theory. Yet what really forced the matter was the concept of libidinal energy. Freud realized that the libido is not the energy of sexuality but sexuality is the manifestation of "a libido," which could be invested and manifested in more than sexuality. *Not every libidinal urge is sexual, but every sexual urge is libidinal*. Following that insight the polarity of sexual *Trieb* versus self-preservation *Trieb* collapsed; instead the concept of narcissism was introduced and caused a major shift in the theory of psychoanalysis (see chapter 6).

The introduction of narcissism forced a revision of a basic concept of the cathartic theory: libidinal investment. Narcissism strongly suggested the existence of a primary stage of the libido that precedes its investment in an object. A primary state of narcissism led in a natural way to exploring the vicissitudes of the *Trieb*, especially after discerning its four constituents of *pressure*, *sources*, *aim*, and *object*. The theory of psychoanalysis turned a very significant corner at that point: instead of a theory of the dynamics of psychical entities such as sex, repression, narcissism, defense mechanisms, libido, and so on, it entered the realm of psychical processes that govern the formation of psychical structures, which in turn generate secondary forms of those structures. In other words, psychoanalysis changed from a theory of *what* "is" to a theory of *how* the "is" comes into being. Three more concepts that were basic followed in Freud's endeavor to revise his theory.

The first that followed was *repression*. Freud discovered that for repression to happen it has to be preceded by a stage where the representation that will be repressed is separated from the *Trieb*: the affect separates from the idea and a cleavage is created between those things. When that happens, repression proper would act upon one of the two separated entities. He called that stage primary repression to distinguish it from repression proper (but did not call repression proper secondary repression). Repression proper maintained its original function of repelling something from consciousness, thus creating the preconscious. Primary repression is completely aconscious, and the cleavage it creates is the source of the entwinement of the primary and the secondary states of the psychical; the entwined could, and only could, be repressed *properly* (i.e., the product of primary repression is still judged inadmissible to consciousness).

The distinction between the two types of repression forced another distinction between the unconscious and the system *Ucs*. Although Freud had the notion of a difference between the two types of unconsciousness from the time he published *The Interpretation of Dreams*, he did not have the clarity of that distinction until he changed psychoanalysis from a psychology of functions and causality to a theory of structures and processes. He stipulated that what happens before repression proper, or in primary repression, creates a psychical condition that is not of the quality to enter consciousness. Hunger is a sensation that could be felt as an uncomfortable *affect* but not sensed before it is transformed into a representation of the affect itself. A representation is admissible to consciousness because it can latch on to the secondary process of mentation, thus acquiring the attribute of a thought. However, entwinement with the secondary process submits to the rules of the primary process and makes the representation—though part of consciousness—difficult to read. The two processes in entwinement become a system. Psychopathology exists within that system because representations keep generating representations and the possibilities are high in misrepresenting the original urge. Finally, Freud came up with three definitions of the unconscious and with the concept of the nonrepressed unconscious. This should have been the final blow to the catharsis theory because it is a theory that acknowledges only the dynamic meaning of unconsciousness or repression proper.

The fourth revised concept was *regression*. In the libido theory, regression was to a point of fixation that was usually considered a point of trauma or an infantile point of gratification. However, Abrahams and Ferenczi redefined regression not to being a return to a *Triebhaft* object or aim but to the totality of the erogenic phase and its zone. Freud added to that important clarification the idea of three forms of regression: *topographical*, *temporal*, and *formal.* About the same time, Freud changed the concept of identification from a pathological process to the process by which the identity—later called ego—is formed. Identification was no longer a sign of pathology but a formative process that under certain conditions could become pathological. He indicated that there is primary identification that comes from assimilating the attributes of the *Triebhaft* object, which would be followed by more complex identifications emanating from the relationship with the object. He also came to the concept of the compulsion to repeat, thus freeing identification from psychopathology and taking it out of the theory of catharsis. The revision of those four concepts happened between 1912 and 1915.

In 1920, Freud came up with a controversial work on a new theory of *Trieb*. Its controversy stems from substituting the polarity of sex and life preservation with a polarity of life and death, replacing defective functional concepts with other debatable functional concepts that would not fit in a theory of psychical structures. The duality of life versus death is a curious one because at first glance it is a banal biological duality. By stretching the concept a little, it represents the primary state of the *Trieben. Beyond the Pleasure Principle* became a turning point in the theory of psychoanalysis—as most analysts claim. Nevertheless, to qualify as such it had to bring more than just the concept of repetition compulsion to the fore because the duality of life and death as such took the theory back to the framework of psychical things and mechanisms. Nevertheless, the new duality completed the revision of the theory of psychoanalysis that started in 1914. It provided the theory of *Trieb* with its primary and foundational state. All the entities in the catharsis theory were given their originating beginning: *Trieb*, repression, identification, narcissism (the replacement of the libido theory), and regression, and now the basic duality that is behind all those entities. As they all had a primary state they could only now be considered in terms of a process that turns the primary into its secondary state.

If the core of another theory of psychoanalysis had not been outlined already and was not stated yet, at least the catharsis theory was no longer viable. However, Freud was unable until that time to give it up (for reasons I will get to a little later). His works after 1920 attest to the obvious impact of the other theory on his mind, except in the two works, the highly praised *The Ego and the Id* (1923b) and *Analysis Terminable and Interminable* (1937c). They were attestation that he regressed to the catharsis theory whenever he found himself swayed from it. He ventured to deal with clinical phenomena that would not have been tenable in terms of the catharsis theory (1918b, 1919e, 1920a) and very significant issues that would not have been possible to acknowledge in terms of "repression of the objectionable" (1919b, 1924e, 1927c, 1930a, 1939a). But the most significant of all those works is *Inhibition, Symptoms and Anxiety* (1926). In that work Freud went back to the origins of psychoanalysis in the *Project for a Scientific Psychology* to show that his starting point was the transformation of the endosomatic stimuli into representations, thus creating the chains of psychical phenomena. Investigating symptom formation in that work led to a formulation that bridged theory and clinical work in a unique way, which reminds us of the role of the state of wishing in creating dreams. In it lies the other theory of psychoanalysis.

The crux of a theory to replace the catharsis theory is three imperatives: to be a theory of the processes of transformation that happen aconsciously, a theory of psychical structures that generate functional manifestations, and a theory of the entwinement of the primary states in the secondary processes generating the psychical material that under certain conditions could become pathological. A theory of processes formulates the way an originator evolves into other forms and the varied possibilities encountered in that evolution (Darwin's conception of the survival of the fittest). In formulating that process the theory puts aside the functional relations between causes and effects and searches for the structural nature of the process because each structure would be just a link in a chain of evolving structures (Darwin's equivalent notion of mutations). The originator of a process has to remain entwined in that process to keep it going even in a state of repetition (Darwin's idea of the establishment of the best form and maintaining it).

Freud's inability to cut loose from the catharsis theory is understandable if not excusable. He took it on himself to produce a theory that has the qualification of a final statement on the subject of the psyche and in particular psychopathology. Having been a physician, his theory had to be consistent with the modalities of formal thought, in particular that of medical formal thought. The theory of catharsis has some of those features; maybe that was the reason it was not a good theory of psychoanalysis. Moreover, the theory of catharsis appeared to be a good deductive theory and thus could gain the acceptance of "rational" thinkers. However, the deductive aspect of the theory was not founded on solid clinical observations to support it (Grunbaum, 1984). In contrast, Freud's most valuable and central discoveries were intuitive (i.e., inductive or retroductive). They did not come from direct observation, which was possible in hypnosis, but they had to "dawn" on him, particularly from deliberating normal psychical phenomena. However, as we will see later, Freud was always able to recover from slipping into total compliance with the catharsis theory and unfailingly corrected his slips.

As was noticed in the discussion group there were disagreements on almost every issue, even though they were all within a psychoanalytic framework. The reason I gave above was the absence of a theoretical line that goes through the exchanged opinions and the lack of agreement on what we are supposed to interpret in the first place: the interpersonal or the intrapsychic. It became very confusing when the interpersonal was considered the replacement for the intrapsychic. The discussion group found itself in a minicrisis because it did not address that issue beforehand. As an example, when the patient indicated at the beginning that she could not develop a relationship with her parents because *they were not ready yet to have children*, no attention was paid to the possibility that the patient was aware that the analyst was still in training and whether she was ready to receive patients. A theory of meaning would have put that statement in the context of the patient's intrapsychic apprehensions. The minicrisis was depicting a picture of a situation where the absence of agreement on the details was not completely nullifying a unifying implicit background. It was a crisis because not defining that background was reason for disagreement but not for deviation. The group's minicrisis reflects the real crisis in psychoanalysis as a whole, a crisis that has been fermenting since the 1980s, and we still hear its echoes.

Most young analysts are not aware of a period of four decades of conflict, acrimony, diversions, and theoretical disintegration that psychoanalysis went through before it settled on the condition it is in now. "The Way to the Crisis" is *not* simply a historical recount of events that psychoanalysis went through; it is a recount of theoretical issues that raised debates, which have been discarded and either not replaced or replaced with even more problematic issues. The result was the disappearance of a theoretical line that could keep us "in line," yet the implicit background I mentioned previously produced a modicum of cohesiveness, but a tenuous one. It came from understanding the crisis but rather from an aconscious assimilation of Freud's other theory.

I believe that identifying the elements of that other theory, articulating and reconfiguring them, would give us a solid Freudian theory that could reinforce the psychoanalytic field and its institution.

I would like to add to the justifications for Freud's adherence to the catharsis theory. The other theory of psychoanalysis was incomplete and unobvious to Freud while he was eliciting its constituents from his patient's associations or getting insights he did not consider before. If we just think of how much time and thinking of other analysts were needed to understand the phenomena of repetition compulsion and aftereffect, and the working of the primary process, we can appreciate the difficulty Freud had in getting those insights and theorizing them too. Eliciting that theory from his text should be the work of many analysts over many years, where any attempt would initiate a better one. Great theories are great because others who are not as gifted as the creators of those theories open their eyes to great potential dormant in them. If we think of the great theories, such as Copernicus's model of the solar system, Darwin's theory of evolution, and Bore's quantum mechanics, and the number of discoveries they initiated in the works of not-so-talented scientists, we could imagine what awaits us in regard to Freud's other theory of the psyche.

Chapter Two

The Road to the Crisis of Psychoanalysis

Freud's definition of psychoanalysis (1923a) was basic if not simplistic, and thus did not rouse disputes. However, with the advancement in practice and diversities in teaching and training his definition is no longer sufficient to maintain the smooth sailing of psychoanalysis. Changes took place in the field, and we now face a situation that requires a new definition. *Theoretically*, there are irreconcilable diversities implying absence of definition more than differences of opinion. *Clinically*, there are some grumbles about the therapeutic efficacy of psychoanalysis that manifest in a significant decline in interest in psychoanalysis as a profession and a mode of therapy.[1] *Organizationally*, the International Psychoanalytical Association (IPA) has intentionally ignored the proliferation of theoretical diversities in the 1970s (as I will show later) and deliberately disregarded the seriousness of abrogating its obligation to check the consequences of such a trend. Every way we look at psychoanalysis, we cannot but notice that it is in crisis. Although psychoanalysis has a history of crises, the crisis it has been experiencing for the past four or five decades is different. The crisis does not threaten psychoanalysis with extinction, as crises in other fields might do, but it sure makes psychoanalysis look staggered, distorted, flawed, and no longer the distinguished intellectual movement that it once was.

Psychoanalysis is an intellectual movement in every sense of the word in spite of the subtle and not so subtle efforts from the majority of psychoanalysts to restrict it to the clinical sphere. I would like to emphasize this point because it has a significant place in discussing the crisis in psychoanalysis later on. Psychoanalysis is part of the German metaphysical philosophies in particular, which had great impact on philosophy on the European continent (see chapter 4) and constituted the backbone of Western culture in general.

Western culture is the culture of the *subject*, and its enlightenment was founded on the search for the meaning of the "person." That search reached an impasse in the 1850s. Freud's contributions introduced new and very innovative conceptions of the individual, the psyche, and the related central issue of human drama. His contributions were essential in managing that impasse and giving means and ways of overcoming it. He framed the "subject" in a novel way that had never occurred to a thinker before. The Cartesian duality of body and soul dominated philosophical thinking for almost three centuries. Duality remained the standard approach to defining the subject and led philosophy to an eventual impasse. His intuition about the subject reversed the proposition: the subject is not a product of duality but is the dualities that distinguish him from any other creature. Freud highlighted the core fact that what is human in the human are the inherent dualities in the subject, which are not restricted to the Cartesian duality.

Psychoanalysis, as a continuation of a bigger and more encompassing endeavor and not just merely as a method for the treatment of psychical problems, requires putting it in the perspective of the human sciences, or what is called the idiographic sciences. Idiographic sciences have a specific methodology and epistemology that is distinct from those of the physical sciences or the nomothetic sciences. Making that distinction would ensure clearer arguments regarding what psychoanalytic theory should be like and avoid futile arguments later about whether psychoanalysis is scientific.

Nomothetic methodology and its epistemology lead to *functional* theoretical formulations, which were the core of the catharsis theory and clinical practice. Functional theories are based on cause/effect relations; therefore they would be judged as right or wrong because the links between causes and effects are judged by their accuracies in explaining. The idiographic sciences, on the other hand, are concerned with the structures of phenomena. Their formulations pertain to the nature and implicit meaning of the phenomenon; hence they interpret events but do not explain them.

This distinction could be confusing because it suggests that *psychoanalysis could comprise two doctrines, of which one is functional or clinical and one is ontological.* Clinicians would not agree that there could be a theory other than their clinical one. However, strangely, they are unable to agree on or define the theory they follow. Their diversities were mostly founded on disagreeing with others more than defining their own (Stepansky, 2009). This situation became a new movement that is known as contemporary psychoanalysis. Contemporary psychoanalysts do not consider their diversities and "divisions" a crisis. They stayed away from confronting each other with their differences, though they all—with no exception—directed their critiques to the Freudian doctrine. They are diverse but united in that they refuse it. Presently (as well documented by Stepansky, 2009) they are trying to find the best way to live with their differences (Cooper, 1999 in [4N2]; Rees,

Willock, 2007). The crisis in psychoanalysis in fact does not exist in the Freudian camp but only in contemporary psychoanalysis because it has no way out of its chaotic theoretical situation, while Freudian psychoanalysis has a way out of the double theories (i.e., by deducing the theory of psychoanalysis from the same Freudian text that produced the cathartic theory).

However, if the Freudian doctrine comprises two active theories that coexist and still maintain a descent status, what is the objection to having more than two or, for that matter, a proliferation of theories and schools of psychoanalysis? The short answer for now is, psychoanalysis—with which we are familiar—comprises two doctrines, one that was used but not practiced and one practiced but not used. *What we need is one theory that can be applied in different fields, not many theories that define one field.*

THEORETICAL PLURALITY AND STEPPING INTO CHAOS

In the International Psychoanalytic Association meeting in Montreal in 1987, the president of the association accepted theoretical plurality as an unavoidable, if not even a preferable, theoretical stance. This was, as a matter of fact, capitulation to the call for revising the Freudian doctrine and a decision mainly to diffuse a worsening situation in the United States between the schools. Theoretical plurality (Wallerstein, 1988) was accepted, at the beginning, as a temporary position that would eventually lead to discovering "common ground," which would become the acceptable replacement doctrine. The common ground, as he suggested, would generate a clinical theory that will eventually unify all those schools. Since Wallerstein's two attempts at containing the situation (1988, 1990), things have gotten worse: the promised clinical doctrine did not materialize, and, as Sandler (1992) warned, there were no promising signs that we have common ground to stand on. Moreover, none of the many theories that emerged proved to be better than the others. All those modifications happened without any disputation, seemingly for political expediency (Wallerstein, 2007). The crisis culminated in a plurality that was supposed to maintain the unity of psychoanalysis and improve its status but ended by creating a chaotic theoretical diversity, a diversity that turned into a serious problem because it kept its momentum because it was accepted and condoned.

At the time, psychoanalysis in the United States was stepping into the problem of plurality, another problem that was fermenting not only in the states but almost everywhere. It was not a theoretical problem. In the late 1970s, a steep decline in interest in psychoanalysis in general had begun. The number of patients who were inclined to seek psychoanalytic treatment as a preferred psychotherapy dropped and has never stopped dropping since. There was a similar drop in young professionals seeking training in psychoanalysis. This second problem caught more attention and overshadowed the first; it was a problem of livelihood to training analysts.

Yet there was no mention of a possible link between theoretical plurality and the deterioration of clinical practice and training. That link was never considered despite a more serious decline in countries where the proliferation of schools of analysis was more prominent, such as in the United States, than in analytic societies that did not have schools or obvious splits. *In psychoanalysis, missing the obvious is not oversight, but repression.* This obvious link was veiled by misleading arguments about the need for and necessity of discarding the classical theory. Those arguments took, and still take, two approaches. One blames classical psychoanalysts, who are characterized as unable or unwilling to coexist with other disciplines, and gives negative impressions about the "typical" classical analyst (Bornstein, 2001; Eisold, 2007; Kernberg, 2006). The condemnation was directed at the trademark Freudian analysts, and the emphasis was put on "bad" analysts who acted as elitists. The other approach put the blame on the psychoanalytic institution in particular. Summers (2008) blames the crisis on "the failure of psychoanalysis as a field to engage its various, and *incommensurable* [emphasis added], positions, and develop a method of doing so" (pp. 419–420). This approach, which indirectly supports theoretical plurality, blames the contemporary schools for being nonconducive or amenable to opening discussions among themselves. This is a true observation. We seldom find among those schools any serious examination of their theoretical foundations (Stepansky, 2009). The attitude to exempt analysts from causing the problem is the other side of the coin: blaming the institution(s) of psychoanalysis for intolerance of diversity (Eisold, 1994). Summers continues his notion of lack of communication between the schools by saying, "Whether psychoanalysis is one theory or many . . . there is no way to justify the one or adjudicate the many. The choice would be between one orthodoxy institutionalized by fear and trembling and many orthodox sects operating in isolation of each other"[2] (p. 420).

Although the causes mentioned above seem opposite and confused, they are basically one. *There could not be good analysis and bad analysts, or bad analysis and good analysts, because one is the function of the other.* If there is a crisis in analysis it is because there is bad analysis practiced by bad analysts. But we still have to make a decision: Which analysis are we talking about: the classical or the contemporary? If it is classical analysis—the Freudian doctrine—are we talking about the catharsis theory or the other theory?

THE ONSET OF THE CRISIS

Analysts of the 1950s were second-generation analysts who were formed and trained by the last of the first generation, without Freud's presence. They were strong advocates of the classical doctrine and to some degree continued the traditional zeal of its eminence. In the 1970s, particularly in the United States, a wave of criticism of the doctrine started. This shift is intriguing because the exact source of dissatisfaction was the same concepts that attracted analysts to psychoanalysis in the first place (metapsychology, the intrapsychic, the *Ucs.*, the concept of *Trieb*,[3] etc.). It has to be noted that a few years prior to criticizing those concepts some analysts endeavored to modify them but within the framework of the catharsis theory since some of them were clearly inadequate to account for very important new clinical discoveries. *Psychoanalysis was admired before for concepts that were considered later in need of improvements, and when the improvements replaced the original concepts the doctrine became too defective to be maintained.*

There is another paradox in the eroding of the Freudian doctrine. The erosion coincided with, and went parallel to, the emergence of the new theories. The two things could have happened separately, but the new theories seemed to have no grounds of their own to stand on and needed the rubbles of the classical theory as a foundation. The emergence of new theories could have happened without the need to modify or distort the classical doctrine. If there was something wrong with the original doctrine and the new theories are psychoanalytical, as they claim, they should have saved psychoanalysis from its current crisis instead of causing it. This happened on a smaller scale in Europe and most of South America. The new modifications and additions improved the theory and gave it another life. It is thus difficult not to assume that the criticisms of the Freudian doctrine were intended to remove and supplant it.

At the beginning, Freud relied on the same concepts (defense, regression, fixation, etc.). They were used in their functional capacity to denote how matters happened and to explain psychical phenomena as functions of those concepts. Freud had not found the proper language to speak about the new understanding of his discoveries. Gradually he integrated his functional concepts, which increased in number and sophistication, and created three metapsychologies (1896, February 13; 1896, April 16). He did not mention any psychology for the new shift, and metapsychology lacked a proper psychological theory (Fayek, 2000; see chapter 8). However, metapsychology talked about the intrapsychic dynamics in terms of the increase or decrease of psychical pressures (economics), the links between the *Ucs.* and the *Cs./Pcs.* (topographic), and the conflict between the different urges of the psyche (dynamics).

Metapsychology seemed at first to be a theoretical framework that could contain the discoveries of the posthypnotic phase. The three metapsychologies are inseparable; we cannot use one without the other two, or when we could not use all of them with the same phenomenon then the phenomena should be deemed poorly investigated. As late as 1937, Freud said, "Without metapsychological speculation and theorizing—I had almost said 'fantasizing'—we shall not get another step forward" (1937c, p. 225). In spite of that clear statement, ego psychologists, who were the most ardent metapsychologists at first, ignored it. Hartmann and his followers called metapsychology "points of view" and added new ones to it. Shortly after, they decided that the structural point of view—Freud's most recent one—could replace the other three, which could be done away without.

Ego psychologists did not only change the meaning of metapsychology, but by that change they deleted the integral conception of the intrapsychic. In no way could we separate metapsychology from the intrapsychic conflicts because *metapsychology is the language of the intrapsychic*. Nemiah (1965) said, "The intrapsychic appears early in Freud's psychological writings, and runs as the leitmotiv throughout the development of his theory" (p. 367). Therefore, the two core concepts were deleted from psychoanalysis. Renouncing the intrapsychic to allow adjusting metapsychology created a need for a substitute or a replacement; it was object relation.

The third target was the concept of psychodynamics. Freud's insight that symptoms are the pathological expression of an intrapsychic dynamic condition was a great advancement from the cause/effect explanations of the catharsis theory. Eliminating the intrapsychic from the theory made psychodynamics redundant, and it was replaced with the personal interchanges with the object. The Freudian insight gave its place to a Kleinian insight. The issue of the intrapsychic was overshadowed by the Kleinian success in shedding more light on object relations. The failure of ego psychology to create a psychology of the ego to substitute for the classical theory made Klein's object relations more appealing. Object relations did not only replace the intrapsychic in the classical doctrine, but it also opened the gates for a flood of theories about those relationships, theories that have no criteria for their correctness or validity.

After lengthy and extensive revisions of the theory, the concepts of metapsychology, the intrapsychic, and psychodynamics were deemed the most controversial, if not totally flawed and redundant. This point of view is now considered settled and incontestable in all the schools, including the new Freudian (Compton, 1981a, 1981d; Edelson, 1988; Grunbaum, 1984; Holt, 1976; G. Klein, 1976; Rubinstein, 1997). The three basic concepts are now missing from psychoanalysis and not missed.

PSYCHOANALYSIS WITHOUT METAPSYCHOLOGY

Klein's successful explorations in infantile neuroses and the ease by which the observations made on infants were formulated lured analysts in a very hasty way to extend those discoveries to the field of adult analysis. It was hoped to understand aspects of the theory that were limited in the catharsis theory. There were two direct failings to that trend. Most of Klein's conceptions were limited to the oral phase and the dynamics of the relationship with mother. All the other stages of development disappeared from her model of development, and she ended with a unifocal concept of psychodynamics and psychopathology. Even her contributions to the practice of analysis were based, almost solely, on the dynamics of projective identification in the transference. The Kleinian model of development—if it could be considered a comprehensive model—has no matrix for specific psychopathologies that characterize adult neuroses and no psychodiagnostic system that would substitute for the missing matrix. The second failing is transferring her observations on the infant/mother relationship to the transference without much concern about the differences. Although her observations were quite discerning, especially in their formative effect on building the intrapsychic, they were not adequately examined to be automatically applied in adult analysis. The analysts who gained more insights into the psychodynamics of their patients' relationships by using Klein's observations gradually disregarded the intrapsychic aspect in those same relationships. *The object relations theory was born as a substitute for the theory of the intrapsychic and ended as a substitute for the whole of psychoanalysis.*

The shift from the psychodynamics of intrapsychic conflicts to the dynamics of interpersonal relationships was paradigmatic and not merely a change in focus or emphasis. Analysts such as Home (1966) and Bowlby (1981) made distinctions between metapsychology, which they called the scientific basis of psychoanalysis, and psychoanalytic therapy that relied on empathy. They did not consider metapsychology an integral part of the theory of psychoanalysis but only a theoretical framework that could be replaced with other, more modern frameworks, such as relational psychology. Thus, they showed that they could function as analysts without any framework, as metapsychology had no place in the object relations theories. Its absence makes no difference to most of those theories (Mackay, 1981; Meltzer, 1978). The place of metapsychology was vacant in the new theories, but it is not clear if this was intentional or the assumed modality of object relations was sufficient without it. However, they have failed until now to produce a replacement to a theoretical framework to encompass their theory. A theory based on the psychopathology of interpersonal relations should have developed by now a psychodiagnostic matrix that corresponds to its basic assumptions. In addition, it is evident that the Kleinian approach to psychoanalysis is narrow and limited to theorizing in the clinical sphere alone and had nothing else to offer. This limitation throws heavy shadows on the *psychoanalyticality* of Kleinian psychology or the interpersonal schools in general.

In early ego psychology, it was almost inconceivable to think of psychoanalysis without a base of metapsychology. Metapsychology was of paramount importance in the works of Hartmann and Rapaport and their disciples. Nonetheless, there were very early signs that the preoccupation with metapsychology was merely motivated by an interest in developing a new psychology of the ego to replace what was termed "the psychology of the id," or depth psychology, which was "thought" to be backed by topographic metapsychology.

Ego psychologists presented two arguments against keeping both the topographic metapsychology and the structural point of view: First, the structural point of view was Freud's latest metapsychology (Brenner, 1980; Gill, 1979; Hartmann, 1948, 1964); therefore, Rapaport (1951) gave it an overriding status and was considered superior to the three other metapsychologies. Second, a distinction between the *Ucs*. and the *Pcs.* was considered immaterial and clinically of no value (Arlow & Brenner, 1964); therefore, they directed attention to the functions of the ego instead of the influence of the id (which they equated with the unconscious). There was also some discontentment brewing in the background about the concept of "instinct."

The criticism of metapsychology by ego psychologists was not systematic or planned or based on fundamental disagreements with its premise (Brenner, 1980). On the contrary, Rapaport and others added two new "points of view" to Freud's three metapsychologies (Hartmann, 1950, 1964; Rapaport & Gill, 1959). Those additions showed that ego psychologists did not understand the purpose and function of metapsychology. Thus, it was easy to replace parts of it with other parts and even do away with parts of it completely (see chapter 8). Freud (1915e) was very clear that understanding the psychical phenomenon "permits" talking about it metapsychologically, meaning that we have to understand the phenomenon first to be able to put that understanding into metapsychological form. He said, "I propose that when we have succeeded in describing a psychical process in its dynamic, topographical, and economic aspects, we should speak of it as a *metapsychological* presentation" (1915e, p. 181). The three metapsychologies thus indicated the existence of one psychology for the psychical process that could be conceived in three ways, not relegated to one particular agency, such as the structural point of view (Fayek, 2000).

Missing this Freudian postulate allowed severing metapsychology from its function. Gill (1979) considered economic metapsychology redundant and believed that only one metapsychology was required. Ego psychologists did not expect that tinkering with metapsychology the way they did to clear the way for ego psychology would bring down the whole system of metapsychology, including structural metapsychology, which they built their hopes on. Holt (1965a, 1965b), for instance, suggested replacing economic metapsychology with a theory of communication. Calling for the replacement of the topographic point of view with the structural point of view (e.g., Gill, 1979) seemed, at that time, merely a matter of preference. Meissner (1981) said that Holt's attempt to replace economic metapsychology meant "by extension and by implication [that] . . . the structural theory had also to be placed in question" (p. 923). For some time, Waelder (1941–1942), and Rapaport and Gill (1959) considered metapsychology the highest level of abstraction in the theory of psychoanalysis. This view assumed that each level dealt with a different quality of material, where metapsychology belonged to the highest level of abstraction (see how this view was revisited years later by Wallerstein, 1988, 1990, and 2005). In fact, stratifying the theory of psychoanalysis invited the prospect of analysts choosing the strata that looked most acceptable to them while leaving the others.

One of the drastic ways of ridding psychoanalysis of metapsychology was a call by G. Klein (1976) to separate the clinical aspect of psychoanalysis from the theoretical aspect, where we find metapsychology, because he advocated that that aspect of the doctrine had no clinical value and no importance to psychoanalysis. This deceivingly innocent call made psychoanalysis an entity or an ontology that had two representations: metapsychology, which was the theoretical scene, and a clinical scene that was an act looking for its own theory. Therefore, it was inevitable that the intrapsychic would be put outside the boundaries of the clinical theory in an attempt to rid ego psychology of metapsychology (Rabin, 1995). However, if that shift were to produce a clinical theory it was predictable that something else would be put in place of the banished intrapsychic that went out with metapsychology. All attempts at finding a better replacement for the intrapsychic without keeping metapsychology have failed. Consequently, Kleinianism, which was once considered in the United States a serious deviation from the Freudian doctrine, got a quick push into the pledge of the clinical theory. What made that replacement even easier was that a clinical theory seemed to change the concept of transference from reliving of the past in the present to a phenomenon of relatedness with the analyst. The interpersonal theory (or theories) was welcomed as an inevitable solution to the crisis of ego psychology, and ego psychology by that time was psychoanalytic practice without a theory and a practice waiting for a clinical theory that *should* not be theoretical.

As if all that was not enough, criticisms of metapsychology were peculiar in their diversity and contradictions. There were allegations that metapsychology was neurophysiological, biological, mentalistic, vitalistic, dualistic (psyche/soma), physical (looking for causes), or hermeneutic (looking for meaning). Those discussions, which were extratheoretical, took on a life of their own (Ellman & Moskowitz, 1980). The problems that were raised were completely irrelevant either to the clinician or the nonpractitioner. They had no effect on the clinician's way of interpreting or reconstructing the analytic material, as they added no extra value to the methods of analyzing the literature, social phenomena, and so on. The arguments became the main subject of the literature in the 1970s and 1980s. In other words, characterizing metapsychology became the subject matter of the field, while identifying or defining psychoanalysis was not considered at all.

Another endeavor was characterizing Freud himself instead of his doctrine. Some characterized him a biologist (Holt, 1965b) and some as a neurophysiologist (Rubinstein, 1997). Some tried to compare his thinking to the influence of certain philosophers such as Descartes or Kant. Those characterizations were futile in adding any insight into what they were supposed to expose. Although Freud was a product of his culture, time, and education, his discoveries were not derived from any particular ready-made hypothesis by any particular thinker and did not follow the thought of any particular philosopher. However, I will show (chapter 4) that Freud was responding, unplanned, to a philosophical impasse in philosophy in general. It was natural, in that case, in the course of formulating a theory about something that had not been identified before. Freud would show features from different intellectual inferences. Freud's discovery was genuinely his own and changed directions according to his maturation.

A third endeavor separated metapsychology from the doctrine itself. At no time during the characterization of the classical doctrine and metapsychology was there any mention of how changing the theoretical foundation of the classical doctrine would affect psychoanalysis as a whole. Replacing metapsychology with other points of view is accepted and still is considered psychoanalytically viable. Holt (1976, 1981), G. Klein (1976), and Rosenblatt and Thickstun (1977) used the vocabulary of theories from different fields to replace the vocabulary of the original metapsychology. The structural nature of metapsychology was missing from their attempts. Their suggested vocabulary had no basic structural quality that is equivalent to the vocabulary of metapsychology (Meissner, 1979a, 1979b). For instance, replacing the sexual instinct (*Trieb*) with sexual appetite (Holt), self-organization with ego (Klein), cybernetic feedbacks with affect (Rosenblatt & Thickstun) did little to "change or improve" the situation. An important missing part of that mosaic of criticisms is that metapsychology provided a vocabulary to express the psychical events in both their individual conditions (the neurotic) and their phenomenal state (the neuroses). Ignoring this characteristic of metapsychology neglects Freud's insights about the unity of the clinical and theoretical fields.

Critiquing metapsychology opened psychoanalysis to all sorts of reconsiderations (Robinson, 1993) and redefinition by philosophers (Grunbaum, 1984; Hanly, 1995; Ricoeur, 1970) and even physicists (Swanson, 1977), let alone psychoanalysts of all affiliations. Under other circumstances, interest of that nature could increase the potentials of the subject, but unfortunately this type of criticism, which was not based on discerning the structural value of metapsychology, left psychoanalysis in shambles.

THE INTRAPSYCHIC AND ITS REPLACEMENT

The Kleinian school initiated the interest in the relationship with the mother (object) and introduced it as a prototype of other relationships.[4] This notion attracted attention to its usefulness in explaining the mechanisms that govern transference and other relationships in adulthood (Fairbairn, 1954; Guntrip, 1971). The impetus of interest in Klein in the United States was in part due to the collapse of ego psychology and partially a result of rejecting what was called Freud's *drive* psychology. In addition, there were varied political dynamics that played a role in both the British society and the American Psycchoanalytic Association that facilitated the sudden acceptance of the object relation theory. Although I will return to this point later, what could be said about it now is that the relational perspective (along with the attack on metapsychology) found in Klein's concept of internalization a great opportunity to shift the work of analysis away from the structures of the intrapsychic to the functions of relations.[5] The means of changing the pathological condition to effect the cure had to be reexamined. A shift from *interpreting* the intrapsychic to *internalizing* healthy relationships with analysts became the guiding understanding (motto) in relational psychoanalysis. Transference as the relationship that could be managed in the *here* and *now* not only prevailed in the end, it was also deemed the product of the psychoanalytic act. It was a paradigmatic shift because replacing the intrapsychic with object relations reversed the link between the structure and function in the act of treatment. Better, making relationships the subject matter of analysis gave the catharsis theory a new disguise: *find in transference and relationships the content of psychopathology and make it conscious, and forget about the structuring power of the neurosis in creating those pathological contents and relations*.

Neuroses and character disorders are expressions (products) of the intrapsychic conditions. This point is based on two irrefutable facts in any psychoanalytic thinking: (a) The perceived external objects are always within the infant's perceptual faculties from birth, but they become objects of psychical relationships only when the infant's intrapsychic structure is ready to develop those relationships and not before. Infants and toddlers perceive sexual organs, but their meaning and impact change only when they enter the oedipal/genital stage. (b) Psychoanalysts know the insignificant value of advice compared to the power of the compulsion to repeat. In psychoanalytic treatment, neither influencing the perception of the object (advice) nor changing the object itself would bring about any curative change. A change in the intrapsychic is a prerequisite for a change in object relations.

The relationists claim that the interpretation of transference, not the intrapsychic, is the core of analytic work.[6] This view ignores the fact that transference, by definition, is moving (transferring) an earlier relationship (infantile intrapsychic structure) to the analytic situation. *Transference is in itself an interpretation of a previous relationship, and interpreting the transference is meant to correct an earlier flawed interpretation.* The analyst is also not an object but a substitute for an object that was created by infantile intrapsychic conflicts. Wisdom (1984) put together what was left of the original psychoanalytic theory as infantile sexuality, the genetic approach to psychical phenomena, and the partial influence of infantile sexuality on the psychical life of adults. Those three basics are hardly recognizable in any contemporary relational theory, that is to say, that whatever the view on what is central in the original theory has no trace left in the relational theories.

The relationists' interest in Klein was mainly in the changes she introduced to Freud's theory of the *Trieb.* She approached that concept from a relational point of view in the context of attachment (love)/detachment (hate). Transforming life/death *Trieb* into a polarity of love and hate was, in the opinion of Greenberg (1986) and Mitchell (1983), reformulated *a drive concept into a relational one.* Instead of arguing their point they changed it into a trivial issue: Is psychoanalysis one-person or two-person psychology? This is a nonissue because we treat the person, not his relationships.

Gedo (1999) attributes the confusion about the intrapsychic and interpersonal issues to having two theories of object relations: one developed by Freud based on his *Trieb* theory and another that sees relationships as the motivating source of psychical life (p. 371). The confusion and differences of opinion in that regard are clear between Balint (1968), Fairbairn (1954), Guntrip (1967), Kanzer (1981), and Meissner (1989). Bouvet (1967) was able, with great success, to elaborate Freud's theory of relationship with objects still based on *Trieb* and the model of the psychosexual stages of development, showing the ultimate fusion of all that in the creation of character.

The relational theory introduced another serious change to psychoanalysis. Phantasy, the fabric of the interpersonal relationship in the Kleinian theory, was considered the corollary to the structural (systemic) unconscious *Ucs.*; thus it could be used to replace it (Isaacs, 1948). This was a subtle reversing of the link between causes and effects because phantasies are products and functions of the unconscious. The Kleinians even differentiated between conscious and unconscious phantasies, by that negating the basic stipulation of phantasy being only unconscious and daydreams being conscious. This change shows that the Kleinian theory adopts only the concept of dynamic unconscious. In that theory, phantasies are constructed from external-world material and based on psychical drama of conscious contents. Accordingly, fantasies are formed from repressed conscious material; this way a fantasy could be conscious and unconscious depending on the circumstances, not the nature of the fantasy. Freud distinguished between primal phantasies (phylogenetic) and genetic fantasies, but he always considered both of them products of the workings of the primary process; hence, they were *Ucs.* and only unconscious.

The Kleinian theory is a theory of psychical contents, where phantasies are the content of the unconscious, while the classical doctrine is a theory of psychical structures, where phantasies are a function of a structuring unconscious. *Trieb* was also configured by that theory as a *content*, suggesting that it colors the interpersonal relationship, changing death *Trieb* to hate (aggression, envy) and becoming operative in a relationship. Freud's *Trieb* has no content and stands only for representing the endosomatic stimuli in the mind, that is, life *Trieb* represents the pleasurable aspect of sexuality, while death *Trieb* represents its teleological aspect. The offshoots of the Kleinian theory (Winnicot, Kohut, Mitchell, and others) offered relational formulations of the mind that, though plausible, were unspecific as well as too general to reflect specific conditions encountered in practice. They were also unnameable to verification or refutation but were convenient, in all cases, to accommodating a wide variety of technical modifications. Green (1998) commented on the flatness of the interpersonal theories by saying, "Contemporary psychoanalysis [relational theories] is in great need of structural differentiation in order not to mix the material coming from different types of patients in a one and only matrix" (p. 661).

At the beginning, the intrapsychic did not constitute a problem for ego psychology. The notion of applying the structural point of view as a comprehensive metapsychology gave the impression that no basic changes had to be introduced to the Freudian doctrine. However, ego psychologists' emphasis on the comprehensiveness of the structural theory forced them to embark on critiquing the other metapsychologies. However, the structural point of view alone, as the only metapsychology left, could not itself sustain the concept of the intrapsychic. Furthermore, the critique of the economic point of view, which discredited the concept of *Trieb*, left ego psychology without an *originator* of psychical activities. Therefore, it had to resort to interpersonal relations and the demands they put on the individual as a replacement for the intrapsychic. In other words, ego psychology pulled the rug from underneath itself when it distorted and rejected the tripartite notion of metapsychology in favor of the tripartite constituents of the structural point of view alone. Ego psychologists did not pay enough attention to the major problems the structural point of view has created for psychoanalysis (see chapter 7).

PSYCHODYNAMICS AND THE STRUCTURE OF THE PSYCHE

Calls for the elimination of psychodynamics from psychoanalysis were rarely open and direct. As far as I know, Guntrip (1967) was the first to be dubious about it, but Schafer (1975) was the first to openly call for eliminating it from psychoanalysis. Schafer's (1976) call was an attempt to create a new language that could replace the language of metapsychology. Most probably, he misunderstood the generic meaning of *dynamism*. Any dynamic field is by definition a self-propelling field, but its active parts are usually not in direct contact with the propelling force; even the moving parts are not directly related to each other. In the dynamic field, the propelling force produces motion through a series of indirect impacts, creating a field of interacting and integrating forces. This description when applied in the psychological field, such as to psychoneuroses, obliges the analyst to consider two things: a causing force such as need or *Trieb*, and the indirect links between the causing force and the action it generates (unconscious links). *Drive* is linguistically wrong to apply in this case not just because it is not the right translation of *Trieb* but because it does not apply linguistically to a self-propelling force (as oppression drives to revolt).[7] Rejecting the notion of a self-propelling psychology, especially infant psychology, obliged the anti-drive theory to find a substitute for the drive. As Gedo (1999) said, "When in the 1970s, these metapsychological postulates were successfully challenged . . . it was incumbent on Freud's critics to propose some novel theory of motivation that would be epistemically and biologically tenable" (p. 45).

First the critics called their psychology a psychology of motivation, followed by building hypothetical "motivational systems" (G. Klein, 1976; Lichtenberg, 1989; Rosenblatt & Thickstun, 1977) to replace the *Trieb*. Then they proposed new terminology to account for motivations, such as sensory feedback loops, affect, schema of motives, a premium of pleasure, or the preprogrammed innate system of attachment. Greenspan (1977) tried a Solomonian solution by making a distinction between preoedipal stages, in which relating is drive propagated, and the oedipal stage, in which relating becomes the propagating force. Peskin (1997), in defense of the drive theory, responded to its critics by saying:

> Drive theory deals with phenomena which are universal; any postulated endogenous drives are found in everyone, though their intensity may vary. It is thus a theory which deals with basic, species-wide phenomena. It has phylogenetic as well as ontogenetic applicability and as such, has tremendous heuristic power. . . . Theories that have attempted to eliminate drives inevitably embody constructs which serve the same function. Relational theories embody an implicit drive to relate. (pp. 385–387)

The most important point to consider about psychodynamics is its subject matter. It is not a matter of opinion that any infantile relationship is initiated by the infant's specific need for it. Children's relationships could not be imposed on them until the need for one reached the stage of its activation. Thus, we could say that the infant's need transforms into relationships and in that transformation a dynamic set is built and becomes complicated. The items and parts of the feeding situation are an example of a need for nourishment evolving into a "very" complex system of significations. The way the need forms and then impels the child to "relate" is depicted well in the Freudian doctrine and is not articulated *at all* in the relational theories. The dynamics of the interpersonal relationship in the relational theories appear to have no reasons to be or no justification to originate in the first place. In other words, the relationists discount that *relationships will always start from a need in the person, not a demand from the other*. Freud put it well when he suggested that the psychological is born during the trip the *Trieb* takes in search of its object (1933a).

THE CRISIS AND THE PRACTICE OF PSYCHOANALYSIS

The prevailing trends in contemporary clinical psychoanalysis were to do away with the clinical guidelines Freud had suggested in his papers on technique and were linked to the fundamental concepts of his theory. Those guidelines were deemed redundant, without serious examination of their significance. In such cases, it was expected that the new schools of psychoanalysis would develop their own techniques of practicing psychoanalysis and particularize what their theories offer as guidelines. This has not happened yet, suggesting that refuting Freud's imperatives was just liberation from the original theory.

The interest in object relationships superseded the interest in the unconscious because we can only uncover the *Ucs.* in analyzing the intrapsychic. Orenstein (1995) stated the notion that relational psychology and intersubjectivity have no use for the concept of the unconscious. He also showed that the lexicon of the classical doctrine is able to deal with the "novelties" proposed by the new schools and that the claims of those schools to originality are unfounded. For instance, dealing with structured anger leads to exploring the intrapsychic formation of empathic feelings. However, dealing with an angry relationship may only initiate change in that relationship without changing anger or anything else related to it.

The notion of one- and two-person psychologies emerged and gradually changed to be replaced with the terms used in the interpersonal psychologies. Those changes were not merely differences in the practice of analysis; they were paradigmatic changes in psychoanalysis itself. As an example, the Freudian doctrine stipulated that transference is not a "relationship" with the analyst but a representation of a previous relationship. What is transferred is an interpretation. Maintaining that view allows us to interpret the false interpretation of the past and effect a change in its internal fallacy in the present. The classical view of transference focuses the work on (a) the experiential material the transference brings to the session, which deserves interpretation, and (b) the working of the primary process that condenses the past in the present and facilitates the displacement of the previous with the current. To give the transference all the time and space it requires for developing and evolving in the analysis, three imperatives have to be rigorously observed: neutrality, abstinence, and anonymity—elementary, old paradigms stipulated by Freud as the basis for the practice. *They are technical stances intended to help the analyst avoid swaying from the analytical role of the facilitator; they are not attitudes but acts.*

Neutrality prescribes avoiding giving opinions about issues such as patients' attitudes regarding certain matters (morality, religion, politics, etc.). Analysts should do everything possible not to add anything to or take anything out of those issues or influence the issues themselves, and restrict themselves to exposing the presentations of those issues in their intrapsychic structures. In other words, the analyst should be merely a facilitating factor in the change of the intrapsychic structures that lie behind those issues. Neutrality is not toward the patient (it is not positional neutrality) but a position taken from the patient's issues and associations (it is technical neutrality). Contemporary analysts have vehemently attacked this clear Freudian psychoanalytic recommendation (Cooper, 1998; Greenberg, 2001; Jacobs, 1999, 2001; Renik, 1996, 1998b; Storolow & Atwood, 1997). Deeming it artificial, impossible, and negative impacted interpreting transference negatively.

Neutrality is not an artificial stance when the patient is informed beforehand that it is what he should expect for reasons related to the therapy. It is not impossible for analysts to keep their opinions to themselves about current events that happen to their patients. Nonetheless, because the relationship with the analyst is transferential, neutrality removes hindrances to the transference. Only if the relationship with the analyst were an issue in therapy, as in severe narcissistic cases, neutrality would be ill-advised, and thus psychoanalysis as a treatment should not be applied.

Abstinence complements neutrality. It sets up the analytic session as a scene of optimal frustration; the patient's demands are not met, causing the infantile repressed feeling to mobilize and transfer onto the analyst. Abstinence is a means to facilitate regression to get some phantasmic form within the transference—a means that avoids the perception of either rejection on the part of the patient or helplessness on the part of the analyst. The analyst's abstinence is also a way of giving the primary process enough room for the patient to interpret the analyst's attitude and reveal valuable unconscious ways of thinking about it. The contemporary schools, which strive to build relationships with patients, avoid frustrating the patient's neurotic demands and adopt an accommodating attitude. Even in the best conditions, as Thomson (1996a, 1996b) suggested, when he discussed the two concepts of neutrality and abstinence, they are considered independent of each other and are selectively exercised.

Anonymity, or limiting the amount of information given to the patient about the analyst, is the third requirement in classical psychoanalysis for maintaining the purity of the transference relationship. A major part of anonymity is a product of neutrality and abstinence. Because transference confuses the past relationship with the present by displacing feelings from old characters to the analyst and condensing characters from past experiences into the analytic experience, the anonymity of the analyst lessens the interferences with the working of the primary process in that respect. The other part comes from the analyst's refusal to reveal or respond to the patient's curiosity about his personal life. Contemporary analysts find anonymity irrelevant because patients can find out a lot about the analyst on their own, especially since the psychoanalytic "community" facilitates the exchange of information about analysts and analysands. However, this understanding of anonymity stems from the contemporary understanding of transference. *Anonymity does not depend on the amount of information the patient has about the analyst but on the amount and the way it is given to the patient by the analyst.* When the patient knows something about the analyst, asks the analyst about it, and does not get a response, the patient's imagination and fantasies will be mobilized to account for the analyst's insistence on anonymity.

Understanding the core idea behind sticking to the intrapsychic would put most, if not all, the issues raised about the classical practice of analysis in perspective (Meissner, 1998). The established trend of considering one-person psychology the antithesis of two-person psychology has made them technically opposite stances and obscured the fact that they are both means to ends. They have become the subject matter of a conflict, leaving behind the original conflict between the Freudian doctrine and the new theories (see Aron, 1990). This change in the practice of psychoanalysis has very little echo in its theory. Wallerstein (1998) said,

> We have moved from an intrapsychically based, one-person psychology, once hegemonic in America, to the inclusion of an interpersonal, subjective, and intersubjective two-person psychology. . . . There are sharp controversies about how this paradigm shift can or should be driven. . . . To what degree should the two-person psychology replace the more traditional one-person view? (p. 1140)

In other words, the practice of psychoanalysis has to be consistent with its core principles, just as the other schools are expected to be internally consistent with their practices. It is rather strange to be critical of the classical way of practicing analysis, when its core principles are improperly defined and are critiqued with no consideration of their merits. It is equally strange to criticize the classical practice of psychoanalysis because it does not cohere with the other schools' practices, when they both are considered fundamentally opposites. The other theories have failed in delineating their own practices to allow comparisons. How could one be critical of the practice of a theory that he does not approve of in the first place?

THE ILLUSION OF THE CLINICAL THEORY

In the early 1960s, long before the present deterioration in the practice of psychoanalysis, the different psychoanalytic institutions started talking about a "looming crisis on the horizon," if not already formed. The impending crisis was "gradual serious changes to the core principles of the Freudian doctrine." Strangely, the first response to the creeping changes to the theory was a call for examining the technique of analysis in the classical doctrine as the means to defining the theory. The very few discussions this call roused ended with agreement on what analysts agreed upon before about interpretation, transference, defense before content, and so on (Simons, 1981).

In the mid-1970s, when metapsychology was considered a redundancy, G. Klein (1976) advocated developing a clinical theory[8] that would suffice for a practice without a *theoretical theory*. This premise was accepted easily and enthusiastically because this way metapsychology would finally disappear. Klein's efforts were unsuccessful, and still are, because professions do not have theories of practice separate from or without a theoretical framework. We now have a crisis in both theory and practice. Wallerstein (2002) summarized the growth and transformation of American psychoanalysis in these steps, showing how the crisis was in a theory that had distorted its practice: (a) the attack of the economical point of view; (b) the rise of self-psychology; (c) the move to Klein's object relations (as an antidote to self-psychology); (d) the emergence of Mitchell's and Greenberg's relationality; (e) the acceptance of pluralism, which led to the approval of the object relations theory (after it was considered anathema); and (f) the transformation of ego psychology through the introduction of new concepts that were not related to its theoretical origin (Greenson's working alliance, Zetzle's therapeutic alliance, Stone's humanization of the analytic situation, Leowald's conception of the analyst as a new object). Those transformations, as Wallerstein presented, were not related in any way to the need for a clinical theory; they were related to the absence of a core psychoanalytic theory and the need for identifying it. I say that, because while those endeavors were indicative of dissatisfaction with where things were after Freud's death, they did not show any serious attempt at reviewing his doctrine and asking/answering this question: *What is the theory of psychoanalysis a theory of?*

The suggestion of a separate clinical theory came at about the same time another wave of discussions about the scientific status of psychoanalysis were replacing the previous interest in one- and two-person psychology. The elusive clinical theory was supposed to make psychoanalysis more scientific, precise, and accurate. The subject of scientifism and psychoanalysis was an indirect review of the Freudian doctrine and its need for major revisions. The contemporary schools were propagating everywhere, but the new criteria of scientifism, or the need for a defined theory of practice, was not applied to any of them. None of the contemporary schools were particularly more scientific than the others or the Freudian doctrine.

Nonetheless, it was paradoxical to pursue a scientific identity for psychoanalysis when the clinical theory is defying formation. Wallerstein summarized the situation well when he said (2005):

> The hermeneutic movement in psychoanalysis arose in response to our difficulties in establishing our credibility as a natural science. . . . Some leading theoreticians and clinicians came to conceptualize psychoanalysis as, anyway, only an uneasy amalgam of two separable, utterly different traditions, the projection of two strands of Western intellectual history. . . . The clinical psychological theory . . . seeks to interpret the reasons of human action, the answer to the "why" questions. There is the general metapsychological theory that seeks to establish the causes of human behavior, the answer to the "how" questions. (p. 424)[9]

By the 1980s analysts did not have much new to say about psychoanalytic plurality, but there was an upsurge of interest in *extratheoretical* issues: Is psychoanalysis scientific or hermeneutic, Cartesian or Kantian, subjective or objective, physicalistic or mentalistic? Superficially, it looked as if there were indirect attempts at defining the core principles of the theory. The preoccupation with the extratheoretical issues of the psychoanalytic doctrine took on a life of its own and headed toward a different crisis based on the previous unresolved ones.

The serious and extensive discussions, which were of a high caliber most of the time, ignored the fact that there were no answers to their questions despite how intelligent the questions were. One of the reasons was that at the time of those debates there was already more than one theory claiming to be psychoanalysis. So which psychoanalysis was meant by those questions? The preoccupation with extratheoretical issues was unrelated to either the theory or practice; consequently they introduced additional confusion to the crisis.

POLITICS OF THE IPA AND THE CRISIS

In 1995, just five years after the IPA lauded plurality it became obvious that Wallerstein's plea did not conceal the seriousness of the passive attitude taken by the IPA. The IPA formed a committee to study the actual crisis of psychoanalysis and to report on it. The committee's report identified four main signs of the crisis: (a) "Signs of decline in the situation of psychoanalysis worldwide"; (b) "Its public image has by and large suffered a great deterioration"; (c) "Patients . . . seek help from alternative therapies . . . [and] fewer and fewer patients accept classical analysis"; (d) "Few people ask for training analysis. Classical psychoanalysis is disregarded and even viewed contemptuously" (Eizirik, 1995, p. 2). Sanville (1995) said in the report, "Unless we make some wise decisions, psychoanalysis may well be dead" (p. 13). The report came to this conclusion: "A plague such as the one we psychoanalysts are facing today is a pandemia comparable to the one that descended on Thebes because of the murder of Laius, the father. And now: could it be the result of the murder of Freud, the father? Will we not discover, like Oedipus, that we ourselves are the murderers?" (Cesio, 1995, p. 2). I know, personally, that the report did not lead to any changes in the stand the IPA took on the crisis, the proliferation of theories, and the deteriorating standards of training. I am also sure that the IPA is not putting any effort into reviving the Freudian doctrine, possibly still waiting for a clinical theory that will unite us.

The most alarming thing in that report is an accurate depiction of a situation that is still the same two decades after its publication. (See *The American Psychoanalyst*, 2002–2007; *International Psychoanalysis*, December 2003; Kernberg, 2006; Summers, 2008). Kernberg (2006) noted an additional dimension to the crisis. He said:

> The membership of the psychoanalytic societies who do not have "training analyst" status have experienced a reduction in the number of patients in analysis in their private practice for a significant period of time. Training analysts, by virtue of a steady stream of candidates seeking analysis, have been relatively protected from the full impact of changes in the social environment. Psychoanalytic institutes only began to react to these changes when they were threatened with fewer psychoanalytic candidates from departments of psychiatry and from medicine in psychology and other professions, including social work and the humanities. (p. 1658)

The crisis started before any serious decline in practice. The absence of a definition of psychoanalysis facilitated the disarticulation of the doctrine and was a major, if not the major, factor in generating the conditions of theoretical plurality. Theoretical plurality led to deterioration of practice and added poorly trained analysts to the crowd. Analysis should have been changed to something else or could have simply vanished as behavior therapy did before. Yet it is still there—a puzzle.

I have traced the crisis of psychoanalysis to the critique of separate elements of the Freudian doctrine and to the efforts to do away with them, resulting in doing away with the only theory that identified psychoanalysis.

Now I turn to the puzzling nature of the Freudian doctrine to put the crisis in perspective so we can discuss a possible solution for it.

Chapter Three

The Puzzling Freudian Doctrine

Critiquing psychoanalysis in the 1960s and 1970s left it neither dead nor alive but in a state of perpetual crisis and at an impasse. Criticisms could not put a complete end to psychoanalysis, as happened to many other theories in the history of knowledge that proved to be wrong or wanting. They only encouraged efforts to replace it with other theories that could usurp its name, none of which managed to replace it. At the same time some classical analysts resolved to save the classical theory not by responding to its critics but by reconstituting the theory of catharsis in the hope of making it adjust to the challenges it faced from the interpersonal theories and contemporary psychoanalyses. They failed in formulating a better theory of catharsis that does not have the same problems the old one had. Freud tried that—in his own way—and came away short of a definitive solution.

Psychoanalysis is puzzling in that regard: flawed but irreplaceable. When we read into the attempts of reviving the catharsis theory we see clearly that the solution is not in those efforts. Moreover, if we rethink the critiques of the nonclinical *thinkers* we easily realize that they indicate the existence of another psychoanalysis precluded from articulation by clinical psychoanalysts. To support this viewpoint I present two attempts at revising the catharsis theory to underline the uselessness of solving the problem in that way. I also present two criticisms of the theory made by two *thinkers* whose criticisms pointed at the real reason for the resilience of psychoanalysis despite certain flaws: *two attempts at reconstructing the classical theory.*

Leo Rangell (2002) attempted to revive the classical theory by reconstructing it to where it was before the crisis, suggesting going back to the point before the criticisms began. He said: "The apex of psychoanalysis is its theory. . . . Looking for its essence, the core that distinguishes psychoanalysis from other social or psychological sciences, I found it in its exclusive domain of 'unconscious intrapsychic . . . process'" (pp. 1109–1110). He continued to say: "I consider the structural view the apex of the psychoanalytic theory. Without it, much of the power of the theory is lost" (p. 1131). He built his argument on the new schools' exclusion of aspects of the theory, like metapsychology, hence having partial understanding of it and concentrating their critiques on isolated aspects of the theory by taking them out of their context in the theory. Although he is right, that what was critiqued in the theory was "aspects" that lose their meaning in isolation, he still overlooked the fact that those aspects were unsound because the catharsis theory was basically flawed. As an example, Rangell talked about the repressed as the unconscious, when Freud designated it as the creator of the preconscious and not the *Ucs.* (see chapter 6). Defending an unsupported theory made Rangell (2002, 2004) contradict himself. Ego psychologists dismissed the economic and dynamic metapsychologies, claiming that their value is preserved in the structural metapsychology, therefore it is enough for the theory of psychology. Although he stipulates that the theory accommodates all three metapsychologies he affirms that the classical theory is only the "structural point of view." Moreover, he maintained that the doctrine has no difficulty including *ego psychology* and *drive psychology* in its fabric. He supports that view by stating that he is not only an ego psychologist but an id and superego psychologist too. It seems that his enthusiasm for ego psychology made him forget that analysts analyze patients, not psychical agencies, and by dismissing the other two metapsychologies he weakened the argument that those agencies have a veritable existence.

Rangell's defense of the theory was more a downplaying of the criticisms and claiming their redundancy but without giving justification. He concluded his defense by saying:

> [The] total theory includes drive and object, oedipal and preoedipal, constitutional givens and environmental inputs; the past and the present; the transference neurosis and infantile neurosis; conflict and deficit; the cognitive and affective; the self and the ego; the intrapsychic and the interpersonal; the internal and the external worlds; nature nurture; and fantasies and seductive trauma. Historical truth and narrative truth all have their place. (2006, p. 232)

Economic metapsychology is basic in a psychology of the drive, and the pregenital issue has to be considered dynamically before anything else. Therefore, by limiting metapsychology to the structural one he loses the grounds on which the classical could accommodate all those issues. A definition like that does not mean anything unless we assume that all those components are equal in significance and *exclusive* of each other, yet exchangeable, all the same. Otherwise they could not fit together in the shadow of the classical theory. A theory that is a collection of issues and has no focal point would eventually seek a theoretical core to give it some needed order. We should note here that all the components in this amalgam of issues are functions of an originator that needs to be identified to consider them all of psychoanalytic value. Generally speaking, Rangell based his defense of the theory on calling for ignoring what came before ego psychology and what came after; this way he did not respond to a very important aspect of the crisis created by ego psychology and ego psychologists.

Rangell's expansion of the theory of psychoanalysis is obviously an expansion of the cathartic theory because he just added to the principle of repressible objectionable material. He went beyond its limitations without making any distinction between those additions, thus blurring the difference between what is functional and requires analysis (obsessive symptoms as acts of doing and undoing) and what is structural and needs reconstruction (the role of *aftereffect* in symptom formation). Not only would Rangell's amalgam of psychical conditions blur the distinction between the functional and the structural in psychoanalysis, it would link two functional concepts without specifying their originator; thus they would not be interpretable. As an example, the link between childhood relations and present interpersonal relations has to be interpreted to reveal the working of the primary process in creating that link, or else the analyst would be merely informing the patient of the existence of a link.

It is impossible to expand the catharsis theory or reconfigure it in a better way if the theoretician does not pay attention to the difference between functional and structural concepts and have the ability to discern them. The reason, as previously mentioned, is that all the conditions Rangell suggested to add to the catharsis theory are of the same functional nature and denote psychical entities resulting from psychical demands (repression, integrating past and present events, etc.), in other words, they are functions of a certain demanding structure. They could be replaced by other functional concepts with no obvious change to the core of the theory. Replacing transference with enactment makes no change to the core of reliving the past in the present. But structural concepts such as primary, duality, process, and representation are almost like transitive verbs and need an object to gain adjectival quality. They have no intrinsic meaning but just change the meaning of other attributes and give them distinct connotations such as primary *process*, primary *narcissism*, and so on. Rangell claimed that he relied on Beres (1965) in making some distinction between the two kinds of concepts, though Beres's distinction was not about the ontological meaning of the terms but on the distinction between the structural theory and the rest of metapsychology; and he was basically incorrect in that regard too. Rangell's attempt to advocate the expansion of the present theory of psychoanalysis to incorporate all points of view kept him from perceiving the core principles of a theory of psychoanalysis proper, and he called for an unwavering support for an overstretched catharsis theory.

Edelson is another advocate of the classical theory. He started his argument from the exact opposite position of Rangell. After acknowledging the existence of a serious crisis due to the absence of a "core theory of psychoanalysis," he said:

> The decision at some time in the history of psychoanalysis to expand the boundaries of its core beyond its interest in the unconscious and sexuality to include "ego psychology" has not proven whatever the gains to the therapy, an unmixed blessing to the body of knowledge. . . . We need to simplify . . . not endlessly complicate, just what it is that psychoanalysis is about, what demarcates it from other disciplines, including other branches of psychology, and any other branches of psychology of the mind. (1988, pp. xiv–xvi)[1]

He stated clearly that he finds merit in the objections of the *intellectual circles* to deriving the core theory of psychoanalysis from only its clinical sphere, because according to him the theory is the dog and its clinical aspect is the tail. Although as a clinician he was not familiar with or was uninformed about the ways to work the theory outside his clinical capacity, he directed his defense of the classical theory to Grunbaum's (1984) refutation of what he called Freud's "tally argument" (see next section of this chapter). Ironically, he did not concede the limitation of a clinician entering an incompatible argument with a philosopher, but the philosopher happened to make the same mistake: critiquing the clinical aspect of the theory. They both should have considered that maybe the clinical tail of the theory is not adept at wagging the theoretical dog, especially that Freud did not come back to the catharsis theory to expound it before he discovered a few "important" things outside the clinical sphere. In other words, despite the great effort Edelson put into his endeavor he did not consider that the core theory of psychoanalysis would not be elicited from clinical work. The absence of a core theory of psychoanalysis was a *lack* and not a *misconception*, hence looking for it where it was missing would only lead to some cosmetic corrections to a misconception.

Edelson's (1988) defense of the theory was of its totality, not about any specific aspects. He stated that he will be searching for the core of the theory from which its varied aspects originated. He begins his quest with three premises about psychoanalysis: that psychoanalysis is (a) a theory of causality, (b) a theory that has core concepts, and (c) a theory that has defining attributes of its scientific method. He stipulated that the core concepts are distinctly psychoanalytic *descriptive entities* and that he would demonstrate that in five steps. The first step was making a distinction between psychical reality and actual events and that his pursuit for causality stood on the preeminence of causes over effects (fantasy over memory, sexuality over relations, etc.). The second step was affirming that psychoanalysis is a psychology of intentionality in the sense that it deals with the causal interrelations of the different psychical phenomena. The third step is moving intentional psychology toward mental representations, which in the fourth step become symbolic representations of the object. In a fifth step he would show that the mind links those symbolic representations to each other in causal relations.

Edelson's approach to the core of the theory of psychoanalysis does not seem reflective of descriptive entities as he proposed. The terms he used to expound those steps are part of the vocabulary of the familiar language of psychoanalysis when talking about the psychodynamics of symptom formation. The steps depict the same issues that the critics of the classical theory are criticizing; therefore the weakness in the theory was not improved on by putting those same terms in different contexts. Second, *reconfiguring* the catharsis theory in this way might obscure its functional features but not totally because causality, which is central in his attempt, is the bedrock of the catharsis theory. So defining the core of the theory in his way is again redefining the core of the catharsis theory, which has been the target of the criticisms in the first place. As an example, he considers the division of manifest and latent and the relationship between them one of the main contributions of Freud's theory; based on that he confirms the concept of causality: the latent is the cause of the manifest. Not only that, but the whole theory becomes a theory of products, a theory of functions. In the context he is proposing there is no explanation of a manifest unless it has a latent that is repressed. So it is reasonable to assume that something latent caused the manifest and that something is also definable a priori (sex, trauma, fantasy, etc.). As we will see later causality is the springboard of Grunbaum's criticism of Freud's clinical argument and the main debate between drive and hermeneutic stands, and what the other theory of psychoanalysis bypasses.

The issue of causality collapses in view of a clinical observation that all analysts, including him, could not ignore: "the inexplicability of the contents of particular mental states" (Edelson, 1988, p. xxv). As he correctly stated causality collapses in front of the fact that the causal link could be between the mental state and its content, or with its putative content, or an incorrect content, and even without a definable content. Nevertheless, he "insists not only on the causal role of unconscious mental contents and processes, but especially upon those having to do with sexual wishes and counter wishes, and especially sexual wishes and counter wishes arising in childhood" (Edelson, 1988, p. xxvii). The psychoanalysis that Edelson is talking about is the one from the period 1900 to 1905. He is *more royalist than the king.* In 1905 when Freud came up with the concept of infantile sexuality he changed a mainstay of the catharsis theory: the concept of repressed sexuality as content of psychoneurotic symptoms. Sexuality was no longer a repressible urge—even in childhood—but a *Trieb* that partakes in character formation (1908a). Infantile sexuality was structured as a *Trieb*, whose aims and objects are not causal, but arbitrary. Freud settled the issue of infantile sexuality and the libido theory on a different basis from the old basis he stumbled on in the hysteria of sexually frustrated young Viennese women during the phase of hypnosis. *He was listening to patients not to find the unconscious sexual cause of the neurosis but to decipher the representation of the erogenic zones into psychical representations.*

Edelson went a little further to defend the use of the old vocabulary to identify the core theory, but he did not deduce or discover a different or a new core. It was the same core of the catharsis theory, albeit with a different arrangement of its main concepts according to a new preference. There was also another problem with his definition. Edelson's defense of psychoanalysis was founded on replacing the flaws of the catharsis theory with better suppositions, assuming that those are the core concepts, then claiming the *correctness of the theory (begging the question).* As he put it, "This set of distinctive answers *the theoretical conjectures, clinical causal inferences*, or *causal explanations* are constituents of the core theory, in so far as psychoanalysis is confident that if any of its generalizations, conjectures, hypotheses, inferences, or explanations are true of its intended domain, these certainly must be among them" (Edelson, 1988, p. xx). This complex sentence could be saying that if we find the *proper* psychoanalytic entities and describe them *properly* we can then formulate questions whose answers will confirm the proposition. He did that in the rest of his endeavor.

He presumed that mental representations are symbolic representations, and without any justification he assumed that those representations are regulated by the pleasure principle. Without any theoretical or clinical verification Edelson built a whole section of the core theory on those presumptions and assumptions. In another place he said, "Fantasies are symbols of conceptions of inner reality, visualized as states of affairs in time past, time present, or time future" (Edelson, 1988, p. 19). This meaning of fantasy changed when he wanted to specify the target of defense: "The target of defense is the content of a fantasy that is sexual wish-fulfillment" (p. 172). His reconfiguration of psychoanalysis was no more than a review of the catharsis theory in a methodical way, replacing some of its functional concepts with pseudostructural definitions (e.g., proposing that the manifestation of defense is not forgetting [repression] but resistance [expulsion of the significance of the repressed]).

In spite of addressing some epistemological issues in the catharsis theory, such as the place of interpretation in psychoanalysis, Edelson was unable to go beyond the already familiar connotations and denotations of those issues; he could not break away from the framework of their meanings in the catharsis theory. In other words, as an advocate of the Freudian doctrine, he was dissatisfied with the influence of the catharsis theory and opted to improve it and reshuffle its concepts but did not pay enough attention to two errors in that approach: (a) The problem with the catharsis theory is not its concepts but its core propositions. Its framework for practice is to reveal the repressed, as its main aim, instead of inducing the meaning that is disguised in a symptom by the working of the primary process (see chapters 9 and 10). (b) The main discoveries that came after relinquishing the hypnosis could not be contained within the catharsis theory (primary repression, word and thing presentations, delayed reaction, anxiety as the initiator of symptom formation, etc.); therefore, he should have guessed that there must be another implicit theory in the Freudian doctrine to account for all those discoveries and that just revising the old theory would not be enough. He embarked on proving the correctness of an a priori conclusion: Freud was right. The problem was in the a priori conclusion and not in the way he went about proving his stand.

It is obvious from those two attempts at restoring the theory of catharsis that it is wasted effort and the solution to the puzzle has to take a different direction. It is interesting that that direction was the suggestion of two critics of the theory who come from the field of philosophy and not from the clinical field.

TWO DIFFERENT CRITIQUES

Chapter 2 summarizes the critiques from the clinical field, which aim to discredit the existing theory of psychoanalysis for the personal convictions of some analysts that there are better theories to replace it. The two critics I present here, Grunbaum and Politzer, had nothing to gain from criticizing the Freudian doctrine; they are two philosophers who dealt with it as *thought* that deserves scrutiny and assessment. I very briefly (unfairly) summarize their views, which were, with their philosophical abilities, very thorough and detailed in supporting every idea they came up with including their a priori conclusions.

Grunbaum (1984) did something unique: he took on the arguments of two other philosophers, Habermas and Ricoeur, who defended psychoanalysis, and built his critique on the weaknesses of their defenses. In a way he killed two birds with one stone: responding to heavyweight proponents of the Freudian doctrine and to Freud's doctrine as such.

Grunbaum started his critique by taking Freud to his word in the *Project for a Scientific Psychology* (Freud, 1950) and almost until the end (Freud, 1933a) that psychoanalysis is one of the natural sciences. Habermas's and Ricoeur's defense of the Freudian doctrine at first rejected Freud's premise that it is a nomothetic science and maintained that Freud did not understand the exact relevance of that term. Therefore, they continued to consider the doctrine valid and solid if approached hermeneutically. Grunbaum insisted that Freud knew what he was saying and should be taken at his word. As such, Grunbaum began by questioning whether the theory of psychoanalysis qualifies as a nomothetic science, a peculiar situation because he was arguing with two thinkers who agreed with him that analysis is not a science. Unexpectedly, Grunbaum admitted that Freud backed down from the notion that psychoanalysis is scientific. He said, "Freud forsook his initial, ontological reductive notion of scientific status in favour of a methodological, epistemic one" (1984, p. 3).[2] Freud's notions of psychoanalysis being scientific were always vague. Sometimes they were merely to give it some credibility as a practice and sometimes to underline his belief that his conclusions are correct and valid. Rarely if ever do we find him make any attempt to relate it to science except indirectly through psychology or psychiatry (Freud, 1913j). Therefore, it was not enough for Grunbaum that Freud had stopped making comparisons between metapsychology and clinical material to remedy the ills of the theory; he actually considered that a different kind of weakness in the doctrine.

Grunbaum could not ignore Freud's incessant oscillation between functional and structural concepts of the psyche, and his oscillation between ontological and methodological arguments. So he quite astutely honed in on the issue of causality in the theory of analysis, which is a groundless issue, as we have seen previously in Edelson's defense of the doctrine. Grunbaum found causality the weakest line of reasoning to easily discredit the whole theory because extrapolating from the modalities of metapsychology to the logic of clinical practice needs too many leaps of deduction. He exploited the flawed concept of repression very intelligently to discredit causation in psychoanalysis, without considering that it was the preconscious. He noticed that the gap between the instigator of the symptom and the symptom itself predicated repression, a gap that justified *an* assumption of a causal relationship between them.[3] In other words, the theory of repression became the basis for adding to causality the notion of *reason*: sexuality was not only cause, but it also became a precondition for the condition.

Grunbaum disputed the evidential approach taken in this model. He doubted the epistemic status of metapsychology and the scientific status of clinical work, and claimed (rightly most of the time) that they were methodically used to verify each other. One of his examples is the place of the correct interpretation in dissolving the symptom. He reiterated that the three indications of a correct interpretation (the patient's acceptance, recall of the repressed, and clinical change) are derived from the theoretical model that is under scrutiny and need to be verified, not used to verify (*the fundamental flaw in the catharsis theory*). He continued to consider metapsychology the shadow of Freud's scientism, which he argued to be separate from his clinical theory, and attributed the scientific aspect of analysis to that theory instead (Grunbaum, 1984, pp. 6–7). He dissected every proof of correctness in the clinical theory by using metapsychological arguments and the viability of metapsychology, if based on clinical evidence, in the same manner: they are in his opinion both methodologically and logically wrong. Grunbaum, like Edelson, was caught in the issue of causation as it is defined in the physical sciences (possibly Freud was in the same plight too). Shrewdly, Grunbaum considered the hermeneutic arguments a change in "game rules" of causality in psychoanalysis because Freud did not build his theory of psychopathology and psychotherapy on the search for meaning. On the other hand, it is conceivable that Freud did not know hermeneutics well enough for him to consider replacing the notion of "the natural science" with it, nor was it developed enough for analysts or thinkers from outside the field to apply to psychoanalysis. Hermeneutics is quite a tempting discipline to apply to the Freudian doctrine because if the doctrine embodies a second theory it is best approached from an interpretative angle, the angle of an absent meaning that gives illusive clues to its presence.

Grunbaum ended his critique of the Freudian doctrine with an interesting and unusual reservation. He said,

> Despite the poverty of the clinical credential, it may perhaps still turn out that Freud's brilliant theoretical imagination was actually quite serendipitous for psychopathology or the understanding of some subclass of slips. Yet, while psychoanalysis may like this be considered scientifically alive, it is currently hardly well, at least as its clinical foundations are concerned. (Grunbaum, 1984, p. 278)

Did Grunbaum sense that what he criticized was not *exactly* the whole theory of psychoanalysis? Did he mean that there might be a second theory of psychoanalysis that would be "Freud's brilliant theoretical imagination"? Is he saying that psychoanalysis is neither healthy as a science nor hermeneutically mature enough to be able to provide unique answers to problems of psychopathology? In my opinion Grunbaum, as a thinker who has studied the Freudian text very well, must have sensed that there is something else in the doctrine that made Freud's theoretical imaginations "brilliant."

Ten years before Freud wrote his last work, Georges Politzer (1928/1994)[4] made a significant distinction within the Freudian doctrine between what he called the *real drama* of the individual and a parallel attempt at *concretizing psychical life* that is illustrated in metapsychology, which, in his opinion, was not different from worthless traditional psychology. Psychology in Politzer's time, and until now to a great extent, was about studying manifestations of cognitive functions (e.g., memory, emotions, personality, etc.). Even in the best psychology of his time, like Piaget's studies in child development, those functions were studied in isolation of each other and off the studied individuals. Psychoanalysis, which Politzer considered the new and upcoming psychology, studied those functions *in* the subject. He admired Freud's explanation of the structure of delusion in paranoia as projecting an undesirable desire on the other, creating misconception, a model of a psychology of the subject and not the function of his condition. Psychoanalysis to a thinker and philosopher represented the hope for a psychology that will eventually explain the drama (not dramas in the Greek sense) of the compulsions and neuroses in humans. Politzer sensed that Freud turned the tables on academic psychology by adducing that the subject is a drama that defines him to others, while his isolated cognitive functions mislead and distance the psychologist from the subject.

Politzer considered metapsychology a limitation in advancing the core of the Freudian doctrine. He goes on to say, "and it is in this spirit that he [Freud] approaches the question at the end of his work [*The Interpretation of Dreams*]. It no longer concerns giving 'analytic' proofs, but about demonstrating that the dream *can only be* an accomplishment of desire" (1928/1994, p. 44). Yet he ascribed Freud's metapsychology to insecurity about building his theory on inductive (retroductive) thinking and a desire to give it the certitude derived from deductive thinking. His distinction between those two aspects of thinking is important in the attempt to discover the theory of psychoanalysis in the Freudian doctrine and the way it eluded many analysts and thinkers until now. Politzer is not different from most clinical psychoanalysts or Grunbaum in decrying metapsychology, but he considered it a necessary stepping-stone in the progress of psychoanalysis. He did think that it does not seem to affect its advancement in a major way and stated the subtle fact that consolidating a discovery, such as the human drama, requires establishing a concrete foundation for it in order to leap from that basis to further horizons. He deemed Freud's metapsychology merely a necessary step. What is amazingly important in Politzer's statement is that even if Freud does not leap from metapsychology to something more, it should have remained the leaping point for future analysts (i.e., metapsychology should remain the background of further developments in psychoanalysis, as I will show in chapter 8).

Politzer was critical of reifying aspects of the human drama in terms of topography, economy, or dynamics, averring that they do not depict the fluid and flux aspects of that drama. However, he indicated that reifications give the chance to secure the temporary "evidence" needed to go beyond the concrete but should not be taken as reflective of the drama itself. He added that instead of dismissing the whole doctrine because of the manner by which metapsychology was used, we should expect that psychoanalysis—the theory of the human drama—is going to outlive its metapsychology. Politzer's critique of psychoanalysis is clear evidence that though he was critical of it he was firmly convinced that the Freudian doctrine contains within it another theory that relates to the psychology of the individual (i.e., the psychology of the human drama).

Politzer's conception of a core of the theory of psychoanalysis was the individual's striving for something lacking in his life and seeking it compulsively and neurotically. This representation of the human drama is very much what Freud was looking for in every analysis (i.e., something lacking in the neurotic picture, not something missing), which we analysts make an effort to find in our analytic endeavors. Politzer says,

> With Freud the induction is different. First of all, we start from a true psychological fact. Let us open any of Freud's writings: the report is always based on individual facts, and what is essential is that the individual character, far from disappearing in the course of the explanations, always remains the main point. (Politzer, 1928/1994, p. 49)

Our analytic work should keep both patient and analyst on the same path of inducing that lack from the present condition they endeavor to change.

Politzer's understanding of psychoanalysis is not just unique among the critiques of the doctrine, but it also puts us face-to-face with what is significant in analysis (e.g., the search for what is lacking in the patient's narrative puts us *inside* his life story). Consequently, Politzer's criticism of psychoanalysis directly and indirectly confronts us with the absence of a theory of that drama, which has to correspond to what we endeavor to reach in our work as analysts—the untold. Better, Politzer identified psychoanalysis as the psychology of human drama but did not consider metapsychology its right expression. However, he gave Freud the excuse that being the pioneer in handling that subject means some errors are predictable. He said, "Errors of this kind always correspond to historical necessities and go beyond the power of individual logic. . . . Freud's attitude represents a necessary step in the evolution which arrives at the evidence of the concrete attitude" (1928/1994, p. 133). The last sentence in his work was "*metapsychology* has lived its life, and the history of *psychology* [psychoanalysis] is beginning" (1928/1994, p. 165).

Both philosophers who critiqued psychoanalysis came very close to declaring the existence of a second theory, which eluded them and they could not articulate.

TWO WAYS OF READING FREUD

What was the starting point of the discovery of psychoanalysis? Some historians would consider the beginning to be the case of Anna O in 1892. Freud and Breuer made some strides in the treatment of hysteria using hypnosis. They put together a theory of psychopathology stemming from a method of treatment that was to inhibit consciousness by hypnosis so patients could abreact what they repressed from consciousness (1895b). It was a clinical theory, or a theory of clinical matters. However, in 1894 Freud stopped using hypnosis and relied on patients' free associations. There should have been a new theory for that shift, but Freud kept the core of the catharsis theory as is: he still expected that patients' associations would reveal something repressed. This stance remained and still remains the basis of psychoanalysis, which is familiar to all.

Other historians would take another later point in the history of psychoanalysis as its true beginning. The breakthroughs that led to the discovery of the Freudian doctrine, clinical and nonclinical, came to him as intuitions about matters from outside the field of pathology and the clinic, and without the help of hypnosis either. They came from ordinary, even commonplace, phenomena such as dreams, slips of the tongue, and jokes. Between 1900 and 1905 he made significant—maybe his most significant—discoveries: the psychology of the wish and the working of the primary process (1900), the fusion of the workings of the primary and the secondary processes in our daily lives (1901, 1905a), and infantile sexuality, highlighting the separateness of the objects and the aims in the sexual *Trieb* and the noteworthy distinction it makes between responding to endosomatic stimuli and physical external stimuli (1905b). Most scholars of psychoanalysis consider *The Interpretation of Dreams* the starting point in psychoanalysis and would add to it the main works on the nonpathological psychical phenomena.

Once looking for something pathological in the psyche to formulate a theory of psychoanalysis ceased, the discoveries that astonished the world came to Freud as a flood. He had valuable insights in literature (1907a), family (1910c), art (1910b), language (1910e), the psychology of love (1910h, 1912d), the primitive formation of social order (1912–1913, 1918a, 1921c), and sociocultural topics (1927c, 1930a). Although those insights affected his conceptions of psychopathology more than they affected his clinical discoveries he remained captive of *the model of repression*. The most important change that happened subtly in the theory was the clearer definition of the intrapsychical structure, its formation and its pathology. Nonetheless, Freud did not show convincing evidence that changing the tool of therapy made him rethink the theory itself. However, he went back to the theory of catharsis and revised three of its most significant concepts: *Trieb* (1915c), repression (1915d), and the unconscious (1912c, 1915c). He dislodged them from being functions of the interplay of the rejectionable/repressible by revealing their structural attributes (Fayek, 2009). The changes he made in those three central concepts were fundamental, although they were seldom mentioned later or used to free psychoanalysis from its obsolete functional connotations and denotations. Those revisions permeated his work after his paper on narcissism (1914c) and were the foundational propositions of another theory of psychoanalysis derived from free association and the interpretation of the "text" of patients' symptoms and transferences. The other theory that eluded clinicians but beckoned thinkers and kept their interest was entwined in those revisions.

Mehlman said in that regard (1970/1976), "Indeed the entire body of Freud's oeuvre is constituted by Laplanche as an elaborately structured polemical field in which two mutually exclusive conceptual schemes may be seen to be struggling, as it were, to dominate—or cathect—a single terminological apparatus" (p. ix). What he meant, and what is a glaring fact, is that the Freudian text comprises two lines of thought: one is guided by the urge to find causal explanation in which an entity (anxiety) is a function of a dysfunction (sexuality); the other is based on eliciting the structural nature of psychical entities (anxiety is an affective condition that generates certain symptoms). The two lines are entwined in a unique theory of the human condition and linked through a few concepts that have structural as well as functional connotations. Better, the Freudian theory is *one* theory of two entwined human conditions, which are distinguished by the subjects of their study. Moreover, although the functional line of thinking, the first one, was not eliminated and was elaborated to integrate with the new discoveries, that line acquired some new features that kept its value alive. Metapsychology, for instance, was by definition a product of a functional conception of the psychodynamics of repression. After the revision of the concept of repression, metapsychology became the language of the intrapsychic. Freud followed those two lines of thinking in his psychoanalytic work: The first was rigorous deductive thinking, which generated the concepts for his insights. The second was retroductive thinking that ensues from unusual intuitions. *His retroductive thinking did not produce concepts but new conceptions of a new order*. Those conceptions were workable within the psychical phenomena, whether in a pathological state or in an ordinary and natural condition, and in individual or generalized cases. For example, Freud's concept of the compromise solutions in symptoms formation was an *insight* based on observations about conditions under which a symptom, which is painful, could lead to a sort of satisfaction. On the other hand, the conception of primary repression and repression proper was *intuitive*; it was about the grammar of the *Ucs.* as it is distinguished from the unconscious as the repressed. The *Ucs.*, therefore, is good to explain the formation of religious convictions in cases of depression and in depressed societies as well (Freud, 1927c).

Highlighting Freud's shift from deductive to retroductive thinking is important because the critics of his doctrine directed their attention solely to his insights and revealed weaknesses in his deductive thinking. For instance, at the beginning, Freud derived his concept of the unconscious mainly from his experiences with hypnosis. He did not care about the distinction between its attributes as a noun and its features as an adjective. He realized later, from what his patients were talking about, that there is not only some psychical content that is unconscious but there are psychological aspects that have no content that remain unconscious. Freud looked into nonpathological phenomena for a solution to that new insight. Between 1900 and 1905 Freud had the intuition that what is aconscious is the process that makes other material subject to repression proper, or to become unconscious. Thereby, Freud put order to the chaos of a topography that was misunderstood by most psychoanalysts (Blanco, 1975).

Missing Freud's two related ways of thinking created two unrelated ways of reading his text: *pragmatically* and *dialectically*. The pragmatic approach reads the Freudian text as a body of knowledge (pragma). From that perspective, the text comprises reified discoveries that could be improved upon and developed further, and may be partially or totally discarded. Within that approach Freud is seen as a historical moment, which could be bypassed and perhaps should be. However, the Freudian text has *only* two pragma, which he himself believed to be "his lot in life to discover" (Jones, 1957): the topographic conception of the psychical system, as it was derived from his intuition about dreams, and infantile sexuality, with its unlimited implications in the distinction between pathology and normality. Those two discoveries were intuitive moments and could not have come from deductive thinking. They became the structural foundation of many functional concepts (insights), which would have been literally impossible or useless without the discovery of the workings of the primary process and the *Ucs*., as those two pragma showed. The rest of his text is the detailed explications of the psychodynamics of those two pragma. The pragmatic approach is mainly concerned with the functioning and content of the psyche and is inadequate in taking us beyond the already actualized.

The dialectical approach reads Freud as a text that has within it a system and method of knowing, that is, an act of thinking and not as a body of thought. It considers the Freudian discovery one and the same, from the *Project* to the *Outline*, despite the few twists and turns in its line of advancement (see chapters 6 and 7). It values the text not merely for the importance of its historical insightful but as a source of renewing insights. It looks for the dialectics of the discovery and establishes a dialectical relationship with it. Moreover, it differentiates between statements of fact and prime tenets. Freud made many statements of fact (contents and functions), which could be refuted without affecting the discovery and its underlying theoretical tenets (i.e., its structure [core principles]).[5]

This approach is similar to the approach we take in listening to patients. We listen to what is said, but we still hear something that is not said and is dormant in the patient's speech and what is weaving all the associations into one texture.

The textual consistency of Freud's theory drew Ricoeur's attention to its dialectical nature. He said:

> A reader familiar with Hegelianism [dialectal philosophy] cannot help but notice the constant use of opposition in the structure of Freud's concepts [which are consistently dichotomous]. . . . It is true that dichotomy is not necessarily a dialectic, and that in each instance the dichotomy has a different sense. But his [Freud's] style of opposition is intimately involved in the birth of meaning; the dichotomy is already dialectical. (Ricoeur, 1970, p. 475)

However, we should warn that the ease by which we could classify the dichotomies in the Freudian doctrine, and the seemingly logical way each class of concepts related, could lead to misconceiving it as a reductionist theory.[6] A closer examination of the emergence and development of concepts in the original doctrine reveals and emphasizes their dialectical nature and not a reductionist quality.

Reading Freud's text in the tradition of dialectic thinking reveals that it was founded on some tenets that organized it from the very beginning and remained its connotative meaning until the end. However, when Freud tended to give an operational formulation to an insight (be scientific) or considered a conclusive articulation of a discovery, he overlooked those core tenets. His *structural point of view* was one of those attempts that led to serious reifications of the psychodynamics of symptom formation and ended up as a theoretical blunder (see chapter 6). Furthermore, keeping in focus the distinction between dialectical dichotomies (unconscious versus *Ucs.*, primary versus primal) and mere reductionist oppositions (drives versus relations, trauma versus deprivation) reveals where *the dormant theory of psychoanalysis* got lost. Reductionist oppositions encouraged and were the source of the diversity of theoretical formulations and the proliferation of psychoanalytic schools. Dialectical dichotomies, on the other hand, maintained the consistency of the theory from start to end. They involved antitheses embodied in the same entity, such as the antitheses of life and death in the entity of *Trieb*, external and internal stimuli in the act of representation, or thing presentation and word presentation in the act of interpretation. Better, though, the dialectical reading of the text hones in on a basic feature of the theory of psychoanalysis and on the foundational, dualistic nature of that theory. Duality creates dialectics that apply to any phenomenon that could be a product of such entities, as social institutions, creativity, and artistic works.

As psychoanalysis is a theory of the nature of the human psyche and not just its pathology, we face a veritable query: Was Freud's other theory of psychoanalysis simply an idiosyncratic gesture of a gifted physician, or does it have a more significant context? Is psychoanalysis, even in its nonclinical form, a chance occurrence, or is there more to it than "it just happened"?

Psychoanalysis came at a time when idealistic metaphysics in Europe reached an impasse, and Freud's other theory was the answer to that impasse. It came, in a way, as a natural and unintentional reaction of a gifted thinker, who happened to be a physician, to his culture's dilemma. In other words, the real theory of psychoanalysis is an integral part of the history of outstanding Western philosophical thinking. Without recognizing that history and placing Freud's doctrine in its context, the theory would remain an isolated flash of insight that does not pertain to anything except the limited clinical field. This is false.

Chapter Four

A Cultural Impasse and the Freudian Solution

The Duality of the "Subject"

We cannot deny that the possibility of another theory of psychoanalysis waiting to be discovered was not enough to maintain the interest of the intellectuals and some classical analysts in keeping it alive. If that potential theory had a role in the survival of psychoanalysis it is because it links it with the much bigger intellectual endeavor of the Western culture, which is thriving and advancing now in part due to some of the contributions of psychoanalysis. The reason I am saying this is because psychoanalytic discoveries, particularly the ones that did not come from the cathartic model, got easily and enthusiastically integrated into the fabric of the culture almost immediately and on an ongoing basis. There is an obvious explanation for that: Western culture is the culture of the subject per se, the person as an entity distinct from its social, ethnic, and religious attributes. The other theory of psychoanalysis is a theory of the subject's psychical life, and, as we will see, it dovetailed with the great progress of German metaphysics.

Psychoanalysis has contributed to Western culture in two distinct ways: First, it exposed the manner in which we educe implicit meanings from the subject's textual phenomena, the equivocality of his expression, the duality in his identity, and the struggles with the link between truth and reality. Psychoanalysis changed that culture's approach to human phenomena and its understanding of their meaning, thus influencing the way the culture considered the person. Second, it enriched old conceptions such as morality, will, volition, and freedom, which were inherited from the scholastic philosophies with little understanding about them except their biblical connotations. It also enriched the culture with new notions such as the unconscious, narcissism, identification, representation, and a few more. It would be useful to find the place psychoanalysis occupies in Western culture in our undertaking to uncover the other theory of psychoanalysis and elicit its very genuine conception of the subject within his cultural background.

Psychoanalysis had a salient place in Western culture, though there is no agreement on the significance or nature of that place (Grunbaum, 1984; Nagel, 1994; Roudinesco, 2002). Some thinkers likened it to the prodigious discoveries that characterized the spirit of Western culture and reflected its qualitative ingenuity, such as Newton's laws of gravity (*Principia*, 1687), Adam Smith's political economy (*The Wealth of Nations*, 1776), or Marx's dialectical materialism (*The Capital*, 1867, 1885, 1894). This point of view makes psychoanalysis a foundational theoretical contribution that had a major impact on the culture through its effects on a wide range of other affairs. However, those theories were correct relative to a certain time and under specific conditions. Therefore, the newer discoveries (neurological, pharmacological, etc.) could be deemed more relevant now than psychoanalysis. This proved to be incorrect until now. Some other thinkers considered psychoanalysis an enrichment of the culture, similar to the major philosophies of the great thinkers, such as Descartes, Schopenhauer, and Hegel. In that sense, it was considered one of the building blocks of the Western mind but not as part of its foundation, thus comparable to similar theories in the field. But no other theory of the human psyche in its normal conditions or psychopathology has gained the status psychoanalysis has.

Notwithstanding all that, psychoanalysis is one of the theories that changed and formed both the spirit and mind of Western culture at the same time, like Darwin's theory of evolution, Copernicus's model of the solar system, and Einstein's two theories of relativity. Those theories changed fixed ideas that were the spirit of that culture for a long time too. Those fixed ideas were replaced with new and better ideas, which created a different spirit and shook the basis of blind and stubborn beliefs. Those kinds of theories are formative theories in that they affect the whole fabric of the culture, not just its concerns.

Formative theories are different from the simply great thoughts and prodigious discoveries in the culture they affect in three respects: First, formative theories *reverse* central convictions that prevailed and were unquestionable in that culture, as in the case of Copernicus's notion that the Earth rotated around the sun and that that was the natural order of things. Second, formative theories come to the thinker's mind as a *complete induction*, which is very much an intuition. Other discoveries evolve gradually through laborious work of deduction and series of insights but remain as new added knowledge, as Euclid's model of heaven, with Earth in its center, was a new knowledge that added to old astronomy. A third difference is that the core of formative theories is irreplaceable or displaceable.[1] These theories are unique in the knowledge they reveal because they are *breakthroughs* that dislodge old givens and unveil a new order of things. Even when they reach the stage where their contributions become indistinguishable and part of the ordinary thinking of their culture, they still remain outstanding. This is the case with psychoanalysis.

Freud's doctrine has all three characteristics of a formative theory. It reversed the way we looked for meaning in human expressions by stressing that meaning is implicitly present within the expression itself; it just needs to be discerned. When Freud was thinking of dreams, their meaning came to his mind inductively, from within the dream text and not from outside knowledge or sources. Moreover, his intuition about dreams turned out to be a full discovery of the relationship between the manifest content of a phenomenon and its latent meaning in all the other psychical phenomena. Freud's doctrine was also intuitive and the source of the rest of his insights into psychoneurosis, human society, civilization, biographical studies, and so on. Foucault (1970) said, "In fact, there can be no true knowledge except by intuition, that is, by a singular act of pure and attentive intelligence, and by deduction [induction is the logical activity in intuitions], which links the observed evidences together" (p. 52). Intuitive knowledge does not show any trace of previous effort to reach it; it just comes to the mind of an intuitive person. It exposes the uselessness of the previous efforts made by other thinkers.

Human knowledge is not attained by intuition alone. Nevertheless, the knowledge attained by intuition, compared to the knowledge derived from experience, experimentation, and working with details, has a specific quality. Intuitive knowledge defies logic at the beginning, sometimes causing serious doubts in the intuitive thinker's mind. Copernicus refused to print his book for more than twenty years, although the church did not prevent him from publishing it. Darwin kept his book unpublished for eighteen years because he felt that it was short on evidential proof to justify the anticipated impact it would have on religious thinking. Einstein, as a physicist, was more sure of his two intuitions. However, he concluded that the laws of physics he had formulated are not correct in a closed and static cosmos (the prevailing conviction in his time) but only in states of acceleration or deceleration. He doubted his equation and worked out, then, a "universal constant" to compensate for this "fact." But when Hubble proved that the universe is expanding, Einstein called his constant *the universal blunder*. In other words, intuition puzzles the intuitive thinker as much as, if not more than, others. Einstein once said,

> There is no logical way to the discovery of those elementary laws. There is only the way of intuition, which is helped by a feeling for the order behind appearance. I could spend weeks in a state of complete confusion. It was only

> with great difficulty that I overcame the stupor provoked by my first encounter with such questions. (cited in Calaprice, 1996, p. 111)

Freud's attitude toward his *Project for a Scientific Psychology* (1950) suggests that he doubted his own intuition. He refused to publish the manuscript, but we are able, now that we have it and his correspondence about it, to value his intuition in its very original form and its correctness (Primbram, 1998; Primbram & Gill, 1976).

Psychoanalysis as an important component of Western culture was subjected to complex and extensive discussions by thinkers and psychoanalysts. Yet, when clinical psychoanalysts dealt with it, they discussed it to judge it, not to expand its boundaries. Most judgments in those circles, as noted previously, were products of major misconceptions. Psychoanalysis is a comprehensive, internally consistent system of thought about specific attributes of the subject's phenomena. Freud's comprehension of that system was the product of a unique intuition that contributed to the formation of Western culture. The rest of his prodigious discoveries were by-products of that intuition. The critiques of psychoanalysis *were critiques of inductive thinking measured by deductive standards*.

As mentioned previously psychoanalysis is a theory of the subject, hence its link with the whole culture of the subject. That culture reached an impasse after three centuries of brilliant philosophical accomplishments, particularly in German idealist metaphysics. To appreciate both the intuition and the rest of Freud's discoveries, it is better to review the course Western thought took to reach that impasse since Freud understood it and unlocked it. As such, we should not look at Freud as merely a member of the medical establishment of Vienna in the nineteenth and twentieth centuries but as a product of a solid cultural and philosophical movement that began a few centuries before his time. He just turned out to be one of its gifted sons.

THE EMERGENCE OF THE "SUBJECT" IN WESTERN CULTURE

The medieval Western European was unable to recognize or consider "something" latent in himself—a thinking person within. He had a communal sense of being. Religion and ethnic affiliation wrought barriers between him and any possible personalized (subjective) knowledge, also between him and his interiority. Each person was an exteriority that belonged to the rest of the exteriorities (i.e., each was barely an object). His world was understood (and understandable) because the nature of things was there in the words that denoted them.

In the fourteenth and fifteenth centuries, Europe went through great political, religious, and social changes, when a gradual emancipation from the feudal system and a movement to the cities changed the individual from a serf to a citizen of a city or state. There was also a renaissance instigated specifically by the revival of the Greek traditions of thinking. The Western European discovered the autonomy of his mind and the responsibility that came with that. She did not accept religious dogmatized knowledge without giving it his own seal of approval. His world changed. Words were discovered to be a personal option. He had to rely less on finding truth (reality) in the words spoken, even in the words of God or the priest, and he ventured to discover what things were and meant. The subjectivity of the sixteenth century was of a subject who is eager to examine the world to make certain of it, after the certainty that signs speak about things dormant in them has evaporated.

In the seventeenth century the problem changed to the semblance between things and their signs (words), and to the importance of revealing the correct analogy between things, words, and meanings. This problem changed to one of uncertainty and the quest for certainty: How could a person believe in his judgment? How could things mean what they are believed to mean? How could the subject deal with his doubt?

Descartes made doubt itself the evidence of and the reference to the existence of "certainty." The certain thing, in that case, was the doubting subject hisself. The subject moved from the certainty of the unity of signs and things to the semblance between intent and meaning. Foucault (1970) expressed the new demand on the subject this way: "To know must therefore be to interpret: to find a way from the visible mark to that which is being said and which, without that mark, would lie like unspoken speech, dormant within things" (p. 32).

The Cartesian duality of body and soul was a major step in metaphysical philosophy and in the scientific revolution that coincided with that insight. The duality of the subject came as a natural result of progressing from understanding a person fused together with the world to seeing the subject set apart from his alienations (i.e., becoming an object of the world and not one with it). It was a primitive duality within a newly discovered object (person) and was just the start of a brilliant series of other suggested dualities of the subject. The current antidualistic views build their arguments on the shoulders of previously identified and well-defined dualities; otherwise, critiquing this duality now, as Damasio did (1994), would not have occurred to anyone.

The eighteenth century witnessed radical changes in the quest for certainty. It became clear that language acted like a veil between the subject and the world. The signs were linguistic representations of things, which in turn had presence only in language; things to the subject were simply and only *representations*. The sign—the word—could be close to or distant from the thing it represented. Furthermore, the link between a word and what it denotes was found to be arbitrary and not natural; yet that arbitrariness did not increase or decrease the value of the sign. "Language is simply the representation of words" (Foucault, 1970, p. 209).

In the nineteenth century, two major shifts evolved: (a) a search for the way the representation is linked to what it represents and (b) treating language as a subject and not as the tool of investigation anymore. The main feature of that period was the gradual shift from interpreting the representation to deconstructing it, an act that led to finding the sought-after meaning. This shift coincided with a rebellion against "reason" (neoclassicism) and the birth of the Romantic Movement. A new type of doubt emerged: it was not doubt about the subject's reason but doubt that reason alone is enough for understanding. The Romantics were intrigued by the way feelings and emotions could make people subjective, unreasonable, and neglectful of physical reality, yet become more true to themselves. The duality between representation and the represented moved from outside to inside; it became an internal duality between a rational person and an irrational person, between the subject who contributed meaning to the world and the subject who was self-deceptive. The link between the representation (the signifier) and the represented (the signified) became probable, possible, and arguable; thinkers challenged previously established knowledge and refused categorical thinking. Meaning, which is implicitly dormant in that link, emerged as the essence of knowledge. It was concluded that representation as much as it reveals also hides, camouflages, and deceives. By then the subject took center stage once again as the creator of the link and the one who should discover it.

The previous dualities between the subject and nature gave way to a duality between a person's reason and his emotions. The subject who was supposed to know had become the object of that which needs to be known, and the process in this way came to a gradual halt; it was an impasse. *The subject had become both a subject and an object of knowledge, and has to know how to know himself. The subject was a duality waiting for someone to find the way to introduce one to the other and unlock that impasse.*

The subject's duality changed from "I think, therefore I am" to "I am, even when I am not thinking." Foucault (1970), in response to this shift in the concept of the subject, said, "The cogito will not therefore be the sudden and illuminating discovery that all thought is thought, but the constantly renewed interrogation as to how thought can reside elsewhere than here, and yet so very close to itself: how it can be in the form of non-thinking" (p. 324). As we will see later, the problem was not in the separateness of two modes of the subject's existence but was rather in where the solution that sustained the subject's duality resides, that is, where was the link between the parties of his dual existence? This is when and where psychoanalysis came with a major contribution.

THE SUBJECT'S DUALITY AND WESTERN METAPHYSICS

Previous to Western culture, cultures searched for and formed conceptions of a world that is separate from the subject; thus both the subject and world were entities with no determined link between them. This conception is embedded in the main three "heavenly" religions, where God lives in heaven, created the world first, then created Adam and Eve, whom he put in it—an unarguable postulate. Western culture is a culture of duality that inadvertently, but also inevitably, raised the question about the subject (i.e., Is he a subject or is he an object?)[2] Laplanche (1997) said,

> Western philosophy, which can be encompassed by the general term "philosophy of the subject," has always stumbled over the problem of the other. For it, the otherness of the external world has always appeared doubtful, problematic, having to be deduced solely from the evidence of subjectivity. . . . The type of otherness proper to the other subject is never recognised as a foundational, originary moment, but always as a barely particularised area in the depth of "my representation." (p. 653)

This point of view concurs with relentless efforts of Western philosophers to solve the problem of otherness within the self and the duality it presents us with.

Duality emerged inconspicuously in Western culture in religious thinking: first as duality of faith and reason (Saint Augustine), then of existence and essence (Saint Thomas Aquinas). It remained that way until the renaissance posed a duality of mind and world. It stayed at that until the seventeenth century when Descartes published his *Discourse on Method* (1637/1999).

Descartes (1596–1650) assumed that relying on the senses does not ensure accurate knowledge because the senses can deceive or misperceive, and "evil" may mislead the senses to false certainties about the world and the self (i.e., *doubt is fact*). But he concluded, with certainty, that "if I am thinking, therefore I am there, because I would not be thinking if I were not extant." The clarity of the idea, in his mind, of his presence in the world put the mind (the attribute of the soul) in an antithetical relationship with the existence of the body. Duality was of the body as matter that extends in space and time, and thinking, which exists outside time and space. But, Descartes's duality posed a question about the connection between the soul and the body since they, in spite of their separateness, coexist in the same body. He proposed that the pineal body is where they connect, that is, the point in the body where antitheses meet. The journey of the duality of the subject has begun, and the soul/body duality brought out the problem of causality, which had been a central issue in philosophy since Aristotle.[3]

Spinoza (1632–1677) founded his philosophy on the single and only substance (nature or God) that has the multiplicity of attributes that constitute the reality in which we live. His monotheistic view had one system that underlay the reality of everything but still had dual attributes: thought and extension. In that sense, the subject is both his mind and body, but in unison. Damasio (2003) put it this way:

> The reference to a single substance [for Spinoza] serves the purpose of claiming mind as inseparable from body. Both created, somehow, from the same cloth. The reference to two attributes, mind and body, acknowledged the distinction of two kinds of phenomena, a formulation that preserves an entirely sensible "aspect" dualism, but rejects substance dualism. (p. 209)

Spinoza had the notion that the mind comprised the capacity to perceive facts but could also perceive its perception (apperception) or become conscious of its own capacity (a more elaborate form of the cogito). He specified another duality based on the previous one: cause and reason. Perception dealt with the world and led to uncovering its causes, while apperception dealt with the reason of things (its grammar!). This dualism reflected a third duality: even though brain and mind were inseparable, they were two distinct entities, physical and psychological. In spite of Spinoza's monotheistic stand, he resorted to the notion of attributes to account for the undeniable dual nature of the subject.

In Leibniz's (1646–1716) world of "Monads" each Monad is perceptive and desiring, and the subject was a duality of both. In that duality, perception, distinct from apperception, was geared toward facts, or the awareness of perception and the reasoning of the perceived. Therefore, the truth of fact refers to the principle of sufficient reason (nothing takes place without a reason). This principle is a passive quality of the mind and just mirrors the factual world around it. Truth of reason, on the other hand, refers to the principle of identity, which stipulates that a thing could not be its opposite at the same time. This principle is innate and an active attribute of the mind (apperception). Leibniz's conception of the dynamics of perception and apperception put the duality of the subject in a context of polarities that are qualitatively disconnected but connected hierarchically (quantitatively). Monads were organized in a hierarchy in which the Monad of the soul, for instance, was above that of the body and exerted control over it. The aspect of desiring in the Monad is unconscious, and it comes back in the form of dreams,[4] for instance. Although this unconscious was not the typical psychoanalytic (*Ucs.*), it was close to the preconscious. Leibniz's philosophy, though monotheistic in form (Monads), was dualistic in substance (each Monad has its own duality).

Kant (1724–1804), as he stated himself, was the Copernicus of philosophy. He shifted the duality of the subject's world into a duality in the subject's mind. In other words, he did not accept that the world imposed on the subject a dual approach to perceiving it; rather, the subject's mind is capable of approaching reality only in a two-stage manner.[5] In his theory, the human mind is endowed with "sensibility," that generates intuition, which is an active quality of the mind and a product of a priori mental categories. The a priori categories of objects are contained in a domain of concepts, thus sensibility could be subject to understanding. Understanding is the limit of interpreting our world as it appears to us and not as "things are in themselves." Kant made duality a structural attribute of the mind that has the sensibility to understand and to intuitively conceptualize its understanding. He introduced the concept of imagination (which transcends perception) as the compromise between sensibility and understanding.

Fichte (1762–1814) took Kant's notion of *I think* as the datum of experience and embarked on a very novel metaphysical trip into the subject's duality. He stated that both the world and *I* are strange to us, though it was the *I* that apprehended both the external (the non-*I*) and its own mental states (the *I*-ness). The *I* that apprehends the mental states does that transcendentally and not by taking the mental as an object of its action because the *I* is not a thing or a substance.[6] It is an activity of self-positing that existed in self-awareness but is continually in a dialectical engagement with the non-*I* (the antithesis), a dialectical negation to affirm the existence of both. The most important outcome of the dialectics of the *I* was Fichte's expansion of the issue of understanding. He considered the understanding the *I* achieves as geared toward causality because causality is an internal understanding, while reason is external (note his reversal of Spinoza's formulation and the existence of the same problem in the catharsis theory).

The approach Hegel took (1770–1831) considered the entire history of human's intellectual development as a continuous effort of the mind to know itself. He apperceived knowledge as a process that is dialectical. At every stage of its progression it unravels the ignorance that preceded and needed to be undone by that same knowledge. Nothingness becomes the antithesis of mere being and forces the mind to discover itself. This dialectical motion produces rationality, which is the equivalent of reality, therefore making anything real intrinsically rational. Hegel's philosophy of rationality and reality was an examination of the duality of the subject's mind and its natural way of knowing, and it was, at the same time, the natural way of knowing the subject's mind.

Schelling[7] (1775–1854) talked about an unconscious that strives toward its negation. He considered the whole purpose of life as being a teleological advancement toward consciousness; therefore the unconscious, in his consideration, was a manifested finality that has a teleological aim to advance toward consciousness. It is not clear to me whether he meant that nature has that quality of unconsciousness or he conceived of nature as the unconscious state of the human mind that strives toward consciousness (see Hegel, 1845/1971).

Schopenhauer (1788–1860) viewed the world as a representation of the way the principle of sufficient reason (Leibniz) is applied in the four root areas of thinking: the physical world we perceive; judgment, or the logical sphere where truth lies; spatial and temporal intuitions (mathematics); and motivation and will. Comprehending the laws of causality led him to understand their conceptual representation (*Vorstellungen*), which was secondary to abstraction. Schopenhauer distinguished between the thing (the phenomenon) and the thing-in-itself (the noumenon). He applied that duality to the subject and came to the conclusion that the noumenal subject was unconscious in nature and that his unconscious was a storehouse of motivations and desires, while the phenomenal subject was conscious, even if only part of himself. In this manner, the unconscious was reflective of the subject's truth and will. Schopenhauer's unconscious was very much the antecedent of Freud's id (a reservoir of the instincts).

Von Hartmann (1842–1906) tried to find the common ground between Schopenhauer and Kant. He agreed with Schopenhauer that the ultimate reality of the subject is unconscious, but he did not agree that it was "blind" will. Von Hartmann considered the unconscious a coordinated duality of will and idea. Will is unable to produce any teleological processes and is accountable for the sense of existence of the "that," or the world. Idea is incapable of objectifying the world and accounting for the "what" of the world, or the nature of that world. He suggested that the conclusion of *telos* is the liberation of the idea from servitude to the will. Therefore, it becomes possible for it to advance toward consciousness.

However exhausted German ideal metaphysics looked in the nineteenth century, it had led to the point where the subject's perception of himself as an object of consciousness and his consciousness of his consciousness revealed an intrinsic and definite gap, if not an abyss, that required bridging. Bergson (1859–1941) in spite of the fading glamour of metaphysics extended thinking of duality a little further. He distinguished between experiences that dealt with static objects (which exist in space and constitute the world of matter) and the experience of nonmaterial objects, such as ideas (which are flexible and exist in a dimension of subjective time). In the former experience, the subject tended to apply reason to understand, while intuition was the subject's approach to the nonmaterial objects, such as ideas. Bergson's approach was a foundation of the twentieth century's perspective of the subject's duality.

Metaphysics in general and the issue of the subject's duality were facing inescapable shifts. One of the most prominent of those shifts was Marx's

(1818–1883) dialectical materialism and what he referred to as turning Hegel's dialectics downside up. He was critical of Hegel's notion that reality is a product of ideas, which made thought process an independent act of the spirit (mind). Marx's penetrating insights into the limitations of Hegel's idealism emphasized that the subject's consciousness and his being were determined by his material social conditions and not by apperception, which is in itself a reflection of the material world.

The shift to materialism led the subject to be perceived more as a product of his material world than as an abstract subject (i.e., as the owner of his consciousness, he forms it from the material world around him). Understanding the subject as an existence in the world—an existence that is understandable only when perceived within its world—dealt his duality a final blow. The phenomenologists and the existentialists (e.g., Husserl and Heidegger) considered the subject more of a dilemma than a duality and saw the subject's being-in-the-world as key to some comprehension of his crisis. The essence of the dilemma was a gap between the subject's consciousness of his consciousness and whatever was not yet in his consciousness (Foucault called it the "unthought"). In other words, duality stood for a schism in the subject that gave him a bi-existence, which was no longer acceptable to the existentialists; therefore they argued that the subject's very existence is that dilemma.

Another product of Western culture was the Age of Enlightenment, which began in France (1730–1800) and spread throughout Europe. It introduced two major insights that allowed a shift in the attitude toward the duality of the subject. The first insight was that the subject's reason is his exclusive means of comprehending the world around him, and that his reason—though it may have a commonality with the reasons of others—is solely his. This means that if we are to understand anything about the dual existence of the subject, we have to find a way to ask him to explain it to us. How can he deduce what is unthought from consciousness? How can he transcend consciousness of the self when the self is partly unconscious? The second insight was about causes. Causes of events were deemed inherent in the events themselves, and the subject's affairs contain their explanations. The external effects mislead the explanations and comprehension of the human act. The rules of a game are part of the game itself and are not an addition from another source (Foucault, 1970). The duality of the subject's self was no longer an accepted concept because it meant a split, with no comprehensible cause or possible bridging or potential resolution. It was a concept that stood in contradistinction to the proposition that causes are part of the event.

The subject must have an other lodged in him, which is neither hidden, nor under, nor behind, but entwined with the visible him. The other in the subject is a double that is neither expressing itself in language of communication nor making itself conspicuous by other means. Although the other is "there" he does not affect and is protected from being affected by external effects. Because the other was (is) not amenable to reflection, it is not material for ordinary thinking; it was inferred to as the unconscious, the noumenon, and the transcendent.

The enlightenment movement gave the "other" the meaning of the subject's counterpart, a concept more suitable to the two propositions of the movement. The counterpart meant that human duality is not the coexistent or cohabitation of another within the person but the presence of an antithesis enwrapped within the self, which makes it seem "in ignorance of itself."

When we talk now of dualities of the subject we do not talk of separate body and psyches (Cartesian duality) but of separate attributes of the subject, to underline the emergence of the antithetical poles of those attributes (endosomatic/representation, intrapsychic/relational, primary narcissism/object love). Therefore, it is a mistake to fault Freud by implying that his psychoanalysis is founded on a Cartesian duality (Damasio, 1994; Storolow & Atwood, 1997).

The gradual decline in idealistic metaphysics[8] in Germany coincided with the emergence of the scientific method, both in physics and the humanities.[9] The new polarity of the subject and his counterpart revealed a dialectical relationship between the subject's positivist status as a subject of study and his tendency to transcend his positivist knowledge and undo it. The issue of the counterpart changed from a purely metaphysical problem to a problem that had to be sorted out first within a polarity of physical sciences (nomothetic) and later in human sciences (ideographic). Capturing the subject in positivistic states is a scientific ambition, while facilitating his transcendence is a psychoanalytic and ethnological endeavor. Foucault (1970) made an important remark about that polarity when he said,

> In relation to the "human sciences," psychoanalysis and ethnology are rather "counter-sciences," which does not mean that they are less "rational" or "objective" than the others, but that they flow in the opposite direction, that they lead them back to their epistemological basis, and they ceaselessly "unmake" that very man who is creating and re-creating his positivity in the human science. (p. 379)

The Western culture impasse was that gap between a subject and an objective other of that subject; therefore the person could not be studied as one or the other, in separation, but has to be studied as both. Psychology was promising some serious formulations of the laws behind the subject's behavior, cognition, and emotions. Yet the counterpart, which no denying exists, was not amenable to the same methods of psychological studies, as introspective studies proved. There was nothing promising on the horizon that could have guided the thinkers to cross the abyss between the subject's positivist quality and his transcendental counterpart. Western culture brought the subject's dualities to an impasse that needed an unusual intuition. Einstein once said, "All great achievements of science must start from intuitive knowledge, namely, in axioms, from which deductions are then made. . . . Intuition is the necessary condition for discovery of such axioms" (cited in Calaprice, 2000, p. 287). Was the intuition to come from the positivistic physical sciences, or was it still going to come from the humanistic interpretative sciences?

PSYCHOANALYSIS AND THE IMPASSE

It was Freud's destiny to get the intuition that made the counterpart talk, define itself, and still maintain its dual properties as a subject of transcendence and an object of study. He uncovered a second and quite different language that the counterpart used in speaking. Freud (1900a) wrote of that intuition (in the preface to the third English edition of *The Interpretation of Dreams*), "Insight such as this falls to one's lot but once in a lifetime" (p. xxvii). Freud's research and practice during the hypnotic phase was supposed to lead him to more knowledge about the splitting of consciousness and the formation of the unconscious source of psychoneuroses. But he was faced with a major problem: the conspicuous lack of causal relationships between the unconscious basis of the symptom and its specific defense mechanism. In other words, Freud could not find an explanation for the formation of the symptom based on its repressed source. This meant that the repressed or the unconscious is not a result of a split of consciousness. He had the intuition that psychoneurosis is not the cause of a splitting of consciousness but the result of a separateness between consciousness and a precondition of unconsciousness. He discovered the preexistence of unconsciousness to the existence of consciousness; therefore they are not made to split but are already split and need to be introduced to each other. This intuition led him to make a very valuable discernment between the manifest and the latent, which gradually replaced the futile cause/effect dichotomy.

Freud's gravitation toward an intuitive discovery happened in the same way all great intuitions happen (see Kuhn's concept of "Disciplinary Matrix," 1977). He took the direction of understanding the link between the repressed trauma (which he thought to involve mostly sexual experiences) and the symptoms, instead of futilely explaining it without examining it. He faced the difficulties expected in such an endeavor: the link was rarely obvious, was not direct most of the time, was misleading and unexplainable, and could be found in some psychoneurotic patients but not in all. He did what genuine intuitive thinkers do: he accepted that the divergence and defiance of the familiar and common, and divergence of causes and effects *is* the core of the phenomenon and its integral structure.

There were several attempts before Freud and all throughout his life to develop psychotherapeutic theories and techniques (see Chertok and de Saussure, 1979, for a detailed and insightful history of psychotherapy before Freud). Medicine offered a variety of theories of mental pathology, as well as models of diagnoses of psychological nature, albeit emanating from neurology. But we know from Freud's early publications and correspondence that neither his experience with Charcot nor what Janet wrote about hysteria left detectable traces or attracted his attention to anything significant in his formulation of psychoanalysis. He was impressed, for a short while, by the splitting of consciousness, but we can notice in his contributions to the *Studies on Hysteria* (1895b), compared to Breuer's cases, that he was attentive and sensitive to the patient's whole story more than being concerned with the direct links between the retrieved memories and the symptoms. He was also able to read more in the symptoms than what was manifestly expressed. In the case of Fräulein Elisabeth von R., he commented on one of her symptoms by saying, "I could not help thinking that the patient had done nothing more or less than look for a symbolic expression of her painful thoughts and that she had found it in the intensification of her sufferings" (Freud, 1895b, p. 152). He even presented a case (Katharina) in which he did not use hypnosis to reconstruct the patient's sexual trauma and relied completely on a brief encounter with her. He mentioned in his presentation of the case history that "[it] is not so much an analysed case of hysteria as a case solved by *guessing* [italics added]" (1895b, p. 133). His intuition expanded to emphasize that the arbitrary link between cause and effect was a product of a psychological process, which could be discerned and deciphered. Freud was examining what the patient's symptoms were revealing, whereas the complaints were hiding. He was beginning to listen to an unfamiliar language the counterpart was speaking.

Freud looked into the characteristic gap within the Western subject's duality and found the means and ways to make the subject and his objective counterpart know each other: he made them talk and listen to each other. We can move now to the Freudian intuition and position it in its cultural context as the solution to the riddle of the subject's duality, the duality of two linguistic modalities used at the same time by the same subject.

Chapter Five

Dreams and the Psychology of the Wish

The Initiation of Psychoanalysis

It was an advancement of sorts to turn the issue of human duality into a duality of a subject and a counterpart,[1] and to consider the "subject" an attribute of the two entwined entities. The subject and his counterpart are neither separate nor joined because although they are two aspects of the same person, they are evidently not communicating or do not know about each other. Even hypnosis failed to acquaint the subject with his counterpart, as it did not succeed in making one listen while the other talked. The transcendence of consciousness and introspection proved useless in that regard too. The gap between the subject and his counterpart had to wait for an intuition to bridge it.

Freud paid attention in his work with hysterical patients to the possibility that symptoms could be "saying" something, unintentionally, on behalf of the counterpart. It remained to be seen how Freud will bridge that gap so that the counterpart of the "subject" could say more about himself—that is, how to make one speak about the other while the other listens. It seemed for a while that studying the symptoms could tell us something about the gap between a subject and his "sick" counterpart, but not everything.

While Freud was immersed in his search for the counterpart of the subject that makes him neurotic, he unexpectedly concluded that "a satisfactory general understanding of neuro-psychotic disturbance is not possible unless one can make a connection with clear presuppositions about normal psychical processes" (1897, May 25).[2] This was a major intuition and a breakthrough in dealing with the problem, because as we will see later, the pathological states blur the link between the subject and her counterpart, and make it more difficult to study their connection. In another insightful moment, Freud realized that dreams, a normal phenomenon and a phenomenon of normality, could reveal the counterpart during sleep; hence, one could listen to his own counterpart speaking to him when he awakes if he can understand his dreams (Fayek, 1980). He turned to work on the gap between himself awake and asleep as a means to understanding dreams and revealing some features of the gap that separates the two conditions.

This idea came around the same time he embarked on autoanalysis, a heroic, though ultimately fruitless, effort. He confirmed that idea to Fliess:

> I will only reveal to you that the dream-pattern is capable of the most general application, that the key to hysteria as well really lies in dreams. . . . If I wait a little longer, I shall be able to describe the mental processes in dreams in such a way that it also includes the process in the formation of hysterical symptoms. (1899, January 3–4)

He considered that understanding dreams is a useful means to bridging not only the gap between the subject and the counterpart but also the gap between normal and abnormal psychical processes. He said, "It is my intention to make use of my present elucidation of dreams as a preliminary step toward solving the more difficult problems of the psychology of the neuroses" (Freud, 1900, p. 104). The notion of looking into the normal processes (dreams) for the nature of psychopathology (hysteria) explains his known doubts about his *Project. In that* Project *he wanted to use neurology to build a psychology and ended with psychology for neurologists*; he faced for the first time the need to think retroductively.

This reversal was, in itself, a major part of his unusual and inventive intuitions, and what led him to what made psychoanalysis a case of unique knowledge. However, the majority of analysts who doubt the classical doctrine do not take into account that shift and appreciate its significance in generating the uniqueness of the discovery of psychoanalysis.

FREUD'S INITIAL INTUITION

Blass (2002) said, "Freud was convinced that his work led him to discover realities that lay beyond the directly observed data. Strangely, those who labeled Freud a positivist do not regard his realism to be contradictory to the alleged positivism, but rather as further evidence of it" (p. 45). Freud's approach to dreams was typical of an intuitive striving that did not start with an a priori notion but unveiled an ingenious a posteriori revelation.

The significance of Freud's intuition is in the distinction it makes between the structure and function of phenomena on the one hand, and induction and deduction on the other. Freud approached the gap between the manifest dream and its latent meaning as a structural gap, a gap that differentiates between dreaming and thinking (remembering, perceiving, etc.). *It is not a gap that serves a function but reveals differences*. In other words he approached that gap as an integral part of the dreaming process and not as a function of an exterior cause (though we will see later that he was tempted to spoil that insight by saying that dreaming is the function of protecting sleep (Freud, 1900, p. 94). Considering a structural gap meant that the manifest is not only different from the latent content but has within it all the attributes that caused that difference. This intuitive idea rebuts any suggestion that the gap was conceived as a function of some external pressure causing it and emphasizes that the manifest and its latent come from the same source that creates the two seemingly disconnected entities. The structure of any phenomenon—the source of the manifest and its latent together—is always obscured by its manifest state because the manifest is merely a representation of that core. However, the core of the phenomena is not the latent but the way the manifest was structured. *The dream is its manifest, while the manner by which it has been created is its latent content.* It is impossible to reach the structural quality of a phenomenon deductively.

There are features in Freud's work predating his major breakthrough in *The Interpretation of Dreams* that suggest a gradual building of assumptions that were his budding inductive thinking. To avoid a tedious retracing of ideas before and after *The Interpretation of Dreams*, I quote part of a letter Freud sent to Fliess:

> Everything seemed to connect up, the whole worked well together, and one had the impression that the thing was now really a machine and would soon go by itself. The three systems of neurones, the free and bound state of Quantity, the primary and secondary processes, the main tendency and the compromise tendency of the nervous system, the two biological laws of attention and defence, the indication of Quality, Reality and thought, the (particular) position of the psychosexual group, the sexual determinants of repression, and finally the necessary conditions for consciousness as a function of perception: all that was perfectly clear, and still is. (1895, October 20)

In that letter he affirms that he was at the doorsteps of a comprehensive theory that would incorporate all his insights, including the catharsis theory (see further discussion of this quote in chapter 9). We could easily note that he anticipated insights that will be of great significance after using free association to replace hypnosis. It is important to keep in mind that his letter was about a comprehensive theory that is not derived from psychopathology because he made that distinction very clear when he said later: "I had not intended to make use of the latter [my psychology of the neurosis] as the basis of reference in the present work. Nevertheless I am constantly being driven to do so" (1895, October 20, p. 588). Therefore, when we come to elicit the psychoanalytic theory from his text we should find out how he dealt with "the shadow of the project," in the rest of his endeavor.

I will mention for now a deductive hypothesis that was kept from the catharsis theory but applied differently when he used it inductively in the theory of dreams. When he was making deductions from neurology to build a psychological theory for the neurologists, he came to the conclusion that "[w]ishful cathexis . . . which involves a complete expenditure of defense are described by us as psychical primary processes; by contrast, those processes which are only made possible by a good cathexis of the ego . . . are described as psychical secondary processes" (1950a, pp. 326–327). This premise suggested that the causes that separated primary and secondary processes in the *neural* cathexis of the wish are the same that separate them in *psychical* life, creating primary and secondary processes. He then tried to form a psychological theory about wish fulfillment based on that same premise but showed an attachment to the old deductive meaning of the wish. Freud said:

> It seems to me that the theory of wish fulfillment has brought up only the psychological solution and not the biological [metapsychological]. Biologically, dream-life seems to me derives entirely from the residues of the pre-historic period of life (between the ages of one and three)—the same period which is the source of the unconscious and alone contains the aetiology of all psychoneuroses. . . . [A] recent wish only leads to a dream if it can put itself in connection with material from this prehistoric period, if a recent wish is a derivative of a prehistoric one, or can get itself adopted by one.[3] (1898, March 10)

Specifying that the fulfillment of a wish in dreams has to come from attaching a recent wish to an infantile *want* has no deductive basis at all; it was purely an intuitive inductive premise, which later had an analogous principle in the aftereffect phenomenon and its role in creating symptoms. The shift from the *Project* to *The Interpretation of Dreams*, without abandoning the structural core of psychic energy, affect, and the wish, is a new utilization of catharsis concepts in structural denotations.

DREAMS AND INTERPRETATION

The evolution of Freud's discovery of the meaning of dreams is seldom examined and is usually narrowed down to the statement "a dream is wish fulfillment." However, the notion of wish fulfillment was only the beginning of his work on dreams, and the rest of *The Interpretation of Dreams* was the unfolding of that starting idea. He ended in that work with an unusual theory of the wish that led to the discovery of the systemic unconscious (*Ucs.*) and, from there, to the discovery of the whole theory of psychoanalysis.

The Interpretation of Dreams strongly suggests that Freud began his theory on dreams with assumptions (principles) and succeeded in validating those assumptions. The clearest and first assumption was that dreams have meaning and are not, as previously thought, merely psychical reactions caused by external or internal stimuli (see chapter 1 of *The Interpretation of Dreams* for Freud's comprehensive refutation of those notions). More properly, he did not start with dreams looking for interpretations but started with propositions that could be supported if dreams *were* interpretable. A second assumption was that uncovering the meaning of dreams is insufficient to reveal the process that hid the meaning or the manner by which that process has worked to hide that meaning. The third assumption was revealing the process behind the formation of dreams (discovering the workings of that process) would be the only natural way to bridge the gap between the manifest and the latent (the subject and his counterpart). Freud's intuition came to him while attempting, for the first time, to *understand* a dream of his own.

On the night of July 23–24, 1895, Freud had a dream, which was for the first time submitted to a full interpretation and which made him state that at last the "secret" of dreams was revealed to him (1900a, pp. 106–121). He dreamed he was in

> a gathering including his patient Irma and some physicians. He blamed her for not accepting his advice and as a result aggravating her condition. However, she complained of severe pains in a different part of her body. He had concerns, in the dream, that he might have missed an organic diagnosis. He wanted to examine her, but she was reluctant at first, making him feel contemptuous of her vanity. She then became more cooperative and allowed the examination to proceed. He found some physical signs to make a proper diagnosis, but he brought in another doctor, who gave an unlearned diagnosis and prognosis, which were confirmed by a third doctor. Those doctors were "directly aware, too, of the origin of the infection," which came from an unclean syringe used by his friend Otto who injected the patient with an unfamiliar medical preparation.

The day before the dream, Freud's friend Otto gave him some bad news about Irma, the young woman whom Freud had treated, with limited success. He considered Otto's remarks "a reproof, such as to the effect that I had promised the patient too much" (1898, March 10, p. 106). He was conscious of his annoyance with Otto's remarks as he was talking to him the evening before the dream.

Freud divided the dream into its main sections and free associated on each section separately. This was a different approach to solving the incomprehensibility of dreams, never used before. The idea was that the dream had more to it than what its "manifest content" said and that he should allow the manifest content to say more. After he had produced his associations about all the parts, he stated that the dream interpretation had been "completed" (1900a, p. 118). Nonetheless, he made an important remark on his interpretation:

> And in the mean time the "meaning" of the dream was borne in upon me. I became aware of an intention which was carried into effect by the dream and which must have been my *motive* for dreaming it. The dream fulfilled certain wishes *which were started in me by the events of the previous evening (the news given to me by Otto and my writing the case history). The conclusion of the dream, that is to say, was that I was not responsible for the persistence of Irma's pains*, but it was Otto. . . . The dream represented a particular state of affairs as I should have wished it to be. *Thus its content was the fulfillment of a wish and its motive was a wish* [all italics added]. (1898, March 10, pp. 118–119)

In this first completely interpreted dream, Freud evinced three important points: (a) A dream is simply a direct presentation of a situation in the present tense. (b) When a dream is interpreted, it reveals a fulfilled wish (1898, March 10, p. 119). (c) The residues of the day before could explain the dream content (the manifest dream) and shed light on the motive behind that particular dream. However, *the fulfilled wish was neither part of the manifest dream nor of the association on the dream but was almost a finding*: "the dream said what I was not able to say to all those people." The wish was induced from the link between the manifest dream and the associations put together; the interpretation was the link.

Freud started with the structural quality of the dream to pave the way to its function (content). Hence, Freud deduced the rule that all dreams were wish fulfillments. This leap needs further investigating because it calls into question the statement that dreams are wish fulfillment.

If Freud's wish in the "Irma" dream were fulfilled, he did not feel such fulfillment while dreaming[4] nor was the wish present in any form in the manifest dream when he was awake. It came to his mind when he was awake, "watching" his dream. Politzer (1928/1994) said, "[I]f the dream, and in general the neurotic symptoms, have a meaning, they have this meaning at the time they are produced; and if the dream in particular is the satisfaction of a desire [wish] it is this satisfaction at the moment it is dreamed" (p. 119). *What does it mean, then, that a dream is a wish fulfillment if the wish is neither there in the fabric of the manifest dream nor in the latent content but only shows itself in the work of interpretation?* Furthermore, Otto's bad news about the patient aroused in Freud the wish to exonerate himself, but the dream fulfilled more than one wish: he wished to accuse Irma of causing her own misery and he did; to have not made a mistake in diagnosis and in the dream he made a right diagnosis; to make fools of his senior colleagues, who proved not to be too senior; and for Otto to be the culprit. How did the dream bring all those wishes together? Possibly by simply making the dream say one overdetermined implicit statement: "I am right and everyone else is wrong."

Although Freud did not raise those questions about the wish, he was quick to recover from what could have aborted his intuition early, that is, giving content to the work of wish fulfillment. Instead, Freud eased himself into the concept of the unconscious to address the issues raised by those questions. He did not assume, until then, that the unconscious was something that existed behind the wish fulfillment. The existence of another process behind the formation of dreams, which brought back some thoughts from the *Project*, caught his attention (he was not looking for an unconscious yet). He had a vague notion of that process in the *Project*, where he said that there is something beyond our perception, which we can still describe only with the vocabulary of perception and conception, and despite its independence, it will remain unknowable.

Freud inferred the unconscious from the emergence of the meaning of the dream in the process of interpretation, which did not exist in the dream before the interpretation. Inference is inductive: it happens when we move from "observables" to their organizing principles or from facts to their essence. As he recognized the unconscious as a factor to contend with in dreaming, he moved from the functional explanation of dreams as wish fulfillments to exploring the nature of fulfilling wishes in dreams (i.e., interpreting dreams leads the dreamer to represent the wishes in a state of fulfillment).

Freud's examination of wishes in dreams (more than fifty of his own and 150 of others') made him less emphatic about the wish-fulfillment formula he proposed as the secret of dreams. He said that "dreams are given their shape . . . by the operation of two forces (systems): and that one of the forces constructs the wish . . . while the other exercises a censorship upon this dream-wish" (1950, p. 144). Thus, the wish is not what initiates the dream because there is another operation or process that constructs the wish first, making it the originator of the dream.

The sudden change in direction divested the dream wish of any fixed quality; therefore there should be a condition, or rather a state, that we could name a wish and that acquires its attribute from the system that produces it. Otto's subtle reproof, the night before the "Irma" dream, set up a state of wishing, which we can easily say was not specific, and Freud, figuratively speaking, had to choose one of many possible wishes in response to Otto's remarks. *It is the state of wishing—not a wish as such—that is the predicate of dreams*. That is, wishing has become the precondition for dreaming and not the condition; it is an unconscious condition that creates the wish, that in turn creates the dream as well as its structural attributes. At that stage of dealing with the unconscious, he considered the wish an experience of frustration that required the dreamer to deal with regardless of what system had produced it.

For Freud's general postulate of wish fulfillment to hold he had to have found a solution to dreams of punishment or frustration. He opted to consider punishment within the scheme of wishes, fulfillment of a wish for punishment. This "begging the question" solution (simplistic deduction) led him to make another major deduction that was quite flawed. He gave wish fulfillment, even of a negative wish, the function of protecting sleep and attributed that to benefiting the ego (1900a, p. 267). It was a blunder, because he turned the discovery of wishing during sleep into a function of no relevance to dreaming per se or to the ego, which could have been bruised the day before.[5]

At that point in his work he showed some hesitation (confusion) about the nature of the "wish." The wish was unconscious, but "the unconscious has nothing else to offer during sleep but the motive force for the fulfillment of a wish[6] (1900a, p. 565). The notion of dreams as wish fulfillment changed to be, in actuality, a step toward understanding the state of wishing. Freud separated the motivational force of wishing from the wish itself and relegated it to the *Ucs*. As such, it was possible to look at dreams as products of impulses (causes to be identified) and also as representations of those impulses (texts to be interpreted). In the analysis of another dream (not his own), he identified two very evident features in all dreams, and when added to the previous thought, they would have deep implications for the field of psychical phenomena in general. He said about the dream of the "burning child," "Two almost independent features stand out as characteristic of the form taken by this dream. One was the fact that the thought is represented as an immediate situation with the 'perhaps' omitted, and the other is the fact that the thought is transformed into a visual image and speech" (1900a, p. 534). The first feature is using only the present tense (the state of fact) in presenting the event, not given a place for any commentary on the event. The second feature is transforming thoughts into sensory images, which are experienced with a high level of conviction in their realism. Psychical phenomena such as dreams or symptoms are "time-less," or time in those phenomena is fixed permanently on the present tense, indicating that its past and its future are considered only in their present states. They are also captured in a sensory form, that is, experienced and not just watched. Those two features are unusual compared to the normal ways of thinking in our waking life, which is not restricted that way.

Any of the three psychical systems (*Cs.*, *Pcs.*, and *Ucs.*) could generate a state of wishing that would be different only in the wish it produces and the demands for fulfillment. Thus, *wishing* has no typical quality; it is also content-less and is amenable to latching to any content or to be chosen by any content to have a chance to reach consciousness. Since neither the nature nor the source of wishing is fixed, we cannot say that the dream is wish fulfillment as such but can say *the fulfillment of a wish (wishing) is a dreamlike state*. We encounter that in daydreams and in neuroses in the form of fantasies, which are dreamlike states too. Symptoms convey wishful thinking, and in their final analysis they are structured like dreams or by the same process that structures dreams.

The conflict within a wish between fulfillment and a "force" working against it (censorship) was one of the exceptionally significant aspects of Freud's intuition.[7] If we go back to the "Irma" dream we can see that Otto's remark prompted the wish to negate it. Freud's wish to negate Otto's remark was the antithesis of the remark; therefore, Freud was right in assuming that each wish creates its antithesis (he dreamed that he was correcting already prevalent wrong ideas about his method). Therefore, we could say—with confidence—that a dream is a compromise between the fulfillment of a wish and its frustration (a statement that we are familiar with in the context of symptom formation). Gradually, Freud moved to the notion that *the wish was no longer the core of dreams; the psychology of wishing became the core of dreaming and the center of the other psychical phenomena that share something with dreams.*

Freud's concept of *censorship* in dreams is deductive. Considering that dream distortions are products of censorship presumed that the censor was an agency that existed independently, did not yield itself to sleep, and had the power to interfere with dream formation. Censorship was introduced from outside the process of dreaming and imparted a realism that conflicted with the teleological nature of the dream theory, a teleology that led him to the unconsciousness of the dream work. However, in spite of the notion of censorship Freud proceeded to examine the effect of the internal conflict between the wish and the probable wish to censor it. He intuited that the obscurity of the manifest dream is a result of that conflict, which affects the proper representation of the wish. In other words, the distortion of the latent meaning in the manifest dream is a function of conflict that distorts the latent content, precluding the recognition in the manifest dream. This view was inconsistent with the dialectical opposition between a wish and its antithesis, which makes more sense than between two different wishes. He said that the dream content is "not a faithful translation or a point-by-point projection of dream thoughts, but a highly incomplete and fragmentary version of them" (1950, p. 281). This conclusion strongly suggests that a wish in the dream creates its own opposition or antithesis, a notion that befits Freud's ubiquitous dualities, which are dialectical and not reductive (Ricoeur, 1970). The emergence of the antithetical wish sets the scene for a process that reveals a link between two antithetical wishes, but not just any kind of link. It is a link that takes us back to the person and her counterpart.

The unconscious nature of wishing and the antithetical conflict within wishing distort the manifest dream and presuppose the presence of a psychical process that works to that end; otherwise there would be no place to interpret dreams. Freud "discovered" the process of dream work. He did not have any notion from his previous experiences of the existence of such a process, let alone what dream work entailed. Blass (2002) said, "What Freud considered to be his revelation was that he could discover the actual connections in the mind that were responsible for the appearance of dreams—the actual connections that were finding expression through it . . . the actual connections that exist within the mind" (p. 49).

Freud's further understanding of dream work specified three of its features: condensation, displacement, and pictorial representation of ideas. Condensation is what makes one of the dream elements stand for several elements in the dreamer's life or several elements of the dream correspond to one element in the dreamer's life. He commented on condensation by saying, "We might conclude that condensation is brought about by omission" (Freud, 1900, p. 281). Blass (2002) attributed Freud's notion of condensation to his technique of dream interpretation, in which free association on each element would produce an abundance of thoughts. This feature showed itself in the interpretation of the "Irma" dream, where Irma stood for, or represented, several other characters in a condensed way (Freud, 1900, pp. 292–293). Metaphor is the linguistic attribute of condensation (Cassirer, 1953).

The next feature in dream work is displacement, which Freud succinctly delineated as follows:

> In the dream-work a psychical force is operating which on the one hand strips the elements which have a high psychical value of their intensity, and on the other hand, by means of over-determination, creates from elements of low psychical value new values, which afterwards find their way into dream-content. If that is so, transference and displacement of psychical intensities occurs in the process of dream-formation, and it is a result of these that the difference between the text of the dream-content and that of the dream thoughts comes about. (Freud, 1900a, p. 307)

The linguistic attribute of displacement is metonymy (Cassirer, 1953). In metonymy, a part stands for the whole (I have a new set of wheels; she is Irish; look at her hair; the yellow beard of Freud's friend stands for his uncle [1900a, pp. 136–145]), or the value of a whole is transferred to a part (she had a firm grip on me). The most intriguing and potentially enlightening statement about displacement is what Freud said about the link between it and condensation: "displacements . . . facilitate condensation in so far as, by their means, instead of two elements, a single common element intermediate between them found its way into the dream" (p. 339). He is stating that condensation and displacement could be a duality in their own right, and each could express aspects of the other. The assumption that something means more than what it denotes, as a feature of dream work, brings us back to censorship. Metaphor and metonymy, which are constituents of our ordinary linguistic expressions (verbal and nonverbal) and the foundation of what later will become the regular way of "saying" things, function differently in dreams than in our waking lives. In dreams, we do not purposely use them to express more than what we have in mind. Metaphors and metonymies muddle up the manifest content of the dream (and symptoms) and distort the expression of the wish, just by the way the primary process utilizes them. Their effect on the manifest dream is what Freud wrongly called censorship. They are not mobilized by another psychical agency for the purpose of censoring something. Therefore, we should examine closely what we mean by "defenses," because defenses are nothing more than variations on the themes of displacement and condensation (see chapter 9). In waking life, on the other hand, we use metaphor and metonymy purposely but only to enrich our thoughts and enhance our expressions. They are main features of literary work. Even in artistic works creative artists know how to adapt their media to use metonymy and metaphor.

The third feature of dream work is "the means for pictorial representation." This feature is determined by the state of sleep more than anything else. The stimulation coming from the five senses is limited, if not blocked completely, in sleep. The means for action, whether motor, verbal, or intellectual, are paralyzed. The only medium for the psyche to perform is the pictorial medium. In other words, if there is a wish in sleep that demands recognition it will have no other means but to be pictorially "shown" as fulfilled. It is intriguing how the notion of the dream as wish fulfillment came naturally from the two attributes of dreams as being only in the present tense and only in a pictorial form. Freud said that a dream has no alternative but to present the wish as being fulfilled because it has no sense of time except the present (1900a, p. 235).

Because dreams have no means of expressing the latent content except by representing it pictorially, they have a difficult time representing adverbs and conjunctions. Freud said, "Dreams have no means at their disposal for presenting these logical relations between the dream-thoughts. The restoration of the connections, which the dream-work has destroyed is a task which has to be performed by the interpretative process" (p. 312). Another aspect in the latent content that resists pictorial representation is abstract ideas, such as secret love, impotence, or honesty. However, Freud noticed that the plasticity of psychical material benefited from the use of symbols to represent those abstract notions (p. 352). He also displayed an unusual inductive ability to find some grammatical rules that guide the dream in dealing with concepts such as if, when, un-, and after. Freud's intuition about dream work—its role as the unconscious aspect in dreams and its formative procedure—was complemented by deciphering its elements and their mechanisms. *It also points to a theory of psychoanalysis that could emerge only from the speech of patients (free association) and not through hypnosis.*

Politzer (1928/1999) said that the latent content of the manifest dream is what a theme is to a play or what the idea of a wish is to an expression of its concrete fulfillment. What he meant was that wishing is like the play that finds its theme in a wish. It could be added that wishing is not only time-less and content-less, it is also form-less. Any wish, such as Freud's wish to be great and blameless in the "Irma" dream, has to borrow a form to be expressed: "I am the only good doctor in the room, and everybody else there is wrong." In other words, if a wish has to borrow a form to be expressed, then a dream has no other means to express that wish except pictorially, showing it as a fulfilled event.

To sum up, Freud's intuition that the "Irma" dream depicted fulfilling a wish led him to a wide range of exploration of the psychology of wishing. The most important was that a state of wishing has to be there for wishes to emerge and take shape. *The state of wishing is time-less, content-less and form-less*, and *Ucs.* Accordingly, the presence of wishes in dreams predicates submitting to the working of the primary process so that they acquire what makes them form the manifest dream.

THE PRIMARY PROCESS AND THE CONSTRUCTION OF DREAMS

In the absence of a psychological theory to support his intuition about dreams, Freud used two neural functions to deal with the discovery of dream work: a primary function, which is disposed to discharging the accumulated quanta of excitation in the neurological system, and a secondary function, which endeavors to keep a constant quantity of excitation stored for anticipated needs. His notion of a similar dichotomy in the field of thought was nebulous until he was able to formulate a concept of psychic energy (later named libido). However, Freud was careful at the beginning to emphasize the link between the two neural functions and the primary and secondary psychical processes, but he later articulated that link (p. 600). The bound and unbound psychical energies were modeled after the primary unbound neural energy and the secondary bound neural energy. This kind of reductionist thinking could have predisposed Freud to abandon his intuition early with superficial and hasty satisfaction. But he became aware that presenting the two processes in that topographical way would give them reified concrete properties and distract from their dynamic interplay. He even warned, in advance, that this outlook would affect understanding the mechanism of repression by making it a force separate from the repressed. His deductive thinking stopped at a point where it needed a change in direction and attitude, especially some change in the way the questions were posed.

Freud's advancement from the simplistic idea of dreams as wish fulfillment to the conception of a state of wishing saved his intuition from fading early. He expressed this significant point of view in an extraordinary allegory, considering that it preceded by a few decades the great developments in the field of linguistics. He said,

> The dream-thoughts [wishing] and the dream-content [the wish] are presented to us like two versions of the same subject-matter in two different languages. Or, more properly, the dream-content seems like a transcript of the dream-thought into another mode of expression, whose characters and syntactic laws it is our business to discover by comparing the original and the translation. (1900a, p. 277)

This notion of a dream language had far-reaching consequences because it meant that a dream should be treated as a "statement," written in a special language and requiring translation to be understood (i.e., interpretation). The psychoanalytic task was, therefore, defined as the act of interpreting what the statement has said[8] and translating it into the secondary language of waking-life thinking. The translation would be from a language of metaphors, metonymies, and pictorial representations of abstract ideas—a language rich in vocabulary, semantically deficient, and syntactically poor, with no discernible grammar. He was rightly likened by Lacan to Champollion, who deciphered the Rosetta Stone and managed to read the hieroglyphic text on it by using one known language to decipher the other. The distinction he made between the primary process and the secondary process led him to realize that they are dialectically linked; for this reason, the conflicting forces in the dream were considered a split between two aspects of the same psychical state.

The first feature of the primary process was the ease by which wishes, ideas, characters, and meaning exist in it, free from the common rules of thinking, and the logic of the relation between cause and effect. This feature made him say that the mind has free play in representing the preconscious (p. 591). The secondary process as the antithesis of the primary process is not an opposing force because dialectically speaking, it springs from it. The opposing force is rather a process that interferes with the freedom of signifying things and forms a manifest dream, which is regularly hard to understand. This subtle recognition controverts his previous notion that censorship is a product of the work of the secondary process that defends the ego. He even averred that the most sophisticated achievements of thought, which belong to the secondary process, are still possible within dreams, independent of the assistance of consciousness (p. 592). Moreover, he alleged that dream thoughts are in themselves *inadmissible to consciousness not because they do not follow the rules of the secondary process but because they are severed from the chain of thoughts attached to the wish.* The primary and secondary thoughts, in that sense, could explain the operation of dream work quite well.

The psychical state of wishing, by remaining in its plastic unbound condition (time-less, content-less, and form-less), could freely latch to different psychical entities, meanings, and representations, thus creating condensations and displacements. The second feature that connects with the primary process is the concept of the state of wishing.[9] Freud considered *wishing a state of necessity* that instigates dreaming. The dream, in that case, is the psychical phenomenon that suits the wish because it allows it to be presented only as fulfilled. Wittgenstein (1982) said, "The representation of a wish is, *eo ipso*, the representation of its fulfillment" (pp. 64–65). In fact, the dream fulfills wishes by virtue of its capability in representing them as actualized. What makes the dream a wish fulfillment is the facility of representation, not the content of the wish. In fact, the wish does not demand fulfillment as such but looks for a form that it could take to simply be expressed or represented. Therefore, it is reasonable to say that dreams, daydreams, and phantasies are nothing but wish fulfillment because the wish would not have the slightest chance of being actualized through secondary processes in those modes of representation and because the wish does not demand change in the external world. Hence it is satisfied in the dream scene. The wish changes into a message and a demand only if it is communicated to the other, which does not happen in sleep.

FROM THE INTERPRETATION OF DREAMS TO A NEW PSYCHOANALYSIS

Chapter 7 in *The Interpretation of Dreams* contains very clear indications that Freud has begun developing a theory that goes beyond dreams and their interpretations. It would be more correct to say that he *used* dreams as his first field to test and come up with the new conceptions of psychoanalysis. This is especially important to underscore because what I recover and the way I recover it in this chapter is what I will do in the rest of the Freudian text to elicit his theory of psychoanalysis.

Freud realized that for a wish to be represented in dream form, it has to go through two transformations: First, it has to acquire a content (from the day's residues) and a form (from a childhood want) to construct the manifest dream. Second, it has to succumb to the imperative to be pictorially presented as demanded by the primary process. Reaching the point of explaining the psychology of the wish, Freud introduced the topographical model of psychical systems of *Cs.*, *Pcs.*, and *Ucs*. The wish has to be located in one of the psychical systems. But which system? We should note that Freud's understanding of the unconscious at that stage was supposed to be the one he discovered in hypnosis; accordingly the wish would be a repressed entity. However, it is astonishing to find instead an elaborate concept of the unconscious of which Freud said:

> The unconscious (that is, the psychical) is found as a function of two separate systems and that this is the case in normal as well as pathological life. Thus, there are two kinds of unconscious, which have not yet been distinguished by psychologists. Both of them are unconscious in the sense used by psychology but in our sense of them, one of them, which we term the *Ucs.*, is also inadmissible to consciousness, while we term the other *Pcs.* because its excitations—after observing certain rules, it is true, and perhaps only after passing a new censorship, though nonetheless without regard to the *Ucs.*—are able to reach consciousness. (Freud, 1990, pp. 614–615)[10]

The unconscious of a new theory of psychoanalysis evinced.

The distinction he made between the *Ucs.* and the *Pcs.* is to be noted for two reasons: (a) The *Ucs.* is inadmissible to consciousness not because of its unacceptable content (functionally) but because of its qualitative difference from consciousness (structurally). This new insight meant that the unconscious is not a function of repression but the preconscious is (see chapter 6). (b) Freud avoided founding his psychology of the wish on a functional basis. He confirmed his structural understanding of the *Ucs.* when said, "Thought-processes are in themselves without quality, except for pleasurable and unpleasurable excitations which accompany them, and which in view of their possible disturbing effect upon thinking, must be kept in bounds" (p. 617).

It follows that Freud's conception of the *Ucs.* meant that the psychical state of excitation has no content and it seeks a form to become meaningful. It is important to note that Freud talked about a "quota of affect" in the book on dreams merely as a manifestation of a sum of excitation. This was before he got his intuition of the overlap between wishing, the *Ucs.* and the primary process. When Freud moved from the *Project* to *The Interpretation of Dreams* it was evident that his neurological framework fit well with the psychical framework of the dream. As such, affect too found a place in the psychology of the wish because the quanta of affect were neither negative nor positive, but depending on its satisfaction or frustration, it could lead to pleasure or unpleasure. Like affect, if the wish persists, it borrows a form that it finds in the conscious/preconscious material. Therefore, the *Ucs.* state of wishing could make an objectionable choice, creating this way its own anti-wish, which has to be censored. Freud said, "My supposition is that a conscious wish can only be a dream instigator if it awakes an unconscious [preconscious] wish with the same tenor and in obtaining reinforcement from it" (1900a, p. 553). This statement could also be reversed and still be right: *an unconscious wish can only instigate a dream if it finds a conscious wish to represent it*. Freud went back to the dynamics of the primary and secondary processes equipped with the new distinction between the *Ucs*. and the *Pcs*. Although he already referred the primary process to the *Ucs*. as its structuring background and relegated the secondary process to the *Pcs./Cs*. systems, there was a much-needed comprehensive configuration of all those details from a psychology of an elaborate psychical system, and of the *Ucs*. in particular, a conception of the *originary* states of all those novel insights.

At that stage of discovering the state of wishing and the psychology of the wish Freud made this statement:

> The exigencies of life confront it [the mind] first in the form of the major somatic needs. . . . A hungry baby screams and kicks helplessly. But the situation remains unaltered, for excitation arising from an internal need is not due to a force producing a momentary impact but one which is in continuous operation. . . . A change can only come about (through outside help) an "experience" of satisfaction can be achieved. . . . An essential component of this experience of satisfaction is a particular perception . . . , the mnemic image of which remains associated thenceforth with the memory trace of the excitation produced by the need. As a result of the link that has been established, next time this need arises a psychical impulse will at once emerge which will seek to re-cathect the mnemic image of the perception and re-evoke the perception itself, that is to say, re-establish the situation of the original satisfaction. An impulse of this kind is what we call a wish; the appearance of the perception is the fulfillment of the wish. (pp. 565–566)

Freud referred the wish to an *endosomatic need* that transforms into something that would represent it by the help of the *other* (i.e., it changes from being a signifier to becoming a signified). The endosomatic need—with the help of the other—is transformed from a somatic pressure into an affect demanding relief. To gain access to consciousness, the state of wishing has to acquire a qualitative form and a subjective flavor (qualia). Without those two qualifications, the state of wishing remains an aconscious demand for fulfillment, and its mnemic image establishes a permanent link with that demand.

A second part of Freud's conclusion is that the wish is a pressure that attracts, or gets attracted to, other events, which by themselves are inadequate to rally the functions of consciousness without its "push." The wish drives those elements to activate consciousness, and in doing so, the wish employs the rules of the primary process to bridge the gap between itself and those other endeavors, a bridge that keeps it disguised, among other things, until the work of interpretation is initiated. Actually, the only unconscious aspect of dreams, symptoms, and the rest of the human phenomena is the process of transforming the wish into conscious endeavors, which could mean something to the other within the boundaries of the secondary processes (i.e., the wish becomes a desire).

It is not difficult to notice that moving from the dream as a function of a wish pressing for fulfillment to the dream as a function of a state of wishing, regardless of the wish, was the only possible way for Freud to move from a sterile theory of dreams to a pregnant theory of psychoanalysis. He invoked the concept affect and its primary and secondary functions in neurology five years before using the same conception in explaining dream work. This insightful invocation allowed him to avoid the unexplainable notion of "wish" (among many wishes), which has no particular privilege to create a dream. It also allowed him to advance the idea that a state of wishing—as the condition of all wishes—is responsible for creating dreams. It is erroneous to say that the *Project* shed his shadow on the whole doctrine of psychoanalysis, and it is more accurate to say that *the* Project *was the embryonic idea of the much bigger project of discovering psychoanalysis that was not cathartic in core.*

Laplanche and Pontalis (1973) said, "If Freud's discovery had to be summed up in a single word, that word would without any doubt have to be 'unconscious'" (p. 474). This sweeping statement is not a frivolous personal opinion. Freud's other discoveries and ideas are meaningful, internally interrelated, and consistent only because the unconscious permeates them all and is fundamental and evident in their fabric. The discovery of psychoanalysis is a result of discovering the unconscious; therefore, the unconscious is not a function of the analytic discovery but the foundation and the structure of that discovery.

Freud had to have a grip on the source of the state of wishing, the primary process that regulates its expression, and the way its expression finds a way to consciousness, issues that the theory of catharsis could not deal with. Even more, this part of his discovery is what has subtly but insistently evolved into the theory of psychoanalysis despite the persistence of the catharsis theory, a theory that could hardly develop beyond its original boundaries and inherent limitations.

Freud tested most of his discoveries in the field of dreams in two other works, one on *Parapraxes* (1901c) and one on *Jokes* (1905c). In doing so he was on his way to understanding the "gibberish" of symptoms, patients' talk, and transference. He entered the realm of the real theory of psychoanalysis without knowing or noticing that the catharsis theory is no longer appropriate or useful.

THE BASIS OF ANOTHER THEORY OF PSYCHOANALYSIS

Freud unveiled three main characteristics of a theory of psychoanalysis from his study of *dreams*, *parapraxes*, and *jokes*: *a theory of psychoanalysis should be a theory of the processes that turn an endosomatic pressure into psychical phenomena, not a theory of the psychical phenomena themselves.* This genuinely unique approach to "psychology" came to make him conclude that the state of wishing (the state that does not change by satisfying the wishes it generates) must have a source, which ought to be constant and perpetual. This quality of the state of wishing cannot but emerge from an endosomatic stimulus. He said:

> The excitation produced by internal needs seek discharge in movement, which may be described as an "internal change" or an "expression of emotion.". . . A change can only come about if in some way or other . . . an "expression of satisfaction" can be achieved which puts an end to the internal stimulus. An essential component of this experience of satisfaction is a particular perception the mnemic image of which remains associated thenceforward with the memory trace of excitation produced by the need. As a result of the link that thus has been established, next time this need arises a psychical impulse will at once emerge which will seek to re-cathect the mnemic image of the perception, . . . to re-establish the situation of the original satisfaction. (1900a, pp. 565–566)

This long sentence describes the way the endosomatic stimulus keeps on being the perpetual source of wishing (the originator) from which both the wish and the recall of the mnemic image of its fulfillment emanate. From a psychologist's point of view I find this elementary fact could not have been said better. From a psychoanalyst's point of view this is a blueprint for a whole theory of psychoanalysis. However, temporarily I will select two ideas from this statement to bring the psychology of wishing to sort of a conclusion: (a) the satisfaction of an endosomatic need *is* a prototype of the wish, and (b) the birth of the psychological from the somatic.

The endosomatic need and the response to it by the caregiver create a memory of satisfaction (mnemic image), and a gap is created between the emergence of the need and the response to it, where the chasm between wanting and getting what is wanted becomes a state of *wishing.* Wishing is the prototype of all human dualities where there is a gap between the wishing person and the satisfaction of her wish (more often it is in the hands of the other); a gap between "me" the wisher and "I" who is the satisfied or frustrated. Psychoanalysis is the analysis of that gap, its creation and the manner of expressing itself to the other. Psychoanalysis is neither a theory of wishes, urges, thoughts, affects, and so on, nor of their frustration/satisfaction; it is the theory of how all those things happen.

The significance of that gap is that similar gaps also exist in other forms: wish and its antiwish, *aconsciousness* and unconsciousness, bound and unbound excitations, primary and secondary processes, and day residues and infantile residues. The psychology of wishing reveals that those gaps are not between different entities but between antitheses, an entity and *its* negative.

The theory of psychoanalysis is founded on recognizing those gaps and their role in creating the "psychical."

The endosomatic source of stimulation that creates the state of wishing emanates from the body and in particular from the erogenic zones. Wishes and their representations are colored by the somatic nature of those erogenic zones. An oral wish will produce oral fantasies and metaphors, and thus will be metonymically conditioned to find in the *Cs./Pcs.* their appropriate equivalents of those metaphors. Notwithstanding the sensibility of that assumption, the problem remains that in our adult lives, it is almost impossible to trace back a dream to a wish, a fantasy or a slip of the tongue to an endosomatic stimulus. Freud did not forgo that difficulty nor did he abandon the intuition of the state of wishing. He addressed this issue by outlining a developmental line, a psychosexual model of development, where the erogenic zones became the seat of the endosomatic pressure on the mind to represent their wishes (*Trieben*, drives or instincts). Yet he complemented that model with a unique and clear understanding of how the endosomatic stimuli continue to be the source of the wish. This development in the theory introduced the issues of sexuality, *Trieb*, narcissism, and the compulsion to repeat.

Freud's understanding of the mnemic image of the wishful experience, as he expressed it, gave the endosomatic source of the wish a prominent place in psychical life in the form of a psychosexual developmental model of the psyche. The psychosexual model of development was complemented by a diagnostic system that related psychopathology to the erogenic zones. The diagnostic system is based on the dynamics of the psychoneuroses, which is the failure of the endosomatic stimulus to create proper ideational images, and thus the failure of bridging that gap (see chapter 6). Although Freud seemed to deviate from that intuition on more than one occasion, he maintained the principle of not resorting to anything from outside the pathological condition to explain psychopathology. He explained the different pathological entities, such as hysteria and the obsessive-compulsive neuroses, from within (intrapsychically) and described their conflicts, defense mechanisms, symptom formations, and sometimes the expected variations in their transferences during treatment, all without resorting to any external factors such as an object relation, a social circumstance, a misconception of the other, and so on. The contemporary psychoanalytic schools do not have a definite theory of psychopathology; consequently they do not have a diagnostic system or concepts of treatment. In those schools all patients have one and the same problem, which is relational failure, and they are all treated in the same way (Green, 2000).

The psychology of wishing forced revisiting concepts of the catharsis theory that needed further elaboration, such as repression and defense mechanisms, and functional insights for which it became possible to consider their structural quality, such as transference, regression, and the negative therapeutic reaction. There were also some clinical benefits from that psychology. The unconscious is problematic in the true sense of the word. Evens et al. (1998), paraphrasing Deleuze, said, "The truth of a problem is measured by its capacity to insist, persist, and return. . . . A problem desires its solution; it [the problem] is the desire for its solution" (p. 270). The unconscious, both in theory and practice, insists, persists, and returns, seeking its solution. On the clinical level, the unconscious is "an absence that is persistent" and without which there could be no veritable meaning for the "present" (the symptom). Every time that absent element is sought after and brought out, it recloaks itself and returns to its state of absence. It has the quality of the wish, which keeps irking the psychical system before and after its fantasmic fulfillment. Most of the time, the analysand tries to capture the transpiring unconscious material and fix it in a conscious context. If the analyst colludes with the patient and agrees to attach causes (intents and contents) to the unconscious material (some analysts even offer such meanings), the act of analysis ceases to be psychoanalysis. The unconscious then is allowed to slip into hiding again, under the guise that it has a conscious bearer, and what stays in consciousness, then, is an empty presence of the unconscious. The solution, as every psychoanalyst learns from "working through" and interpreting the transference, is to achieve (together with the analysand) an understanding that the wish is transient but returns continuously. There is no final analysis after which there will be no unconscious. The psychology of wishing with its parallel *Ucs*. furnishes a very important clinical concept and clarifies a puzzling area of practice, the problem of termination. It is a puzzling problem (as I will show later), which remained so until now, and even led Freud to make his second (and last) psychoanalytic blunder about that subject (Freud, 1937a). The richness of *The Interpretation of Dreams* in intuitions and insights gave it the prominent status it occupies in the psychoanalytic literature. However, there is another feature in that book that makes it an outstanding psychological work: Freud's conclusions about dreams, and later about the other psychical phenomena, came from actual psychological observations on real dreams of real individuals.

Contrary to academic psychology, the psychology of wishing came from wishing individuals who dreamed their wishes and not from dreams of wishing or from wishing dreams. The individual was always present in all the meanings and explanations he reached. This feature is worth special attention because *The Interpretation of Dreams* was not about dreams but about the person who "dreams" the dreams, and later about the neurotic who produced his neurosis. This idea is clearly expressed in Freud's papers, "The Handling of Dream-Interpretation in Psychoanalysis" (1911e). He underscored that interpreting dreams in practice is not an end in its own right. Interpreting dreams is part of understanding the patient, a means to an end. His recommendation to the beginner in the practice of psychoanalysis was not to "retain his interest in the *content* [italics added] of dreams" (1911e, p. 91). Freud stayed at the level of the "first person" in discovering the *Ucs.* (the counterpart) and did not sway from that attitude at any point in his discoveries. The fact that he asked the patient to talk about what he (the patient) claimed not to know made the story of each neurosis a personal one. Moreover, the *Ucs.* meant to Freud that it was missing in the narrative of the patient but was not lost; hence, the *Ucs.* was lost within the person himself and could not be found outside him, and he can retrieve it.

Chapter Six

The Structural Core of the Freudian Doctrine

The Theory of Trieb *and Narcissism*

Around the same time Freud made his breakthrough in *The Interpretation of Dreams* he had a second intuition, or the second part of his first intuition came to him. He wrote to Fliess that a theory of sexuality might be the next work after *The Interpretation of Dreams*. A few months later, he wrote to him again saying, "I am putting together the material for the theory of sexuality and waiting till some spark can set what I have collected ablaze" (1899, January 3–4). It took five more years for that spark to ignite the theory of sexuality. The link between the book on dreams and the one on sexuality had a lasting effect on Freud's mind. Jones (1957) once asked him about his favorite works, and he pointed out his two books on dreams and sexuality in particular (p. 384).

Freud's work on hysteria in particular led him to formulate an etiological theory of psychoneuroses based on the sexual life of patients (1895d,1896a, 1896c, 1898). That theory had three features: (a) Symptoms were responses to sexual frustration or trauma that had caused the patient to repress aspects of it. (b) The energy (libido) of the repressed sexuality was transformed into symptoms. (c) The link between the sexual causation and the symptoms it produced was repressed. It was a plausible etiological theory reflecting the understanding of psychoneuroses at the time. Nonetheless, there were hints in Freud's writings, at the time, that he was becoming aware of "childhood sexuality." Until then he considered infantile sexuality a problem that should be kept merely as an addendum to the theory of catharsis. He understood his patients' recollection of their childhood experiences as products of adults' seductions. However, by 1897 (1897, May 25) he discovered his patients' recounting of their sexual trauma was not especially accurate and that childhood fantasies had almost the same impact on neuroses as on actual events.[1] He did not recognize the significance of infantile sexuality yet to include it in the general theory of psychopathology. His early etiological theory had to be reviewed and revised for that to happen.

Accepting childhood sexuality as a reality was the first step toward revising the causal effect of sex in psychopathology as formulated in the theory of catharsis. He realized that he used repression of sexuality as an explanation for neuroses, but with the existence of infantile sexuality that explanation had to be changed.

SEXUALITY AND THE PROGRESS TOWARD THE CONCEPT OF *TRIEB*

Freud shifted from using sexuality to "explain" psychoneuroses to sexuality as a subject that needed explaining (1905d). This shift is a reminder of the shift he made from the wish as the cause of dreams to the state of wishing as the structure of dreams, a shift that allows understanding dreams as functions of wishing and not as psychical events aimed at fulfilling a wish. However, Freud turned the issue of sexuality upside down in a slightly different way than he did with the wish. Sexuality in the first etiological theory was supposed to be the structure and grammar of the neuroses. However, with adding infantile sexuality and infantile sexual fantasies to sexuality, sexuality became a function of the psychoneuroses. In other words, he shifted the accent from sexual experiences as causes of the neuroses to the patient's particular sexuality as a product of his psychoneurosis. This change announced the start of some deeper explorations into the way it is expressed and manifested as neuroses.

Sexuality, before acknowledging its presence in childhood, was defined as a biological urge that develops quietly until it reaches its maturity, prompting attraction between the opposite sexes aimed at a union between them. This "normal picture of sexuality" was not compatible with several common sexual behaviors, such as sexual deviations, and did not have a place or existence in childhood. Freud's analysis of sexuality in those sexual conditions led him to make a distinction between the sexual object and the sexual aim, of which either becomes the seat of deviation in sexual behavior. The distinction made was influenced by common observations in infantile sexuality, where the sexual aims and sexual objects start unrelated and get connected in the course of maturation. It was a major insight into sexuality, which had been up until then a function that expressed its own purpose, that is, it was both an aim that determined its own object and its object defined its aim. In other words, Freud stipulated that normal sexuality is not separated from its abnormal forms. Different sexual behaviors—normal or abnormal—are determined by sexual preferences or broad inclinations toward different sexual aims and sexual objects. After a reasonable consideration of various types of sexual perversions—deviations in the sexual aim and the sexual object—he concluded,

> Perhaps the sexual instinct itself may be no simple thing, but put together from components which have come apart in the perversions. If this is so, the clinical observations of these abnormalities will have drawn our attention to amalgamations which have been lost to view in the uniform behavior of normal people. (1905d, p. 162)

This insight about the intrastructure of sexuality did not make Freud abandon his etiological theory of sexuality completely. He still felt that there was some merit left in it and said:

> All my experience shows that these psychoneuroses are based on sexual instinctual forces. By this I mean that the energy of the sexual instinct [libido] makes a contribution to the forces that maintain the pathological manifestations (symptoms). I mean expressly to assert that that contribution is the most important and only source of energy of the neurosis and that in consequence the sexual life of the person in question is expressed—whether exclusively or principally or only partially—in these symptoms. (1905d, p. 163)

He tried repeatedly and in vain to give sexuality a new perspective, a place within the etiology of the psychoneuroses. In one attempt, he considered the psychoneuroses the negative form of sexual perversions, begging the question of a unified sexual instinct behind all behaviors. In another attempt, he suggested that symptoms are symbolic expressions of the abnormal sexual life of the patient. He was of the opinion that the psychoneuroses do away with the boundaries of the sexual object to fulfill the perverted sexual aims. Then he reversed the link between sexuality and psychoneuroses, by conceding that an instinct constituted of component elements, such as sexuality, would not be by definition of a primary nature; therefore, there should be a primary instinctual condition from which those components emerge. Henceforth, he proceeded directly to define what he meant by instinct (*Trieb*) and to clarify the possible confusion about the primary and secondary "instinctual" conditions.

He moved the "accent" from sexuality as such to instinct (*Trieb*), the same step he took to move from wish to wishing. His concept of *Trieb* as an originator of activity gave activities a structure and separated the originator from those functions. This distinction has a double significance: The first is that the originator of activity, *Trieb*, is a continuous source of stimulation from within (endosomatic, physiological demands), contrasted with the interruptible stimuli that come from without (external physical world). Therefore, sexual desire is a condition that could not be created by an external object and that fades away after its satisfaction; it does not end by satisfying its excitation. It is also capable of "representing" its endosomatic stimuli psychically and without the instigation of any particular object; it keeps transforming the somatic stimuli into mental representations, thus predisposing it to becoming psychological. This is significant when considering the *Trieb* a continuous source of representations because its place on the frontier between the mental and the physical makes it the foundation of psychical life. Freud (1905d) wrote: "The simplest and likeliest assumption to the nature of *Trieb* would seem to be that in itself an instinct is without content (italics added), and so far as mental life is concerned, it is only to be regarded as a measure of the demand put on the mind to work" (p. 168).

Trieb, as a content-less entity, varies according to the particular organ it is representing, its stimulation of the mind. Freud called those organs erogenic zones. Yet, the source of the *Trieb* is always just a pressure on the mind wherever it originated. That pressure does not differ in its nature but differs in its aims and its corresponding objects that facilitate the discharge of the pressure. This way a *Trieb* could acquire content: the mind has to represent what it receives from that particular erogenic zone because the pressure of a specific zone would produce representations specific to the functions of that zone. Oral representations produce the mental equivalents of incorporation or fantasies of introjection (see Isaacs, 1948). It seems that Freud's development of the concept of wishing affected his conception of Trieb *because its content-less nature gave it, in the theory of sexuality, the same status wishing had in the theory of dreams. Freud moved from an etiological theory based on sexuality as an entity of a definable impulse or a desire that* ***is subject to repression*** to a sexuality that is a manifestation of a more complex structure of several components that have to get integrated.

THE ENDOSOMATIC SOURCE AND THE *TRIEB*

Freud noticed the obvious about sexuality but understood the implicit in that obvious: sexuality is dependent on the participation and the urges arising from several bodily zones that all participate in sexual satisfaction. He called those zones erogenic. He also noticed with a very acute insight that those zones in childhood are main sources of endosomatic stimulation and play a vital role in the child's relation with body and in developing relations with the caregiver. Those two points that Freud reached in his dealings with sexuality allowed him to separate sexuality from its common meaning as an urge that emerges only in maturity in what looks like a final form.

Putting sexuality in the context of *Trieb* allowed Freud three important insights about its link with the endosomatic stimuli. The first insight was that the existence of sexuality in childhood implies that sex is not a static construct (not *Instinkt*) but a developing, evolving entity that starts from a state of primitiveness to reach a state of maturity. It begins with disorganized components noticeable in childhood and aims toward their integration, changing from simple representations to complex psychical structures. The most important characteristic of a developing *Trieb* was the role its earlier forms play in its later organized mature stages. The domination of the genital organ in sexual activities in adulthood is a product of organizing all of the early forms of the sexual attributes.

The second insight is that an intermission in the evolution of the *Trieb* happens around age seven, for a period he called latency, where some amnesia envelops its early experiences, before it reemerges in puberty. The third insight concerned the changes infantile sexuality undergoes during that latency period, such as establishing moral and personal objections to some of its aspects, and the sublimation of some others. Those characteristics showed that the content-less *Trieb* was not just looking for a quality to acquire, but it also develops into the source of a great many human qualities that later define the social meaning of sexuality. Those qualities contribute to structuring a sense of "I-ness" and bring together the attributes of the objects of infantile sexuality and integrate them in a character formation attached to an erogenic zone. In other words, the sexual *Trieb* is not just a complex representation of an endosomatic stimulus; it is also the seat of the sense of I-ness (the person-ality).

The representation of the endosomatic stimulus of each zone integrates with the representation of the stimuli of the previous zones. In this way, a wider and richer attachment to the sexual objects and the external world as whole gradually gets built. By representing the endosomatic stimuli in the mind, the sexual *Trieb* achieves its aim in the most intriguing way: representation functions as a searchlight that discovers, creates, and gets attached to the objects that pave the way to satisfying the aim of the *Trieb*. The basic and final function of the sexual *Trieb* is to copulate, thus procreate, but in doing so it also creates our psychological world with its subjects, objects, values, and significance. In an unusual explication of the origins of psychical life, Freud (1933a, Lecture XXXII) said that the *Trieb* becomes operative psychically on its way from its source in the erogenic zone to its aim, which is satisfaction, passing by the appropriate objects. If that is the case—and it is—then the transformation of the endosomatic into psychical representation is the precondition of the psychoneuroses, or better, the psychoneuroses reveal anomalies in the normal process of mental representation.

Those insights should have convinced Freud (yet did not) that there is no sexual *Trieb*, but that sexuality is available—as content—for *Trieb*; there is no *Trieb* of sexual qualification, but sex could become a *Triebhaft* content. Sexuality in that sense is the urge for representing the emerging powers of the preservation and procreation of life, which starts from infancy and takes place under *Trieb*-like conditions.

Freud had the insight about a link between the endosomatic stimuli and sexuality. As mentioned above, there was no one particular endosomatic source for sexuality. He said: "At its origin it [an infantile sexual manifestation] attaches itself to one of the vital somatic functions; it has as yet no sexual object, and is thus auto-erotic; its sexual aim is dominated by an erogenic zone" (Freud, 1933, Lecture XXXII, pp. 182–183). The pressures of the endosomatic stimuli, which are all the same in nature whatever the source, have one aim (a wish), which is to discharge. This aim could get temporary relief autoerotically. Nonetheless, autoeroticism does not achieve the final aim of the *Trieb*; therefore, the *Trieb* has to discover the object that will help satisfying that aim. This transformation imbues the wish in the other, where it becomes a desire, a wish for the other to wish to respond to that wish. Desire is a wish that has discovered its object, with all the required phantasies about him. Freud expressed this idea by saying, "[The sexual aim] consists in replacing the projected sensation of stimulation in the erogenic zone by an external stimulus which removes that sensation by producing a feeling of satisfaction" (1933, Lecture XXXII, p. 184).

At the beginning, the sexuality attached to the oral vital activity derives pleasure from the satisfaction of the need for nourishment. However, after establishing a pattern of satisfaction for the oral needs, sexuality separates from the vital aim (nourishment), gets attached to the object of that function (the breast), derives its pleasure from it, and makes it the new aim. Sexuality evolves from sucking the breast for nourishment to sucking it for pleasure too and finally using "sucking" only for pleasure (sucking gets unlimited meanings in the daily life of an adult). This understanding of the link between satisfying the vital needs and sexual pleasure raises some questions: Why did Freud label the incidental pleasure that comes from satisfaction sexual, especially since it is usually not more than a decrease in the pressure of somatic need? Doesn't that negate the specificity of sexuality and neutralize it? Why instead, do we not restrict sexual pleasure to the manifestation of the strict discharge and release of sexual pressure? Freud's insight concerning these accompanying queries brings out something unique in the theory to psychoanalysis.

Freud realized that the link between the endosomatic and the sexual was reversible. He said:

> if for instance, the common possession of the labial zone by the two functions [sexuality and nourishment] is the reason why sexual satisfaction arises during the taking of nourishment, then the same factor also enables us to understand

> why there should be disorders of nutrition if the erogenic functions of the shared zone are disturbed. . . . A good portion of the symptomatology of the neuroses, which I have traced to the disturbances of the sexual processes, is expressed in disturbances of other, non-sexual, somatic functions; and this circumstance, which has hitherto been unintelligible, becomes less puzzling if it is only the counterpart of the influences which bring about the production of sexual excitation. (1905d, pp. 205–206)

Granting that the sexual *Trieb* signifies an endosomatic stimulus allowed recognizing that the endosomatic stimulus is amenable to be represented by the sexual *Trieb*. This insight answers the questions about the sexual nature of pleasures. If the two functions reciprocate in the process of representation, it is irrelevant to assign different pleasures to each.

If we put infantile sexuality, sexual perversion, the natural components of the sexual *Trieb*, and the content-less-ness of the *Trieb* all together, it would be difficult to assign all that to the function of sexuality, especially if sexuality is specified as merely a sign of biological maturity and attraction between members of the opposite sex who seek genital union. While Freud was putting all those pieces together he faced a major problem: If sexuality is a *Trieb*, what is *Triebhaft* (instinctual) about it?

THE LIBIDO THEORY: SOLUTION OR PROBLEM?

Freud continued his efforts to find a place for sexuality within a theory of *Trieb*, ostensibly to hold on to his theory of the sexual etiology of the neuroses. The appeal of the sexual etiology of the neuroses was its simple functional formula of providing causation for the "intra-structure" of the neuroses. However, this appeal was incidental and misleading because the sexual cause in that etiology was seen as related to fixed links between sexual events and the neurosis. Understanding of the neurosis this way controverted the notion that the link between the aim and the object of sexuality is arbitrary. The discovery of infantile sexuality and the introduction of the concept of *Trieb* were supposed to obviate falling into the theoretical trap of having a clinical understanding that contradicts its psychopathological model. Although infantile sexuality played a role in avoiding that trap, its result was not fully successful.

Freud's persistence in finding a place for sexuality in a theory of *Trieb* drove him to look for a concept of energy that could adapt to the different transformations of the *Trieb* in its movement from one erogenic zone to another and was plastic enough to conform to the aims and objects of each zone. He also had to discover another *Trieb* that could stand counter to the sexual *Trieb* and become its antithesis. An antithetical *Trieb* was indispensable to explaining the formation of symptoms in terms of conflict, which is the psychoanalytic paradigm of the catharsis theory. He chose the Latin libido, which means “lustful wish,” and is used as the energy of sexuality. He said: “We have defined the concept of libido as a quantitatively variable force which could serve as a measure of processes and transformations occurring in the field of sexual excitation” (1933, Lecture XXXII, p. 217). Hence, the theory of sexuality gradually became a theory of libido, and Freud draw a distinction between it and another libido that belongs to vital functions.

The sexual *Trieb* was contrasted with a *Trieb* that manages life functions. He had to tackle the difficulties presented by the libido theory in regard to the source of the life *Trieb*. He presupposed that both the sexual and the vital libidos originate from the same source and primarily coexist undifferentiated at the source (1923b). The source of both libidos, as he concluded, was the erogenic zones and their difference was chemical (although he admitted that difference was not detectable or verifiable, and it still isn’t). As they activate they begin the process of differentiation; the sexual function splits from the vital function, and each takes a different course of development. But that conception faced a significant obstacle. Each time the child moves to the next erogenic zone, we should assume that the two libidos start in an entwined state to separate once again, and so on. This view creates many theoretical difficulties because the movement from one stage to the next would happen—in that model in leaps—since the separation of the two libidos is voided in the next stage. Are there different libidos for each stage of development?

Libido is a term given to the energy of both functions—sexual and vital—in their original entwined condition. The vagueness in their different natures led Freud to a very unfortunate theoretical formulation that had a lasting impact on psychoanalysis (see chapter 7). Instead of examining the mistake of giving *Trieb* different contents he referred the distinction to the libido. The distinction he made was that the libido in its original condition is one and is invested in the ego and called the ego “the great reservoir of libido from which libido is sent to objects and which is always ready to absorb libido flowing from objects” (1905b, p. 218). The libido diverges soon after and gets invested in objects, seeking pleasure, which he called object-libido. To clarifying the matter, he said, “We thus reach the idea of quantity of libido, to the mental representation of which we give the name ‘ego-libido,’ and whose production, increase or diminution, distribution and displacement should afford us the possibility for explaining the psychosexual phenomena observed” (1905b, p. 218). It is not clear whether what he meant by libido was the sexual energy or an energy that would differentiate later into sexual and vital energies. He proceeded to call the vital functions with their libido “ego-*Trieb*” and changed the name a little later to “self-preservation *Trieb*” (1910c, pp. 213–216). Freud was obviously struggling with finding a suitable vocabulary that fits a model emerging in his mind of sexuality as an evolving function emanating from erogenic zones. He set up the vital functions of those zones as the antithesis of the sexual *Trieb* (reminds one of the wish creating its antithesis in dreams). He envisaged the two libidos in conflict because they differed in their aims: one aimed to satisfy the vital needs and the other to pleasure. This model was not only without a suitable vocabulary, but it was also confusing: Was he on the verge of a new libido theory in which one libido would have two states based on where it was invested, or was he doing away with a separate theory of sexuality (1923a)? Freud even raised that question earlier: "Would not the postulation of a single kind of psychical energy save us all the difficulties of differentiating an energy of the ego-libido from the ego-*Trieb*, and ego libido from object libido?" (1914a, p. 76). However, he continued with the two kinds of libido because he insisted on differentiating between ego-*Trieben* and sexual *Trieben* (1914a, p. 77). The libido theory that came to solve the problem of what was *Triebhaft* in sexuality proved to be a problem in its own right.

Sexuality in the libido theory hit two main snags. First, the concept of self-preservation did not fit the attributes of the *Triebhaft*. In self-preservation, the internal relationships between the source (nourishment), the pressure (hunger), the aim (feeding), and the object (food) were direct, static, and unconditional; self-preservation was therefore more of an Instinkt than a *Trieb* (Holder, 1970). As a result, the sexual *Trieb* was in a precarious situation, being a concept without an antithesis. The second snag was in the sources of infantile sexuality. Because infantile sexuality was no longer an addendum to the general theory of sexuality, it became the raison d'être of the sexual etiology of the neuroses and sexual perversions. Freud attributed infantile sexuality to (a) the reproduction of a pleasurable experience that was associated with a physical process (anaclisis), (b) appropriate peripheral (external) stimulation of the erogenic zones, and (c) the expression of certain "instincts" (such as the scopophilic instinct and the instinct of cruelty), whose origin was not yet completely intelligible (1905d, pp. 200–201).

Those sources raise very important questions about the place of sexuality in a theory of *Trieb*. The first erogenic zone could be considered *Triebhaft*, because the satisfaction of a vital function such as nursing could produce pleasurable sensations; later, when the satisfaction is separated from its function, it would take on sexual significance as an aftereffect process (differed-action, see Freud, 1905, p. 141, n. 46).[2] An external stimulus is not capable of instigating *Triebhaft* reactions before the erogenic zone is ready for it, and that indicates that *Trieb* could not have an exo-somatic source. Content-less *Trieb* in an erogenic zone acquires its content from that zone but only after the zone has been prepared earlier by external stimulation, a stimulation that remained meaningless when it first happened. Although it is true that external stimulation of an erogenic zone in childhood could bring about pleasurable excitations, those excitations would contribute only to psychopathology in an aftereffect process.

The third source introduced a new set of *Trieben*, which from the outset were without an endosomatic origin. It is acceptable to presume the existence of other sources of excitation in infantile sexuality that are felt in other parts of the infant's body, such as touch, smell, and sight, but those excitations should be attributed to a *Trieb*-like source because their initiators are external objects and not endosomatic sources. Within the limits of a concept of *Trieb*, only touch could qualify as *Triebhaft* in infantile sexuality, while the other two, being of a different nature, do not qualify.

Identifying of the sources of infantile sexuality in this manner suggests that Freud was not applying his conception of *Trieb* and was still preoccupied with the issue of sexuality as he understood it in his early discoveries in hypnosis. After a few years of groping with this issue he said, "In my opinion . . . the question of how far we are to carry the undoubtedly justifiable separation between the sexual and self-preservative instincts is not of much importance for psycho-analysis. Nor is psycho-analysis competent to answer the question" (1916–1917, p. 413). For the sexual theory to remain a theory of etiology the sexual libido should maintain its sexual quality, whether it is invested in an object or regressed to reinvest in the ego.

Freud endeavored to solve this problem by introducing a new idea of development that interlocked with the model of the erogenic zones. He said: "[F]urther development . . . has two aims: the abandonment of auto-erotism, or the replacing of the subject's own body once more by an outside object, and secondly the unification of the various objects of the separate instincts and their replacement by a single object" (1916–1917, p. 329). The new idea was based on a previous notion that the "sexual libido" supposedly advances from the point where it was entwined with the vital in the ego toward a bodily zone of the body. The libido theory, although still hanging on to sexuality, was no longer able to avoid its basic problem: deciding whether the libido defines its object or the object defines the libido. Better though, is sexual energy or sexuality merely one of the manifestations of an energy that is no different from the quota of affect (1894a)? Freud said: "The concept of the quota of affect corresponds to the instinct in so far as the latter has become detached from the idea and finds expression, proportionate to its quantity, in processes which are sensed as affect" (1915a, p. 152).

The libido theory was flawed because the content-less *Trieb* that was established to be endosomatically formless was transformed into a psychical function simply by separating from the ego in search of content. Laplanche and Pontalis (1973) said, "The notion of 'ego-libido' does in fact entail a generalization of the libidinal economy so as to embrace the whole of the interplay between cathexes and anticathexes, while whatever overtones of subjectivity the term 'libido' may have had hitherto are attenuated; as Freud acknowledges, the libido theory becomes frankly speculative" (p. 240). Libido was introduced to support the plasticity of sexuality but ended up stuck in a fixed sexual modality.

The difficulties the libido theory encountered and also created resulted from setting up a series of awkward dualities between ego interests and a sexual *Trieb*, sexual *Trieb* and self-preservation *Trieb*, and self-preservation *Trieb* and ego-*Trieb*. Finally, Freud settled on a duality of ego-libido and object-libido. This was the least challenging duality from a metapsychological point of view but more of a theoretical challenge than expected. It meant that instead of the libido identifying its objects, the objects identified the quality of the libido, and we could have one libido in two forms decided by where it is invested.

When Freud introduced the concept of narcissism he said:

> I should like at this point [of arguing the separation of the two libidos, ego and sexual] expressly to admit that the hypothesis of separate ego-instincts and sexual instincts (that is to say, the libido theory) rests scarcely at all upon a psychological basis, but derives its principal support from biology. But I shall be consistent enough [with my general rule] to drop this hypothesis if psychoanalytic work should itself produce some other, more serviceable hypothesis about the instincts. (1914c, p. 79)

The notion of narcissism came from a libido that takes the self as its object (i.e., it longs for itself, as Narcissus longed for himself in the myth).

NARCISSISM: RETHINKING THE LIBIDO THEORY

The idea of the libido being originally a property of the ego that differentiates later to invest some of it in sexuality means that it could also go back to its initial condition in the ego. The notions of an original singular libido invested in the ego (*Ich*, I) and a possible regression to that origin after its differentiation forced the concept of narcissism on the libido theory.

We should bear in mind that some transformations and changes happen to the libido when it separates from the body (ego) to invest in an object. Therefore, it is not the same libido when it regresses to be reinvested in it. The regression of the libido from the breast to the thumb would treat the thumb as a substitute for the breast and would yearn for the thumb as it loved the breast. This longing for the thumb is not possible before the infant "knew" the breast. Freud called that regressed libido "narcissistic libido." Although the libido theory put in focus the issue of progression and the succession of psychical events (ego before object, or life preservation before sex, pleasure before reality, etc.), it did not address a major problem implicit in those dualities: Is the sequel a function of the prequel, or are they unrelated. Is the sexual *Trieb* a function of or does it have a functional link to the ego-*Trieb*? This problem could be regard as frivolously academic, but it is not: Is psychoneurosis a sequel to sexual causes with libidinal contents, or is the sexual content of psychoneurosis a sequel to psychopathology?

The difficulties of the libido theory forced Freud to do what he did before: abandon the functional thinking about it and seek a structural understanding. He did that by using narcissism beyond its limited libidinal connotations and was disposed to formulate a theory of psychopathology set up on narcissism instead of a psychopathology caused by sexuality. The new budding theory incorporated the human subject and his psychical makeup in the fabric of a formative process instead of as isolated causes; he did that in an ingenious way.

Freud suggested that the libido in its singular condition or the autoerotic phase (ego libido) does not move to attach to an object (object libido) at once. It passes through a narcissistic phase first where the body (self) becomes a primary object. The libido then moves from the narcissistic investment in the subject to an external object. The theory of narcissism necessitated replacing sexuality with a theory of progression from the primary states of affairs to their secondary forms, passing by an intermediate phase. Temporarily, and until I deal with this point in detail later, narcissism was a theoretical change in which the primary state of affairs included the wish, affect, *Trieb*, and sexual libido. The secondary forms were desires (wishes gained objects), representations (*Trieb* produced mental contents), and a narcissistic libido (libido moved from its initial autoerotic base or regressed to it after it progressed).

The mere change of the term "sexual-libido" or "ego-libido" to "narcissistic-libido" would not, as is, have changed anything significant in the theory. However, it had an unintended significance of far-reaching results. If the ego is the reservoir of the libido and its transformations start from there, then the ego must have existed before any libido was ever formed—another major theoretical paradox. Freud was no longer able to brace the mechanical model of "an ego defending itself" or a psyche produced by the success or failure of strengthening the ego. It became clear that ego was becoming problematic because Freud tried hard to find a place for narcissism in the catharsis theory and he took the ego as the crossing bridge.

The innocuous existence of a narcissistic stage in every developmental phase revealed to Freud the necessity of dealing with the formation of the ego, the libido, *Trieb*, and even narcissism itself. It made more sense to consider the ego a product of narcissism rather than assume the existence of the ego prior to any and all other psychical events, phenomena, or systems. He wrote:

> I may point out that we are bound to suppose that a unity comparable to the ego cannot exist in the individual from the start; the ego has to be developed. The autoerotic instincts, however, are there from the very first; so there must be something added to autoerotism—a new psychical action—in order to bring about narcissism. (1914c, p. 76)

It is peculiar that though Freud agreed to the idea that the ego could not be the primary component of the psyche, he did not pursue this issue any further. The ego was neither the whole individual nor none of the individual, or could be taken as a particular aspect of the individual. He deduced instead that narcissism must have a primary state, which accounts for the fluctuations of libidinal investments, a process delegated before to the ego.

REVISION OF THE CORE CONCEPTS OF THE CATHARSIS THEORY

If we intended to direct our attention to Freud's method of reasoning and not his declared thought, we will notice that every time his functional thinking produced an erroneous conception he managed to deduce the right concepts or to induce a totally new understanding of matters. He realized the limitations of the functional conceptions of the psyche and went forward toward a structural approach and a purely psychoanalytic theory. The breakdown of the libido theory and the emergence of the concept of narcissism necessitated revising the core concepts of the catharsis theory.

The near collapse of the libido theory required a revision of the four main functional concepts of the catharsis theory: *Trieb*, repression, the unconscious, and making changes to the concept of regression to match those revisions. *Trieb* is indispensable in a theory of the transformation of something originary into a representation. The failure of the duality of sexual/self-preservation *Trieben* required reexamination to find another duality that could replace the old one. This had to wait for five more years before he came up with the duality of life/death *Trieben*. Furthermore, the method of free association eventually revealed that repression was no longer enough to explain all that happens to the "unacceptable urges." Freud discovered that the unconscious is not a function of defense; accordingly, its function as a defense mechanism had to yield to a new understanding of what happens to the endosomatic stimuli before they become targets for repression. This was a step toward reviewing the unconscious not because repression looked capable of creating only the preconscious but because clinical observation asserted that some material is unconscious though not repressed (later Freud called it the non-repressed unconscious; 1923b). The revisions of those three concepts put psychoanalysis on a different platform: a theory of psychoanalysis is about the way things happen and not why they happen. One other old functional concept that needed a structural revision was regression; Freud came up with a very ingenious understanding of that process, which, in a peculiar way, fit right in with his new theory of psychoanalysis.

Trieben (1915c)

Freud went back to his original and fundamental intuition of *Trieb*: it is an endosomatic pressure on the mind to represent its source in order to gain its aim through an object. He dealt with those four constituents, emphasizing that the sources are fixed and limited in flexibility compared to the wide range of flexibility the aim and the object have. With this recapitulation of the concept Freud introduced two changes. First, *Trieb* was no longer attributed to a certain urge such as sexuality but to somatic sources, of which sex is one. Moreover, the aim that should choose the object of the *Trieb* could be influenced or tamed by the availability of the object(s). Second, *Trieb* in light of this description is subject to a wide range of vicissitudes. In other words, *Trieb* has moved from being the function of representing a specific urge to being the structural basis of the process of representation (in general), which is endowed with rich potentials for selecting the representations. He complemented this fundamental modification with a significant idea: *Trieben* start fragmented but eventually and through development and maturation they integrate into a holistic entity under the domination of one organizing bodily zone. This addition came from his preoccupation with sexuality as the heart of *Triebhaft*, but it fit well in the model of identification, which was subjected to a parallel revision around the same time. Identification starts as fragmentations of the me and the I to end up in a unified I that stands metaphorically for a bodily zone, me (oral, genital, etc.).

In spite of Freud's inability to give up the first duality of sex/self-preservation when and while modifying the concept of *Trieb*, his departure from the functional concept to its structural attribute exposed more weakness in that duality. The vicissitudes he mentioned (reversal to opposite, turning upon the self, repression and sublimation) do not fit the sex/self-preservation duality. Instead of a detailed explication of this point I will just say that if somehow those vicissitudes could be observed in sexuality, they cannot be envisaged as antithesis in the self-preservation *Trieb*.

In a roundabout way Freud introduced feelings in the evolution of narcissism in which self-love advances to loving an object as a substitute for the self and as an intermediate step toward object love. He was thus able to deal with new clinical phenomena such as love/hate, masochism/sadism, and ambivalence.

The revision of the *Trieb* concept was overlooked by most analysts and to a degree by Freud himself. The revision uncovered the structuring process of the *Trieb*, which determines the nature of several other psychical phenomena and is not a product of some psychical event. Better, *Trieb* denoted what happens to an endosomatic stimulus, whichever, after it succeeds in initiating the mind to action.

Repression (1915d)

With the demise of the duality of sex/self-preservation *Trieben*, the concept of repression was left in a precarious state: If it is not the mechanism of expelling the undesirable sexual urges from consciousness, what would its function be in a theory of *Trieben* that has no content and is almost totally structural? Freud (1915d) raised some logical contradictions in a concept of repression that could be just a function of frustrating the satisfaction of a *Trieb*. He went back to his two papers on "The neuro-psychosis of defense" (1894a, 1896b) to bring out the notion that the representation of the *Trieb* comprises an idea and an affect, which are both not permitted entrance to consciousness (i.e., repressed). This notion implied the necessity of separating those two components and targeting the ideational element to prevent it from entering consciousness, yet allowing only its derivative to do that, and under some conditions, where that is not met, they will be "properly repressed." He says in that regard:

> [W]e have reason to assume that there is a primal repression, a first phase of repression, which consists in the psychical (ideational) representative of the instinct being denied entrance into consciousness. With this a fixation is established. . . . The second stage of repression proper, affects mental derivatives of the repressed representative, or such trains of thought as originating elsewhere, have come into associative connections with it. . . . Repression proper, therefore, is actually an after-pressure (1915d, p. 148).

The recognition of the two phases of repression is an important revision because it dealt with a process that starts internally to limit the entrance of the *Trieb* to consciousness by first separating its two components, allowing the ideational to generate derivatives and permitting the derivatives entry into consciousness. In the second stage those derivatives would submit to a process of repression similar to what is exercised when stopping an external stimulus from entering consciousness. The fact of the matter is that Freud did not revise the functional concept of repression but discovered a precondition for repression (proper) to happen, which is structural in nature. He says: "Psycho-analytic observation of the transference neuroses, moreover, leads us to conclude that repression is not a defensive mechanism which is present from the beginning, and that it cannot arise until a sharp cleavage has occurred between conscious and unconscious mental activity" (1915d, p. 147). This precondition happens, as he says, in "the dark" and is not subjected to any conscious judgment; it almost happens spontaneously, unconditionally, even predictably. Nevertheless, what is even more significant in this statement is the separation of the conscious and the unconscious before any repression takes place, which means that the unconscious creates repression and not the reverse, as it is in the catharsis theory. Moreover, the conscious and the unconscious become structures that predate imbuing them with any content.

The psychoanalytic observation that led Feud to the existence of a primal repression led also to two other significant observations. Primary repression is a process that creates derivatives of what is kept unconscious, while repression proper is a defensive measure. The productions of the derivatives of the unconscious keep going and establish more links with the originary repressed (ideation or affect). The more distant the derivative from the original source the more likely it will find a prospect to enter consciousness. Better, primary repression is the process that distances the repressed from its derivative. It applies the working of the primary process to do that. Therefore, primary repression is not an event that takes place once but an ongoing process that keeps the repressed indecipherable by distancing it from its origin as long as it is generated endosomatically.

In another observation, as he says: "[S]ome other element representing the instinct has to be taken into account, and that other element undergoes *vicissitudes* [my emphasis] of repression which may be quite different from those undergone by the idea. For this other element of psychical representative the term quota of affect has been generally adopted" (p. 152). The distinction Freud made between the two attributes of the *Trieb* is significant in more than one way. The *Trieb* is considered exclusively, for the first time, in its structuring quality (i.e., the originary of the process of representation). As such, it is the term to use when talking about the emergence of anything psychical, whether ideational or affective, and even the link or the missing link between them. The main issue, as it seems from what Freud has revised, is not the repressed but how repression happens and whether it is as simple as it was used in the catharsis theory. He added a statement:

> The quantitative factor of the instinctual representative has three possible vicissitudes, as we can see from a cursory survey made by psycho-analysis: either the instinct is altogether suppressed, so that no trace of it is found, or it appears as an affect which is in some way or other qualitatively coloured [pleasure or pain], or is it changed into anxiety. The two latter possibilities set us the task of taking into account, as a further instinctual vicissitude, the transformation into affects, and especially into anxiety, of the psychical energies of instincts. (p. 153)

We could say that the "wish" is the affective condition of the *Trieb* because it signifies the state of pleasure and displeasure depending on its fulfillment or frustration. It is clear that the revision Freud made to the concept of repression dovetails the revision he made to the concept of *Trieb* because without that the notion of vicissitudes would have been a clinical conjecture, with no theoretical foundation.

The Unconscious (*Ucs.*) (1915e)

Knowing what we know now about the unconscious we realize that Freud discovered the preconscious by using hypnosis. When he began to listen to his patients' associations and moved to the study of dreams and recognized another unconscious that was mostly unrepressed, or as he said later: "The unconscious has a wider compass: the repressed is a part of the unconscious" (1915e, p. 166). Most importantly, he realized that the unconscious is not a function of repression but a psychical structure that has its own way of functioning. This was a shift in the meaning of the unconscious, which was formulated before the characterization of the wish in dreams. It is the originary that generates a corollary such as the state of excitation. Although his first revision of the system of unconscious in dreams was a major, if not the major, discovery of the whole doctrine, it was not yet suggestive of what was to come later because he still gave the wish the generic content of what he found in the preconscious. Yet, as usual, he came up with a most puzzling conclusion from his store of dreams by stating that a conscious wish has to have a link with a childhood wish to instigate a dream (1900a, p. 553).[3] Intuitions like that keep one wondering what could have generated them: Were they there originally, or did they unexpectedly emerge at the realizing, mistaking a mistake?

Freud reached his revision of the concept of unconscious through an examination of the function of consciousness, concluding by saying: "[W]hat is proved is not the existence of a second consciousness in us, but the existence of psychical acts which lack consciousness" (1915e, p. 170). In other words, he concluded that the unconscious is structurally (substantively) distinct from the conscious and preconscious systems (adjectivally); he assigned the abbreviated *Ucs.* (italicized) to that unconscious to distinguish it from any other meaning of unconscious. This conclusion was evoking the topographic system, in chapter 7 of *The Interpretation of Dreams*, with a noteworthy difference: The differences between consciousness and the unconscious is not quantitative; they are qualitatively distinct, or as he said: "[C]onscious and unconscious ideas are distinct registrations, topographically separated, of the same content" (1915e, p. 176). The topographic attribute of the mental system is the foundation of the very significant and intriguing process of aftereffect (see chapter 10).

Freud answers the question of what could be aconscious, and the answer was the *Trieb*, which can never become conscious. Positioning *Trieb* within a new conception of *Ucs.* led to understanding what happens "in the dark" in primary repression. The emergence of an endosomatic stimulus pressuring the mind to represent it faces the problem of not being admissible to consciousness not because it is objectionable (there are no moral criteria in infancy regarding what is objectionable, let alone objectionable endosomatic stimuli). It is inadmissible because as pressure it is indistinguishable from any other; thus would have to get an ideational form first to enter consciousness and its affect (sensation) to be transformed into wish. Therefore, Freud offered a "psychological" interpretation for that split: the ideational transformation of the *Trieb* requires its pressure to be associated with a thing and represent that thing first (sexual pressure represented in the thing penis). The door opens for the *Trieb* to keep changing that representation until it reaches the stage where words stand for things. The derivatives of the endosomatic continue substituting things with words, newer and better ones (or worse), until a fixation interrupts that process.

In the early conception of the unconscious (in the purely catharsis theory) Freud was talking about the dynamics that creates it, as it was considered a function of the interplay of the power of urges and the power of suppression (i.e., it was dynamically unconscious). When he reintroduced the topographical conception of the psychical system with its three entities of *Cs./Pcs.* and *Ucs.* he gave the *Ucs.* a topographic meaning in the sense that it became a registry in a separate "location" in that system, which colors its nature by the working of the primary process (i.e., a topographical unconscious). However, under the influence of the catharsis theory he looked at the unconscious from the angle of the distribution of the cathexis invested in its content compared to what is invested in the other two systems. A third meaning of unconscious was established (i.e., an economical unconscious). Those three implications became the basis of metapsychology as Freud defined it later.

In this seminal work (1915e) Freud introduces a very different conception of what we listen to in free associations: We listen to a patient saying two things in the same sentence and by the same words. He talks consciously of what he chooses, intends to say, and unconsciously expresses the derivatives of the endosomatic representation that seeps through the same verbal network. It does not enter consciousness not because it is unacceptable and has to be disguised but because it says things that were formed "in the darkness of infancy and childhood" and were configured in a primary process language, which is not understandable in secondary language formations and needs time and a tour of associations to lead to its origin.

Freud's revision of the concept of the unconscious allows a psychological formulation of the concept. The *Trieb* splits into affective and ideational component as the means to getting the chance to be represented in the mind, first by a thing and then by a word, followed by entering the domain of human relations. Its affective component will have another course of evolvement (see chapter 6), hence the notion of primary repression.

Regression

Freud introduced the term regression in *The Interpretation of Dreams* (1900) to explain the pictorial nature of dreams. The notion was that a wish that is barred from the psychomotor facilities tends to go back to its sensory (hallucinatory) state; in this way it regresses topographically to an earlier period of its initiation. He published a paper on the metapsychology of dreams (1917d), which was "used" to deal with the issue of regression and expand it. After a comparison between dreaming, hallucinating, and reality testing he made distinctions between three modes of regression: topographic, meaning returning to an earlier stage of the function (sensation before attention); temporal, meaning going back to an earlier phase of development (infantile period); and formal, meaning a primitive quality of the process (primary process attributes). It is not difficult to notice the parallelism between the tripartite division of regression and the three meanings of the unconscious not only in number but also in quality. Regression was no longer, in this revision, a function of repression but a condition of an internal structuring process producing different psychical phenomena.

This revision postulates a new theory of psychoanalysis derived directly from the patients' associations, or coming from nothing else but those associations. The patient's speech displays those three formats together. The symptom demonstrates the failure of a function in meeting its expectations (topographic), and its content relates to some earlier and infantile experience (temporal) and reveals the working of the primary process in its structure (formal).

The four concepts, in their revised form, introduce a different angle for looking at psychoanalysis. Since *Trieb* is obliged to deal with its ideational attribute separately from its affective attribute and is endowed with the capacity to represent each differently, the *Trieb* was liberated from an a priori content, as sexuality, to become the origin of representing its particular endosomatic source (i.e., being the structuring force behind representations). Therefore, the *Triebhaft*, or the urges, are not subject to rejection and repression but are subject to the working of the primary process as their means to get represented since they are not repressible. Repression is no longer a mechanism of preventing the *Triebhaft* from entering the conscious but of preventing a derivative of the ideational aspect of the *Trieb* to enter unmodified by the primary process. The formation of derivatives of *Trieb* is the core of the topographic unconscious (*Ucs.*). First, it is a-conscious,[4] meaning that as a process its onset is never conscious and does not give indications of its existence before it produces the first features of a derivative. Second, its formation within the boundaries of the primary process leaves an indelible important imprint on the production of the future series of derivatives; hence, it unconsciously determines the character of the individual. The *Ucs.* in that way is not something to work on to reveal and eliminate but an aspect of the individual that requires exploring and rearranging. If there is regression to any point of fixation, it will be a regression to a *Triebhaft* structure, whose derivatives were stemming from a structural point of regression and corresponding to an appropriate repressive mechanism.

Those revisions came about after realizing that their functional connotations were no longer satisfactory in light of the decline of the libido theory. Freud moved from the clinical basis of his catharsis theory to the "natural" condition of those concepts, which he encountered in free associations and ordinary speech of people. He noticed the way they are and not the way they are not, as it happens in pathological conditions.

Freud's attempts to revise the four core concepts of the catharsis theory was to "improve" that theory. They revealed the concepts' structuring capacities and a new view of the psyche. Although there is no convincing evidence in Introductory Lectures on Psychoanalysis (1916–1917) that Freud utilized those revisions to revise the theory of psychoanalysis, the absence of the catharsis conceptions is noticeable in two important papers that came after the revisions (1917c, 1919h). The real significance of the revisions would be appreciated more, and the features of the new theory of psychoanalysis would get clearer if the revisions are put in the context of the meaning of the psychical: What is psychical, what is not, and how could we identify that?

NARCISSISM AND REPETITION COMPULSION: THE ISSUE OF IDENTIFICATION

A few years after including narcissism in the theory of psychoanalysis, Freud published a puzzling work: *Beyond the Pleasure Principle* (1920a). It introduced a new *Triebhaft* duality of life and death to replace the previous duality of sex and self-preservation. Freud pronounced two reasons for that shift—one clinical to understand the phenomena of aggression, sadism, masochism, hate, and ambivalence, and the other theoretical to account for the phenomenon of the compulsion to repeat. The clinical reason was conspicuously weak. Strangely, those phenomena did not constitute any theoretical problems before and seemed to have had some explanation in the catharsis theory. They were even explainable in terms of the first *Triebhaft* duality. Besides, they did not get substantially clearer in the new duality of life/death.

Nevertheless, Freud raised some interesting issues about primary sadism and masochism, suggesting that they might be dormant conditions in humans waiting for an occasion to sprout content and express themselves. This was a far-fetched suggestion but plausible in light of the theory of *Trieb* and the old concept of bound and unbound states of excitation (1895b). The phenomenon of the compulsion to repeat is worth looking at more carefully because it was not a new clinical discovery that needed theorizing; it was a commonly shared factor in all the psychoneuroses. Before giving it this exact denotation, it came under the term fixation, which although it implied a sort of pathology was also used obliquely to mean a point in the natural progress of the libido.

Freud talked about fixation in that dual meaning, but in 1920 he distinguished it from the compulsion to repeat and assigned the pathological condition to the latter. It looks as if suddenly Freud had an insight that fixation and the compulsion to repeat are two separate things. But Freud's insights have proven before to come from silent (dormant) recognition of the existence of right answers behind the previous wrong observations, a latency that gradually sprang into action with retroductive revealing of the right order of things. We should consider the turning point of the 1920s, which included the distinction between fixation and the compulsion to repeat in the context of what happened between 1914 and 1920. In those six years Freud discovered the formative nature of identification and the concept of narcissism, revised the core concepts of the catharsis theory, and recognized the need for a new configuration of the theory of psychoanalysis. Therefore, we should ask: Is there a link between the revisions Freud made and the distinction between the compulsion to repeat and fixation? If so, what is the order of the few things he initiated before coming to the theory of life/death duality? It is important to underline that the concept of the compulsion to repeat does relate in a definite way to the new *Triebhaft* duality of life and death.

The first theory of *Trieb* displayed a dynamic interplay between the preservation of the specie (sex) and the preservation of the individual (self-preservation). An improved version of that duality portrayed the conflict to be between the power of pleasure (sexuality) and the strength of the ego (restriction). The problems created by that duality, even in its "improved version," boil down to the loss of its dialectical nature, where one is the antithesis of the other. The libido, as the theory of narcissism showed, is not qualitatively distinct or different in the two poles of that duality. In other words, duality as a cornerstone of the Freudian doctrine seemed to be losing its mooring in the theory. But Freud's heuristic explorations in *Beyond the Pleasure Principle* have the characteristics of a search for something. Despite the need to pay attention to the phenomenon of "emergence" in a theory of psychoanalysis, he still kept duality within its functional importance. He was looking for something that should be there to explain something that has been discovered but is waiting to be defined.

Freud intuitively approached life and death as the bedrock of human duality, which explains the most basic phenomenon in human nature: the ongoing state of becoming, evolving, and dying. Although this might sound ambitious, speculative, and not psychoanalytic, it is actually an elaboration of Freud's insight about the life and death *Trieben* as "the instincts par-excellence." Better, as he said, the most valuable knowledge to us is the common characteristics and possible distinctive features of *Trieben*, for which we would not find a duality to get us there better than the duality of life and death. There is a subtle but unquestionable puzzle in the duality of life and death (1920g).

Life *Trieb* (Eros) is expressed in love, self-preservation, attraction, the propensity to unite, and the pleasure of relating. Those attributes carry the shadow of narcissism, even in the popular, simplistic conception of the word. Yet narcissism is, at the same time, the source of the hatred of what interferes with self-interest, the propensity to withdraw into one's self, "selfishness" in relating to others, and enduring lifeless relationships. It is also the psychical state that we encounter ambivalence and the emergence of contradictory *Triebhaft* tendencies. Narcissism presented potential dualities that stand between life and death; this way needed to be structuralized.

A life *Trieb* is easier to accept if only because it denotes something we know and observe around us. The problem with the death *Trieb* starts with the name. It is supposed to denote what is before psychical life, and what is after it ceases to function. However, there are no manifestations that could specify any of its different attributes beside its finality. It is also difficult to distinguish the psychical representations of the death *Trieb*, even in its symbolic forms, because aggression, hate, sadism, and masochism are not representation of that *Trieb* are its behavioral manifestations. Moreover, defining it in terms of source, pressure, aim, and object is only possible (if it is possible) through speculation. The concept has created a great deal of arguments, and most analysts relinquished it for various reasons, mostly related to its clinical irrelevance and the relative ease to understand the so-called derivatives like sadism and aggression, seperately. We do not see in Freud's purely biological evidence of the death *Trieb* a psychological equivalent that relates to our practices or its other applications. However, as we are in a speculative area of the theory we should keep our speculative abilities sharp and rely on them to determine whether we could or should keep the death *Trieb* in the theory.

As pointed out before, the death instinct emerged after narcissism had taken a significant position in the theory, if not because of that. Therefore, we might find something in narcissism that could shed light on the death instinct. Given that the term was derived from the myth of Narcissus[5] to illustrate a psychological case, I would like to do an exercise in psychoanalytic thinking. Tentatively I will work from the myth back to the theory of psychoanalysis, with the assumption that if I do that correctly I might find in the myth what I am looking for: the link between narcissism and death. I might discover in this exercise what prompted Freud to suggest, in a casual manner, a link between the two concepts.

The underlying theme in the myth of Narcissus is a theme of love that ends in death (see note 5): Echo loved first and faded away in her voice and vanished. Her death is symbolic of the death of the self in the futile act of communicating with the narcissist or the other as counterpart. Narcissistic patients do not have the ability to act directly on their desires; they need to find (create) a counterpart who would tell them what to act upon. The patient most likely splits himself into the false self and its counterpart and is demonstrated from what we regularly hear from our patients: "I said to myself you better do . . . or as I always say." Narcissus's death came after falling in love with that other in the lake (his counterpart). Narcissus withered away into his image and vanished, not knowing that he had known himself. His death was an imaginary death because as he died his image also went with him. Echo died as a subject that had no counterpart, and Narcissus died as an imaginary counterpart who had no subject.

The phantasmic aim in narcissism is a symbol of an absence in a presence and a symbolic presence in an absence. The narcissistic patient lives as an I that has no me, as an I without something to suggest that it pertains to the person. In this manner, when he talks about his self he talks about someone who is absent. He is a person without a desire to articulate because if there is a desire to be mentioned it is something for which he waits for the other to suggest to him (I said to myself). The I of the narcissist is a creation of another who has no genuine desire because it is what the other wanted him to have (mostly imaginarily), and as it sometimes happens, the opposite of what the other articulates. The narcissistic person is psychologically dead: he cannot live in the absence of his me and only through an I that represents this lack and can only be a false counterpart for another. Narcissistic attachment illustrates the impossibility of an I that has no me to attach to the other because the absence of the me denotes a serious deficit in the ability to address the other as an-other and can only be him as a counterpart; hence the narcissistic patient lacks something in everyone he relates to. Grunberger (1979) argues that narcissism could be a defense against the death *Trieb*. He said,

> One question comes to mind is whether the subjective value of the Eros-Thanatos hypothesis does not lie in the fact that it serves as a shield against the narcissistic wound of death as organic deterioration (arousing the fear of disintegration), an implacable process that sneaks up on us and to which each of us must succumb. (p. 241)

Another Angle to Link Narcissism with Death

The reason we do not find the psychological equivalent of death in Freud's new *Triebhaft* duality is his conception of the ego (see chapter 7 for a detailed discussion of this point). As mentioned earlier the ego (I), in Freud's conception, would be the whole individual or none of the individual. Although the *Ich* should have a *Mich* as its source and both would constitute the ego, Freud gave consideration to the *I* (*Ich*) alone, the nominative pronoun, the ego. Ego psychologists regarded ego's unconscious component to be the me. Even the id is considered the counterpart of the *Ucs.*; therefore, the ego in that theory was everything. Under all circumstances if there is a system called ego it comprises both the I and the me, constituting a duality in which the ego is a nominal person. Contrary to the prevailing belief in psychoanalytic circles and public views narcissism is not a type of relationship with the other but is the nature of the relationship within the self; narcissism is caught between the subjective I and the objective me,[6] not between the ego and the other, or the id and the super ego. Narcissism is a problem of identification.

A tense and conflicting relationship between the *I* and me is the narcissistic condition and the background of repetition compulsion. A patient whose I is lacking roots in a me, or a me that is distorted in the I's expression of its aspirations, keeps looking for an-other to make up for the absence of harmony between those two psychical entities. However, this search is useless because there is nothing else that could replace the lost authenticity in that lack. It is important now to note that repetition compulsion in psychoneurotic symptoms and in object relations are the same.

The concept of narcissism, as Freud talked about, was founded on the revision of the concept of identification (more than on the revision of the duality of sex/ego *Trieben*). Identification was regarded as a preliminary object choice, and it became the initial point in relating to the other. Hence, narcissism came into the theory as a complementary concept to the new and widened concept of identification. It is important to reemphasize that in the classical theory, identification had to happen first for a relationship between the subject and the object to be established, and not the other way around, as is the view in relational theories. The compounded concept of narcissistic-identification was, at first, a simple intermediate period between two major phases in the movement from autoerotism to object-love (Freud, 1916–1917, 1917c).

However, Freud added to that conception a very important distinction between two types of identification that are related to narcissism. In the first, the libidinal cathexis is withdrawn from the object, forcing the subject (the I) to identify with the object instead (1916–1917). This type of identification is perceived in events of death or loss of the object, where the object cathexis is withdrawn from it. Yet that cathexis never gets immediately reinvested in another object. The withdrawn cathexis is first invested in the self before it is reinvested in a replacement object later. Altering the ego, in his terms, to substitute for the lost object establishes a regression to an earlier identification with the lost object. The loss of the object precedes narcissistic-identification. If the subject becomes aware of his independence of the lost object and chooses to look for an identity that is aligned with his new awareness, the identification will be healthier. For instance, regression after the death of a parent leads to a sense of independence from the parental figure, and the new identity puts the subject on the course of a new and more advanced identification. The withdrawal of the cathexis from the object would not create a pure narcissistic condition but rather a narcissistic identification. It "invests the libidinal cathexis" in a self that is temporarily a substitute for the object, that is, a self that has temporarily become the object. However, if the subject chooses to identify with the lost object as a remedy for losing it, we encounter then a pathological identification. Psychopathology, therefore, could only be actualized in an identification that went wrong.

The second kind of identification entails directing a libidinal cathexis toward the object that is identified with the his-self (the I). This kind of identification chooses an object that is "identical," which becomes the I, thus making it narcissistic. This type of identification is encountered in the inability to relate in certain ways to others who are different, ranging from prejudices against specified people to falling in love with persons who are "like" one.

This distinction raises several questions: Is there any identification that is not narcissistic in essence? Is there a narcissistic condition that is not also founded on some sort of identification? How do the two types of identifications—identifying with someone or identifying someone with one's self—influence the formation of the psychoneuroses?

The relationship between the object (he) and the subject I is profoundly different from the relationship between the objective me and the subjective I. I could possibly see the signs of discomfort, cheating, or tenderness in the other, but I should know whether I am uncomfortable, cheating, or feeling tenderness. He could be himself or not himself to me, but I should always be me to myself. Of course, the possibility exists that I am not always exactly what I think I am because I can only be conscious of the I—the speaker—which is presumed to represent me truly. There will always be a gap within my identification between what I am conscious of and what is unconscious within me. The duality of the I and the me is the formative aspect of identification and the structural core of narcissism. The degree of the pathological condition will relate to the width and distortions within that gap.

Freud did not sufficiently consider the link between identification and narcissism, and did not mention the significance of that link. Despite that failing, and as Ricoeur said (1970): "[I]t is in identification itself, the structuring process par excellence, that Freud sees a narcissistic component" (p. 450). We can elicit that link in his writings even though he did not notice that he made that link. Every stage of psychosexual development contains the differentiation between subject and objects and between I and me. Therefore, narcissism accompanies all the strata of our experience; it is not only a period of immaturity that needs to be surpassed but it is also "the ever-renewing companion of all life" (Andreas-Salome, 1962, p. 16). The relationship between the self and its image, in any stage of development, is a natural narcissistic configuration. This notion in the classical doctrine makes it stand separately and quite distantly from all contemporary theories of psychoanalysis, whether they include or preclude narcissism in their fabric.

Laplanche and Pontalis (1967/1973) asked about the function of the compulsion to repeat (p. 80). This is a tangential issue because the compulsion to repeat neither has a function nor is a function; it is a manifestation of narcissism and does not cause anything specific. In repetition compulsion, the libidinal pattern sticks and continues to be repeated in the life of a person without ever successfully achieving any aim. Therefore, it is not part of any *Trieb*. The psychodynamics of the link between the two concepts of identification and narcissism had to be revisited in light of their contemporary reformulation. If fixation fails to establish an anchoring point for the self at one of the stages of development, the failed intrapsychic structure becomes a source of psychopathology. It forces features of the psychodynamics of that stage of development to keep repeating themselves in the form of symptoms or character pathology, which can be detected in the interpersonal relationships with others.

The theory of *Trieb* succeeded in forming a workable theory of libido, at least for a period of time, but it also managed to lead us to discover narcissism. The concept of narcissism was instrumental in initiating the new understanding of identification as a formative process and not as a psychopathological process. This shift put us in front of two major issues in "the turning point of the 1920s": Is there a theory of psychoanalysis that could replace the catharsis theory? Is there a psychology for metapsychology?

Chapter Seven

Ego Psychology and the Second Theory of Anxiety

A Psychoanalytic Blunder and Its Correction

The new conception of identification as a formative process, the metapsychology of narcissism, and the four major revisions to repression, the unconscious, *Trieb*, and regression, in addition to the distinction between fixation and the compulsion to repeat, when put together, as they all came connected, constituted a turning point in the evolution of the theory of psychoanalysis. Nevertheless, Freud reached that turning point, with some help from Abraham and Ferenczi, but did not take it. He still aspired to integrate those major revised concepts in the theory of catharsis by using the structural basis of those concepts in some functional mode to fit the old theory. The most far-reaching result of using structural concepts in a functional mode is reifying its basic notion and blurring its main characteristic as an active forming notion.

Freud's persistence in using the catharsis model led him to reify the subject (the person) by partitioning him into three entities, ego, id, and superego, instead of considering him a product of the formative process of identification. The formative process of identification has no ultimate form, but at best, it would have basic dynamically interacting components engaged in forming and reforming identity. Two other changes take place in a subtle way when structural concepts are used functionally: losing the actual connotation of the concepts, allowing it to relate imprecisely to other entities, and slipping into reversing the relationship between causes and effects. As we will see, the id (which is the none-*Ich*) related in the new topography, in a flimsy way, either to *Trieben* or to the unconscious. Similarly, Freud had a major difficulty deciding whether the ego is the cause of psychical events or its effect. Psychology of the ego suffered from all those defects. In this chapter, I will give a critique of Freud's highly praised work *The Ego and the Id* (1923a) to shed light on its unfavorable effect on not taking the turn in that turning point that started in 1914 and peaked in 1920.

The editor of the *Standard Edition* called *The Ego and the Id* Freud's last major theoretical work (1923b, p. 4). This work was supposed to offer a new topography to replace the one of the three systems of *Cs.*, *Pcs.*, and *Ucs.* At the beginning of that work Freud expressed his wish to make a change in the theoretical structure of the theory but did not give a clear reason for that change. He began by emphasizing the significance of the division of the psychical into conscious and unconscious as the only way of understanding psychopathology. A few paragraphs later, and after declaring his puzzlement about unconscious resistance, he said:

> The consequence of this discovery [unconscious resistance] is that we land in endless obscurities and difficulties if we keep to our habitual forms of expression, and try for instance, to derive neuroses from conflict between the conscious and the unconscious. We shall have to substitute for this antithesis another . . . the antithesis between the coherent ego and the repressed which splits off from it. (1923b, p. 17)

The reason he gave in this statement (the unconscious resistance) is not convincing to justify a reformulation of the theory of psychoanalysis. Unconscious resistance is a long, relentless theoretical problem (1896c, 1915e, 1916–1917) and was not so because he did not have the theoretical formulation for it but because he did not, and we still do not, understand it well. He assumed that the new duality of the coherent ego/the repressed could lead to understanding this problem, but this duality embodies contradictions that undermine its logic. Is the ego originally coherent, but some negative psychical elements interfere with that coherence and accordingly have to be repressed for the ego to maintain its coherence? If so where do those elements come from? If the ego originally comprises coherent and incoherent elements, how does it initiate repression? And how would repression know what to repress?

Previous to *The Ego and the Id* Freud did not keep good track of his notion of the ego as a coherent psychical agency that resorts to repression to rid itself of the disorganizing elements. On the contrary ego was an inherently incoherent agency that resorts to repressing its disorganization to get coherent. However, he kept oscillating between repression as a function of the ego or the ego as a function of repression. His solution of a duality of ego/the repressed is nondialectical, like the rest of his dualities, because it does not respect the cause/effect or the structural/functional relationship.

He casually mentioned another reason for writing that work: a desire to come up with a final synthesis of the psychoanalytic doctrine, which in his opinion would be difficult using just the old topography. Nevertheless, this attempt proved more complex than he bargained for. It required him to create three greatly reified psychical agencies and changed psychoanalysis from a psychology of the subject to a psychology of objects (ego-id-superego) (i.e., from the psychology of the drama of the individual to a psychology of three agencies that took over and replaced him). The theory of the "person" became a theory of impersonal psychical agencies, psychical conflicts, and dynamics of abstract forces. The outcome of that drastic change has been overlooked when dealing with the crisis of psychoanalysis and should have been considered a theoretical error that caused the invalidation of the rest of the modified theory.

There is another equally serious issue with *The Ego and the Id* pertaining to its clarity. Although it was meant to synthesize the doctrine in an orderly way, it demonstrated a great deal of uncertainty regarding what was functional and what was structural in those three agencies: Are the three agencies initiators of functions, or are they initiated functions? This uncertainty related more to how to account for the unconscious aspects of the psyche within this framework. It became obvious shortly after raising the argument that it is necessary in order for the three agencies to initiate psychical functions and remain relevant as a theory of psychoanalysis to assume that each entity incorporates a miniature version of the old topography. In an attempt to explain the paradoxes in this work the editor of the *Standard Edition* provided his own explanations. He claimed that Freud wanted to consider each of the three entities as more than just a function, although he fell short of proving that they were structures (ironically Freud's modification was called the structural point of view). Contrary to many of Freud's previous warnings about associating ego with consciousness, the editor suggested that Freud's view was that the first thing differentiated from the unconscious was the ego. This is a serious theoretical flaw because in the old topography it is consciousness that splits from the *Ucs.* and not the ego. A duality of unconscious and ego, or a duality of id and consciousness, could bring down the old and the new topographies together.

Freud stated that each of the three agencies of ego, superego, and id has its distinct method of operating to merit giving the new connection the status of structure. In fact, stipulating this as fact makes them, by definition, functional entities (the eye has the function of seeing because it is built to fulfill that function, yet its basic neurophysiological response to the external stimuli is shared, to a great extent, with the other senses). Inadvertently, Freud refuted the notion that his last topography was a structural theory by giving each agency the same mini-topography.

The failure of the new topography to account, in any shape or form, for the richness and complexity of the process of symptom formation forced Freud to go back to that subject and give it an explication in another major work, which I will review next. For now, I would say that the new topography turned the psychoanalytic theory upside down by delegating to those three agencies certain new psychological functions, which were in essence nothing more than manifestations of the presumed functions and not the functions themselves. Moreover (as we will see), it wreaked havoc with his attempt to use academic psychological issues such as memory, perception, and cognition to justify the functions of the ego.

Freud eventually became aware of the problems inherent in his new topography and said: "Now I am prepared to hear you ask me scornfully whether our ego-psychology comes down to nothing more than taking commonly used abstractions literally and in a crude sense, and transforming them from concepts into things by which not much would be gained" (1933, p. 60). I would say that if Freud had utilized his revisions of repression and identification he would not have attempted to give a final formulation of the theory of psychoanalysis in that way, and he would have actually turned the corner toward a purely psychoanalytic theory.

THE BLUNDER OF THE CONCEPT OF EGO

Freud starts his monograph by giving a brief account of the theory. He made two mistakes. He stated that dynamically speaking all that was latent is unconscious, and attributed this psychical condition to the pressure of repression. So he forewent the revision he made in 1915 and annulled the distinction between the *Pcs.* and the *Ucs.*, a distinction he was very specific and particular about before (1912g, 1915e). Nonetheless, this major declination from the original discovery did not make it any simpler to replace the old topography with the new one. For those three agencies to function or even just meet common behavioral criteria their material has to comprise *Cs.*, *Pcs.*, and *Ucs.* elements, although Freud had refused, categorically, the difference between the *Ucs.* and the *Pcs.* To be based on a gradation of consciousness to unconsciousness he had to exclude the system *Ucs.* from the new topography (1923b, p. 16n). The replacement topography was flawed from the start.

The second mistake was a direct result of the first. Because the unconscious was still the repressed in his new topography, he stated that repression had become to psychoanalysis the prototype of the unconscious. Nevertheless, Freud recognized that repression is only one of the defense mechanisms, but his obstinate fixation on the catharsis theory made him reemphasize its indelibility as the origin of the concept of defense. The notion of defense remained a prototype of any mechanism that protects the ego from undesirable material (I will get to this point when I present his second theory of anxiety). In this way, all defense mechanisms seem to serve the same purpose of repression by keeping something away from consciousness. This is theoretically indefensible and clinically incorrect because what is "defended against is sometimes very conscious," as Freud said in the same work. As such, repression cannot be a prototype of defense mechanisms and their originator too.

Freud's effort to replace the three systems with the three entities got in trouble because the *Ucs.* does not coincide with the repressed; it is true that all that is repressed is *Ucs.* but not all that is *Ucs.* is repressed. He said so himself:

> A part of the ego too . . . may be Ucs . . . and this *Ucs.* belonging to the ego is not latent like the *Pcs.* . . . When we find ourselves thus confronted by the necessity of postulating a third *Ucs.*, which is not repressed, we must admit that the characteristic of being unconscious begins to lose significance to us. It becomes a quality which can have many meanings, a quality which we are unable to make, as we should have hoped to do, the basis of far reaching and inevitable conclusions [all italics added]. (1923a, p. 18)

Having bypassed the centrality of the concept of the *Ucs.* from the old topography, he had to find another way to distinguish between the three systems of the original topography, because he still needed them in his new topography. He resorted to the previous very appropriate idea of representation (1914a). He proceeded to use thing-presentation and word-presentation as a new way of distinguishing between the conscious and the unconscious, and endeavored to use that distinction to identify the ego. But, initially, each representation was a function of the system that created it; therefore, it was inappropriate to use them as substitutes for the systems that they originated from. The *Ucs.* is a system that is able to create only thing-presentations. The *Pcs.*, on the other hand, deals only with the symbolic nature of things, of which words are its most important facet. Freud had to enter the field of psychology, which at that time was not advanced enough to explicate what he needed to explicate. Psychology at that time was just starting to study cognition in systematic terms in the United States.

Freud tried to view those two types of representations thematically by looking for the input of psychological processes that are hardly related to psychoanalysis: memory, mnemonic residues, and perception (*Pcpt.*). This shift complicated the picture because in psychology those processes are studied detached from their causes. He reified functions by declension and used hypotheses as certainties. As an example, he stated that word-presentations are residues of memory and therefore concluded that they are extensions of perception. Despite the incorrectness of this hypothesis (in terms of psychology proper), he proceeded to explain how internal things could connect with word-presentation by saying: "Anything arising from within [apart from feelings] that seeks to become conscious must *try to transform itself* [italics added] into external perception: this becomes possible by means of memory-traces" (1914c, p. 20). An endosomatic arousal cannot turn into perception by itself and assuming this happens is not an explication of the matter.

He did not explain how an internal thing could transform itself, specifically if no other psychological processes cofunction and perform that transformation. In the best circumstances, memory traces might be able to transform an internal thing into whatever those traces originally were, but they would not be able to do the reverse (i.e., make an internal thing create a memory of itself or a memory create a memory). Freud ended with calcifying some basic ideas about the new concept of ego, making the system *Pcpt.* its main attribute. He said:

> Whereas the relation of external perceptions to the ego is quite perspicuous, that of internal perceptions to the ego requires special investigation. . . . [A]re we really right in referring the whole of consciousness to the single superficial system Pcpt.-Cs[?] . . . Let us call what becomes conscious as pleasure and displeasure a quantitative and qualitative something in the course of mental events [internal]; . . . [T]he question is whether this something can become conscious in the place where it is, or whether it must first be transmitted to the system Pcpt [all italics added]. (1914c, pp. 21–22)

It is difficult to fathom what Freud meant by "transmitting pleasure or displeasure to perceptions." Either he meant having a certain sensation in its own right (feeling) equals perception or that there are processes that perform that transformation (an issue he did not address, mainly because it has no place in general psychology). He said the ego is the mental agency that supervises all its own constituent processes (1923b, p. 17) and therefore attaches consciousness to the ego as the seat of the cognitive functions and makes it the entity that controls the approach to motility. Yet he could not deny the presence of the unconscious elements in the formation of the ego.

When we review the whole notion of the ego in ego psychology we realize at once that ego was a puzzling agency, because Freud did not take into consideration the distinction Spruiell (1981)[1] mentioned. He indicated that *Pcpt.* played the more important part in differentiating the ego from the id (p. 25). Still it was unclear whether the *Pcpt.* was a function of the ego that separated it from the id or a separate independent function that acted upon the ego, causing it to split from the id.

Freud put most of the emphasis on the coherence of the ego and on its conflict with the incoherent repressed content. Presumably those incoherent elements were once part of the ego before it supposedly worked on severing them from itself. Coherence of the ego in that event is a function of repression and not one of the ego's intrinsic attributes. Even if we assume that the ego manages to have the "brains" to repress what interferes with its coherence, we are faced with the weakness and incompleteness of this argument. A coherent ego is, at best, relative and impermanent in coherence, as Freud indirectly suggested (1923b, p. 14).

He also considered the ego to be the source and the agent of repression, a function displayed in the form of the puzzling resistance to treatment. This viewpoint contradicts his previous firm notion that the ego is a function of repression and one of its products. Moreover, this new explication of the ego implies that we should consider the ego an agency that functions from outside the dynamics of the psyche and not as one of its components or participants.

Freud addressed a new function in the formation of the ego, which he related to the Oedipus complex and the process of identification. He stated that there are two reasons for addressing that subject: a clinical observation about the existence of an unconscious sense of guilt and the phenomenon of identification. He concluded that an unconscious sense of guilt interferes with the progress of treatment and is responsible for negative therapeutic reactions. He added that identification plays a role in the formation of that sense of guilt, stating, "The considerations that led us to assume the existence of a grade in the ego, a differentiation within the ego, which may be called the ego ideal or super-ego, have been stated elsewhere" (1923b, p. 28). He should have reconciled superego formation with his original and crucial notion of narcissistic identification in the movement from autoerotism to object love. By not doing that he failed to recall the revisions narcissism forced on the catharsis theory; thus he caused a major theoretical blunder. After elaborating the relationship with the parents and their role in separating the ideal from the regular ego, he concluded: "The conflict between the ideal and the ego will, as we are now prepared to find, ultimately reflect the contrast between what is real and what is psychical, between the external world and the internal world" (1923b, p. 36). The ego was put, this way, in a precarious position because if its *Pcs.* attribute was harboring more than just what is real, we have to conclude that the superego is the only psychical aspect of the individual left.

However, the concept of superego was presumably Freud's solution to resistance and the negative therapeutic reaction. This presumption added confusion to the picture because of what Freud said regarding the impact of its formation on the ego. He said that the establishment of the superego subjugates the ego to the id (1923a, p. 36). His view was that the intrinsic resemblance between the id and the ego ideal in terms of their link with reality make them both conflict with the ego because the ego is the only agency that represents both the real and the psychological. The establishment of the superego required explaining the source of the power it exerts on the ego. Freud introduced the parental authority as the explanation. But he could explain that source only through religion and phylogeny. In other words, the second psychical entity of superego in the new topography was no less problematic than the first.

Freud's handling of *Trieben* in that work was equally confusing. He recounted the dualities of the *Trieben*, emphasizing the latest duality of life/death, but housed them both in the id. In the very first approach to the subject, he revoked his basic premise that the two sets of *Trieben* are dialectically antithetical and belonged to two qualitatively conflicting aims because if they both occupy the same psychical entity, the id, there should be a way to accommodate their oppositions. His solution was that instincts could fuse together and use each other's way of discharge to reach their own aims. Distorting one of the basic constituents of the theory of *Trieb* was forced on the theory to accommodate the notion that the reservoir of *Trieben* was the id. It even made the distortion, itself, a new meaning of instrinct. This twist raised various difficulties that were not part of the original theory of *Trieb*. As a solution he suggested ambivalence as the manifestation of the fusion of the two classes of *Trieben*. This solution ignored that ambivalence is the state of affairs in the domain of affect, not an indication of two antithetical affective cathexes. It is the manifestation of one unbound cathexis alternating between the positive and negative charges. Besides, ambivalence does not agree with the nature and function of mental representation, which is the essence of the *Trieb*. In spite of the many arguments against that solution we should not lose sight of Freud's desperate effort to integrate his previous discoveries into the new topography, of which he had serious doubts (Blanco, 1975, chaps. 3–4).

After a little discussion of the possible fusion and diffusion of the two antithetical *Trieben*, he proceeded to pose a query about whether there could be intrusive connections to be traced between the three structures he assumed existed, on the one hand, and the two classes of instincts, on the other! Furthermore, could the pleasure principle, which dominates mental processes, have any constant relation to both classes of instinct and to the differentiation that is drawn in the mind (1923a, p. 42)? To answer this query, Freud did two things that were detrimental both to his new topography and to the psychoanalytic doctrine as a whole. First, he neglected the difference between causation, or motive, and result, or function. The id became the reservoir of the *Trieben* but was also a *Triebhaft* agency. This notion contradicted his previous claim that the ego was the reservoir of the *Trieben* (for a detailed account of this contradiction, see Strachey, Appendix B, pp. 63–64 in *The Ego and the Id*). Second, the id that accommodated fusing the *Trieben* was considered capable of ignoring the specificity of the *Triebhaft*. Freud had to turn back to the concept of the one neutral energy emanating from narcissism, a notion he rejected before in his theory of narcissism (1914a, p. 44).

Moreover, the id had no place for the representation of the *Trieb* as attribute and was only a place for cathexes and their discharge (Green, 2000). In other words, Freud continued sacrificing the core of his psychoanalytic doctrine to suit the new topography, in spite of its tentativeness, paradoxes, and confusing notions. The proof that Freud embarked on a misguided task is the confusion he instituted in the theory of psychoanalysis, the existence of the old catharsis theory and a promising new one that did not materialize. His argumentation for his new topography resulted in the ego losing significance instead of the unconscious, as he suggested (1923b, p. 18). The ego was no longer the seat of consciousness, and it contained a nonrepressed unconsciousness. Yet, with all its cognitive faculties, it could not recognize the nonrepressed unconsciousness within itself.

He had hoped that a new topography could solve the problem of the existence of nonrepressed unconscious, but it did not; on the contrary it is that topography that underscored that fact. The statement he made about the unconscious that actually fits the ego attests to his doubtful understanding of the most significant, if not the most remarkable, of his discoveries (see Strachey's unconvincing argument about Ferenczi's pertinent remark to Freud about his changed conception of the unconscious in *The Ego and the Id*, Appendix A, pp. 60–62). Freud discovered three types of unconsciousness (not three meanings) in his work on dreams, which were reconfirmed and reformulated in his two papers on the subject (1912g, 1915e). If he was clear about the distinction between the *Pcs.* and the *Ucs.*, he would not have been surprised two decades later to find the systemic unconscious staring at him while he was going to officially deny it in his structural point of view.

His approach to the second topography seemed to take the direction of building a theory of psychology instead of reaching a synthesis of a psychoanalytical theory as an original objective.[2] He proceeded to give extended views, mostly speculative, on mental functions such as perception, memory, representation of things and representation by words, external reality and internal sensations, and finally how the *Ucs.* and the *Pcs.* connect. He concluded by regarding the ego part of the id modified by the system of Pcpt., and not by repression (1923b, p. 28). If we accept that conception, we have to accept that the id must have had access to cognitive functions such as perception to separate the ego from it. This notion contradicts if not all, then most, of Freud's previous conceptions of the id as being merely the reservoir of the instinctual aspects of the psyche.

The theoretical formulation of the new topography got more untidy when he said: "For the ego perception plays the part which in the id falls to instincts, because perception is a response to stimuli and not a constituent of the ego, while the instincts are supposed to be the content of the id, if not the id itself" (1923b, p. 25). In fact, Freud had four very different conceptions of the ego and two of the id in this work. It was natural that when he talked about the ego's contact with the id, we are left with a major question: Which creates which? Is the id the origin of everything (the old concept) and then perception comes (from nowhere) to modify part of it to become the ego? Or is it the ego that creates the id by modifying itself perceptually to adjust to the external world (again, where does that ego come from?), thence severing the rest of it to become the id?

Freud ended his exploring of the new topography by defining six important functions of the ego: reality testing, using thinking to postpone motor discharge, judging what to let pass, treating the id as an external reality that needs to be controlled, withdrawing the libido from the id and transforming the id's cathexes into ego structures, and drawing on the stored past ages in the id phylogeny (p. 55). Accordingly the ego is required to serve three masters: reality, id, and superego. I have a problem finding a place for the *Ucs.* in this topography, even as a mini-old-topography assigned to each of the three agencies. In the original theory the ego was a function of psychical processes, but in this new point of view it became a structure, but a structure without a specific, if not unspecific, functional manifestation. Because of that confusion, Freud talked about the ego as a psychical metaphor.

The Ego and the Id was a failed attempt at synthesizing a theory of psychoanalysis because there was no true place for the concept of the *Ucs.* in it. It would not have been a proper theory of psychology either because it was supposed to integrate with the catharsis theory and give it a new look. Ego psychology was a psychoanalytic blunder. Exonerating Freud for his failure to understand the *Ucs.* (something that I personally wish to do and also have good reasons to do) makes me say that a synthesis of the theory would have been impossible without three things: (a) having the whole Freudian text available so that his intuitions could be assessed within the totality of that text; (b) having several scholars (e.g., Laplanche, Leclaire, Lacan, Blanco, and Bion), who were able in a gradual and incremental way, caution about some slippery and deceiving meanings in the text and show its strength in different and particular ways; and (c) having at hand the accumulated knowledge of linguistics, the structural theory, the new theories of logic, and semiology.

THE SECOND THEORY OF ANXIETY

Freud discovered the unconscious in its structural sense but found out that those revisions do not integrate well in the catharsis theory. He seemed to have put them aside, especially in the psychology of the ego. However, his ingenious intuitions never failed to help him recover from his blunders. I will address Freud's recovery from the blunder of ego psychology by reviewing what he did in his next work, *Inhibitions, Symptoms and Anxiety* (1926), a work that just came about, unconnected to a particular problem and without any apparent reason.[3] The corrections he made in this book to the "libidinal" theory of anxiety were correct to make anxiety fit in a theory of psychoanalysis. I will try to show in that work how what was lost in the psychology of the ego was to some extent recovered in the second theory of anxiety and how it pointed us in the right direction toward the "turning point."

Inhibitions, Symptoms and Anxiety is a difficult work to follow (as the editor of the *Standard Edition* also averred) because of two main features: First, it is a work that has a heavily heuristic approach without a clear objective. Second, Freud was tentative at the beginning to consider anxiety, its main subject, a symptom in its own right or a cause for the formation of symptoms (Freud, 1926d, p. 144). In the meantime, it is not possible to ignore that he presented a new theory of symptom formation that totally revised the libido model of symptom formation in the catharsis theory. He needed, thus, to write a long epilogue to end the whole work with a conclusive statement about anxiety as a core for a new conception of symptom formation. The new theory of symptom formation was a return to the characteristic approach in the classical theory of psychoanalysis and a correction of several issues that were badly mangled in *The Ego and the Id.* Freud went back to the analytic approach of using the noticeable functionality of the manifest to educe from it its latent structure.

Freud totally reversed the catharsis theory's way of conceiving of symptom formation by a new theory of anxiety that is not based on the transformation of the stifled libido into symptoms and the differential manifestations of defenses into the different psychopathologies. Anxiety in the catharsis theory was a symptom of unfulfilled and repressed libidinal urges and was a nosological entity group of hysterical psychopathology (e.g., hysterical anxiety). But in this work, he affirmed that anxiety is, at least, a first stage in the formation of symptoms. He added an important idea that was never acknowledged before: psychopathologies create their defense mechanisms and not the reverse (the old idea was repression is the source of the rest of the defenses).

He approached the subject of anxiety by making a distinction between inhibitions and symptoms, which until then was not a very striking issue in the doctrine. However, he used that distinction to show that symptoms were manifestations of unusual and impaired ego functions, while inhibitions were merely increased restrictions on those functions. Right after making that point, he stated that an ego function is renounced if and when it becomes erotically charged, a reason for repression proper to avoid further conflict with the id or the superego. There are several arguable issues pertaining to that conception, but I will concentrate on only two. The first issue is the powerless ego giving a signal of displeasure, or anxiety, in response to the danger of a pending eruption of an erotic component stemming from the id.

Freud does not suggest a source of the energy that gives that signal and is not specific about to what the signal is directed. This is an obvious flaw because if the signal originates in the ego, what other agency has the capacity to receive it? In other words, Freud did not stipulate whether the ego produces that signal or receives it. If it is the latter, what or who would perceive the danger and give the signal? The second issue is the ego modeling its dealings with internal dangers on the pattern of dealing with external dangers, that is, by withdrawing the cathexis from the object of danger. This issue produces a contradiction. The withdrawal of cathexis from an erotic object like the withdrawal of interest from an external object should result in lowering the intensity of cathecting rather than increasing it. As a result, the cause of anxiety becomes paradoxical: Is it an increase or a decrease in cathecting an eroticized object? Freud acknowledged that contradiction when he said: "How is it possible, from an economic point of view, for a mere process of withdrawal and discharge . . . to produce displeasure and anxiety, seeing that, according to our assumption, displeasure and anxiety can only arise as a result of an increase in cathexis?" (1926d, p. 93). Hence, he stated clearly that the problem could not be solved from an economic point of view and therefore does not belong to metapsychology and its solution should be sought elsewhere.

Interestingly, Freud suggested that we consider the inherited reaction to danger as a prototype of anxiety, as it is a constitutional endowment of all living creatures. Although this feature is credible in its own right, it does not account for anxiety in terms of overcathecting or undercathecting the source of danger. The notion that anxiety is a function of a sense of danger is not viable and could not substitute for the economic point of view or justify excluding anxiety from metapsychology. After suggesting a phylogenetic origin for anxiety he discovered that it fell short of turning that phenomenon into an entity of significance in its own right. At this point Freud recalled his revision of the concept of repression and went on to think psychoanalytically about anxiety once more. He returned to the concept of primary repression to explain the quantitative factors in excitation that result in the endosomatic breaking the barrier created by primary repression. He said, "It is highly probable that the immediate precipitating causes of primal repression are quantitative factors such as an excessive degree of excitation and the breaking through of the protective shield against stimuli" (1926d, p. 94). He was still tentative about his new suggestions because a shield is to protect from external and not internal stimuli. It is obvious that he did not want to give up the core idea of the catharsis theory: a rejectionable urge that has to be dealt with.

The failure of the psychology of the ego to explain repression or its relation to anxiety led him to conclude that symptoms form as a result of the unfeasibility of repression, or at least the impossibility of a perfect repression, which means the inevitability of the repressed finding the ways to reveal itself. We should therefore ask: What could initiate a defense, especially before the formation of the superego (the function of judgment)? Is repression the mechanism of differentiating ego/id and creating a defense, or is it a natural outcome of development and the maturation of the psychical structures? Is the logic behind the concept of defense mechanisms that the form-less and content-less *Trieb* constitutes a danger to the ego? If so, what is the nature of that danger (see Freud, 1926d, p. 193, n.61)?

The concept of defense signifies repressed forbidden drives, not *Trieb* as such, because *Trieben* have no content that could be considered objectionable or constitute a danger. Even if we stay at the level of the sexual *Trieb* and ego *Trieb*, we cannot consider the sexual *Trieb* (pleasure) dangerous until it chooses an object or an aim that is reprehensible to the ego/superego—that is, until it represents the forbidden drive. If we understand repression in that way, we have to reconsider the nature of primary repression. Primary repression, in that case, is a repression exerted on impulses before they acquire objects or aims. In light of this insight, we should think of primary repression and possibly repression proper as natural products of psychosexual development and not as mechanisms that serve functions. It could be, and maybe should be, considered the result of the development of the secondary process, which stands against the primary process and counters its workings. In other words, what have been called mechanisms in the service of defending the ego are no more than the natural conflict between the primary and the secondary processes, and its compromise solution (see chapter 9 for an elaboration of this idea). At this stage of the discussion, Freud questioned his own views about the weakness and strength of the ego. He confessed that his narcissism prevented him from admitting that his past formulations about the ego were not correct (1926d, p. 96).

Freud moved to review the two cases of Little Hans (1909) and the Wolf Man (1918b) to support his speculations about symptom formation and anxiety. His examination of Hans's phobia brought out a rather complicated and unexpected view of symptom formation (1926d, p. 103). His understanding of symptom formation led him to realize that different defense mechanisms are behind the differences in symptoms, which is an old insight (1896b). By realizing that defense mechanisms are products of the different psychoneuroses, psychopathology was no longer explainable in terms of the push and pull of the tripartite agencies of ego, superego, and id, or even as the struggle of repression with the undesirable urges of the unconscious. They have to be considered in terms of expressing specific deviations in a normal course of development or according to what Freud mentioned at the beginning of the section on "deviations in the ego's functions" (1923a).

In spite of that, Freud still found it difficult to relinquish old concepts and approaches; he looked for causes for the formation of symptoms, or better, for structures that would classify symptom formation as their functions.

However, while doing that he formally relinquished the libido theory and should have known by then that he was finished with the catharsis theory. He renounced the sexual etiology and replaced it with the Oedipus complex and its castration anxiety, and considered them the base from which symptoms originate. He said:

> I must admit that I thought I was giving more than a mere description. I believed I had put my finger on a metapsychological process of direct transformation of libido into anxiety. I can now no longer maintain this view. And, indeed, I found it impossible at the time to explain how a transformation of that kind was carried out. . . . The anxiety felt in phobias is an ego anxiety and arises in the ego, and . . . it does not proceed out of repression but, on the contrary, sets repression in motion. (1926, pp. 109–110)

Reversal of that nature should have made Freud review and reformulate ego psychology in its totality and do the same with the theory of defense mechanisms and psychotherapy. It is easier to recognize that now, but we should give Freud the excuse that he was still struggling with the old theory collapsing without a clear replacement.

A whole section of the work (section 5) came about as Freud was freeing himself from the libido theory. It was not a full return to psychoanalysis, but it was a departure from the damaged doctrine of ego psychology. He was able to get into some fruitful debates with himself and formulate a solid theoretical explication of the different psychoneuroses. He engaged in detailed theoretical formulations, away from their metapsychological counterparts. First, he dispensed with the libido theory, which was fundamental for the tripartite agencies to be maintained. He was able to put the concept of libido (psychic energy) back in its proper place as a function of the *Trieb*. Second, he reformulated his early theory of psychopathology on the basis of a clearer, though more sophisticated, understanding of symptom formation. This last point revealed, in a surprising way, his clear understanding of resistance as a product of the working of the primary process. In a comparison between hysteria and obsessional neurosis, Freud showed that the trauma in both cases has two different destinies and forms two distinct kinds of symptoms: the former produces amnesia and the latter creates isolation and undoing. He put the link between cause and effect in the right way when he stipulated that defense mechanisms do not cause the neuroses but rather the psychoneuroses dictate the choice of defense mechanisms.

In the search for an organizing mode for symptoms, Freud borrowed some observable phenomena or events from family dynamics and gave them two names: the Oedipus complex and castration anxiety. Using the family dynamics as a field of observation, Freud deduced that the child wants to own his mother and that he probably produces some sexual phantasies about her too, which would lead to hating his father and wishing him out of the way, a deduction based on very shaky facts. Those drastic motives are rarely manifested or expressed, even if we assume they existed in the first place. They do not constitute an organizing principle of family structure but could only be one of its functions. If they are manifested in a family they would be of a failing and dysfunctional family structure; they manifest in symptoms but could not be the foundations of symptoms. There were anthropological attempts to test and verify the universality of the Oedipus situation (e.g., Lévi-Strauss, 1966, 1973; Malinowski, 1955; Mead, 1955, 1961). Those studies confirmed the universality of the triangulation of child-mother-father (or father figure) as the structuring principle of the family and that its implicit aim is to systematize incestuous prohibitions in society. It seems that Freud's conception of the Oedipus complex was just the Western model of that triangulation. However, using family dynamics as "fact" or content that justifies inferring from some possible childhood daydreams does not lead to the structuring principle of symptomatology. The Oedipus complex and castration anxiety are the metaphenomenological configurations of the triangular structure of a specific culture. At the same time, the implicit mode of organizing family psychodynamics could be read as a text that has a meaning, which if turned into a noun, like the Oedipus complex, would become a function without a structure that explains it.

When Freud's heuristic investigation reached that point he had an extremely significant insight. He recognized that ordinary psychopathologies of everyday life proved that anxiety was not a precipitating factor in their formation (1926d, p. 129). In other words, if anxiety is not a factor in forgetting a name or misspelling a word, it should not be considered a factor in the formation of major symptoms either. Acknowledging this fact should have directed Freud, at that point, to restate his new theory of anxiety, especially since he previously considered anxiety a function of castration fear (1926d, p. 130). Instead, he still looked for a cause for anxiety. This time he resorted to the fear of separation and loss as the causation; anxiety became a function of those situations. He said, "It [anxiety] appears to us as a reaction to a loss, a separation" (1926, p. 130). This slight change led him to conclude that the fear of death molded castration fear and manifested in the ego's reaction to the abandonment of the protecting superego (the powers of destiny). Freud's lack of distinction between functional and structural concepts made him miss a most intuitive understanding of his latest *Triebhaft* duality (life/death) and the multitude of its functional representations. Anxiety is molded into the fear of losing the other, which means the I would be without a counterpart (i.e., anxiety is the fear of narcissistic death).

By the end of section 5, Freud had objectified the Oedipus complex by talking about it as a factual family situation and about the fear of castration as a real childhood fear. Considering these phenomena as structuring factors—at least—kept them still within the psychoanalytic context instead of letting them belong to the sociology of the family or the psychology of infantile imagination.

Naming the Oedipus complex and castration anxiety as the bases for symptom formation presents us with a problem. Symptoms define the ego (e.g., I am anxious; I am obsessed). They are also the mode of the ego's functioning (e.g., I cannot cross the street; I cannot stop counting the windows of buildings). In other words, symptoms imply limitations of the ego, which could be considered figurative manifestations of its castration. Nonetheless, they do not mean that a castration of any sort has taken place. On the contrary, if anything, they indicate the negation of castration or that no castration has taken place but was replaced with symptoms. In the most exaggerated form, it could be said that the child's fear of his father's disapproval creates the symptoms that signify the loss of the power of the father's approval. Self-doubt has much to say about imagined castration, especially in connection with infantile genital curiosity (Freud, 1923b). Castration is a metaphor of a desire without the means of satisfaction; it is a term that concretizes a meaning.

We still have a major question to answer, because there is no support for an actual castration imperilment coming from the father: What then is castration anxiety? I will invoke two small issues to answer this question. First, contrary to Freud's approach to phobias, where he considered fear an outcome of conflict, it is better to consider fear as an attribute of conflict and not as its function (1926, p. 127). Second, it is equally important not to consider moral castration the outcome of the Oedipus complex, as Freud suggested (1926d, p. 128), but rather as the foundation of structuring the family's triangulation as an Oedipal triangle in a Western culture. Moral anxiety is the fabric of the parental relationship, or what makes the child willing, spontaneously, to please his parents and what makes him feel upset if he fails. Moral anxiety creates a triangulation similar to that presented in the myth of Oedipus: rage, parricide, and incest. More specifically, I am referring to rage that is not actualized (Laius's murderous intent toward his son, which did not materialize), parricide that is not intended (Oedipus kills a stranger who happened to be his father), and incest in a marriage that is not accepted by son or mother (when they both knew of it). Nevertheless, when we remind ourselves of the gap between the me and the I, we can reposition the Oedipal triangle and castration anxiety in a better theoretical framework, which facilitates reaching a better metapsychological formulation, which is missed in the second theory of symptom formation.

Freud returned to the concepts of narcissism and the death instinct. It was his way back to giving the me a new life after its demise in ego psychology. His new formulations made identification the formative process of the ego (replacing repression of the id), a process that guides the cognitive functions and contact with the external world. The ego became a composite (as it should have been from the beginning) of the internal (the endosomatic, or the me) and the external (identification, or the I). The ego was, to a great extent, a product of what is assimilated from the psychodynamics of the family and was meant to express the parent's own identifications of their child. Three scenarios could be envisaged in that regard: (a) the mother identifying her son as a substitute for his father, whom she is not happy with; (b) a father setting up his son as his competitor (due to the same lack of harmony with the mother), configuring the elements of the Oedipus scene and their implications; and (c) parents who are in harmony, identifying their son as the future of the family. The child's I in the first two scenarios will be a false representative of his me, a me that neither wishes nor aspires to replace the father. In the third scenario, the me will have the freedom to identify itself with the father, with no moral conflicts (no castration anxiety), and therefore acquire a free I to choose its love objects in the future.

CORRECTING THE BLUNDER OF EGO PSYCHOLOGY

Freud was still under the influence of ego psychology when he started the second theory of anxiety. *Inhibition, Symptoms and Anxiety* is maybe the best heuristic work he has written because he starts from a vague point to reach a point that put together most of his intuitive conceptions that would lead to his "other theory." To clarify this point I will go through the ten parts of the book step by step to show the course he took, from the vague starting point to the point that obliges us to put together the foundations of the "other theory of psychoanalysis."

Freud starts his work with a distinction between inhibitions that restrict ego functions and symptoms that change those functions, being rather a surprising distinction that does not resonate with any noticeable difficulties in the theory. Therefore, for the ego to avoid conflict with the id, it gives a signal of displeasure (anxiety) as a warning. Consequently, the cathexis is withdrawn from the object of displeasure or anxiety. This conception of ego functions raised several questions: Where does the energy of anxiety come from? What psychical agency is supposed to receive that warning signal produced by the ego? How does the withdrawal of cathexis, which means lowering of the energy in the ego, create anxiety, which is presumed an increase of energy? Those questions led Freud to more difficulties regarding repression, the inadequacy of the concept of defense, the strength or weakness of the ego, and the place of these factors in the compromise solutions of symptom formation (1926d, p. 95). However, when he reached that impasse in building his theory of anxiety, he reverted to the revisions of the three concepts and their feat in revealing their structural significations. That paved the way for Freud to free himself from the restrictions of ego psychology.

He corrected the concept of repression twice within a psychology of the ego to make it a function of the ego and not its originator. He said: "Repression proceeds from the ego when the latter . . . refuses to associate itself with an instinctual cathexis which has been aroused in the id" (p. 91). Shortly after, he reversed that notion by saying, "The anxiety felt in phobias is an ego anxiety and arises in the ego, and it does not proceed out of repression but, on the contrary, sets repression in motion" (p. 110). In light of this change, primary repression is a process that has nothing to do with keeping something out of consciousness because it is a formative factor in symptoms, meaning that what is primarily repressed is not a content that is objected to but a structure that cannot become conscious and has to get modified to get to that system. So Freud stipulated the contradiction and found the solution in the revision of the catharsis theory.

The theory of symptom formation gradually evolved from a theory of castration to a theory of castration anxiety, which advanced to make anxiety a fear of death. The fear of death was, in turn, considered a function of the loss of the object and of the protection of the superego. After that sequence of changes Freud eliminated the notion of a specific motivational content as etiology and restated the condition of narcissism as the dreaded loss. But what is the possible loss in narcissism? The loss of the superego and its moral support is equivalent to a loss of the I and the authority of enunciating the demands of the me (i.e., the death of the me). It is obvious that moral castration as the disharmony with the superego is a loss within a narcissistic duality and has nothing to do with morality itself. There is little to add to Freud's intuition when he said:

> The high degree of narcissistic value which the penis possesses [as a concrete representation of the identification with the father] can appeal to the fact that that organ is a guarantee to its owner that he can be once more united to his mother i.e. to a substitute for her in the act of copulation [another concrete representation of the father's privilege]. (1926d, p. 139)

He gave the penis a symbolic value that puts it within the province of narcissism; in this way we were free from the myth of the Oedipus, and we can reflect on its symbolic meaning.

Freud was more direct and obvious in making mistakes but was very subtle in recovering from them. This is because the nature of meaning is problematic, especially in the humanities. Most of the time, uncovering the meaning of a phenomenon overlaps with discovering its cause. Elder (1994) expressed this idea more succinctly when he said, "The uniqueness of psychoanalysis consists and is manifest in the uniqueness of its grammar and the peculiar logic of its concepts. A large measure of this uniqueness consists precisely in its identification of meaning and causes, in its conception of meanings as causes and causes as meaning" (pp. 68–69).

Whenever Freud discovered the meaning of a phenomenon he was quick to consider it its cause. This way, it was imperative for him to find its functional attributes. But, because functional attributes are dead ends and can hardly allow any further development of a theory, his retreat from the cause/effect formulations was always subtle.

In section 10 of this work, Freud recovered the essence of the psychoanalytic doctrine and undid what ego psychology had done to it. He denied anxiety the status of causing symptom formation and thus kept symptoms as an issue of meaning rather than the effect of a cause. He stated that the ego seldom succeeds in undoing its repression, which meant that the ego was not what initiates repression in the first place. Moreover, repression resists being removed, a fact that was inferred from resistance. But what unconscious is resistant to removal? It is primary repression, because it is not the work of the ego but of the primary process, which distorts the endosomatic in radical ways (i.e., resistance is the time and effort needed to uncover the working of the primary process and understand their interference with the secondary processes).

Freud (1926) tried to account for the sources of anxiety by attributing anxiety to an involuntary reaction, prototypical of the situation at birth, and a leaning to inoculate the ego against disintegration (p. 162). But he immediately recovered from that presumptuous theorem and said: "Anxiety [Angst] has an unmistakable relation to expectation; it is anxiety about something. It has a quality of indefiniteness and lack of object. In precise speech we use the word fear [furcht] rather than anxiety [angst] if it has found an object" (pp. 164–165). Freud came back full circle to the psychology of the contentless wish, the objectless *Trieb*, the unbound psychical energy, the endosomatic me, and tried and succeeded in stipulating that anxiety is unspecified.

Freud's reversal of his previous views is a spontaneous recovery from vacillating between his intuition and the proper conception of psychoanalysis. It is also a way of restating his functional formulations structurally, giving them a proper definition within a classical Freudian doctrine. Therefore, we can return to Freud to redefine the functional formulations of the catharsis theory. This endeavor is not, in any way, similar to the criticisms prompted by their imperfections. I am returning to Freud's own restatements, which he made either to correct his mistakes or to introduce the structural side of the issues, lest it could be missed. That also happened.

Freud's last main theoretical contribution did not only correct the blunder of ego psychology but provided us with the opportunity to put his whole doctrine into two distinct perspectives. The first perspective is the nature of the human psyche: It is structured as a series of dialectical dualities, and, if we define those dualities wrongly, we would before long find it impossible to understand what we intended to understand in the first place. The second perspective is the permeation of those dualities in every aspect of our psychological lives and their ability to enrich or obstruct our understanding of the psyche. The difference between the two states is whether we will deal with dualities as functions within structures or take them, as mentioned in chapter 4, as the structure of what we are investigating.

Chapter Eight

The Psychology of Metapsychology

Toward a Theory of Psychoanalysis

In spite of the obvious problems Freud encountered with the concept of ego and the clear flaws in a psychology of the ego as a theoretical conformation, Freud continued to consider it a credible reformulation of the theory of psychoanalysis. Originally, he disregarded that he meant it to replace the old topography of psychical systems, implicitly abandoning the catharsis theory. He failed. In other words, he could neither *completely* get rid of the catharsis theory nor hold on to initiating an ego psychology. The four decades from the mid-1920s to the mid-1960s is the life span of ego psychology. They were spent by and large in political strife that looked to be about that theory but were not really.

Freud's ego psychology was emphasized by Anna Freud's *The Ego and the Mechanisms of Defence* (1936). Around the same time Melanie Klein was introducing new visions of the psyche from a relational angle in English psychoanalysis. In France, Nacht, who was analyzed by Hartmann, led a second generation of analysts and adopted ego psychology as the classical theory (with a French flair as Bouvet's work would show). He established the Paris Society on that tradition. However, by the early 1950s divisions started in the Paris Society. Lagache (analyzed by Loewenstein) and Boutonier were both classical analysts and, figuratively speaking, ego psychologists. They were joined by Lacan and split from the Paris Society. When Lacan went his way, Lagache and Boutonier and a good number of analysts with leanings to the classical theory appeared to have maintained their loyalty to ego psychology in their new society. However, it is hardly possible to find any French analyst after the death of Nacht in 1977 who would call himself an ego psychologist.

In the United States ego psychology was a definable, theoretical entity since the early 1940s to the late 1960s and was the only acceptable psychoanalytic doctrine. However, during that time, different from what happened in Europe, any call to rethink matters, to criticize, to reconsider, or to espouse a different point of view was "strictly" condemned, which reached some acrimonious levels when Bion was invited to the West Coast. However, when ego psychologists began tinkering with their theory, uncovering its weaknesses and flaws, and discovered that it cannot be saved, they started looking for a substitute theory. They created a crisis, and their attempts at solving the problem failed, as I showed in chapter 2. They ended with a psychoanalysis that needed a theory.

There are three question about that situation: Why did not Freud and his followers, and the second generation of exceptionally gifted analysts, notice the difficulties with ego psychology?[1] Why were all the replacement theories of ego psychology relational in one form or another? Why were all the replacement relational theories still captive of the notion of unacceptable repressed entities (urges, intentions, defects, misconceptions or misperceptions, etc.), a notion inherited from the catharsis theory?

My conditional response to these three queries is based on an observation. Notwithstanding the efforts of the philosophers to *describe* the nature of the subject, they did not consider that he is a product of an intrapsychic structure. Freud's initial theory was the first theory about the structure (or what structures) the *intrapsychic*. No one before him even considered giving it a thought, and he formulated a theory of the intrapsychical structure of hysterical patients. His first theory of catharsis was a daring attempt, which he complemented with a theory of the structure of dreams and other normal psychical phenomena. The problem with his first theory was its functional explanations of entities that constitute the psychical structure. After wearing that theory down to integrate his burgeoning insights and intuitions, he felt that he needed a new theory. Still captive of the functionality of the theory of catharsis he considered a theory of psychical agencies, ego psychology, to replace the theory of psychical systems. The analysts' need for a new intrapsychic theory encouraged accepting ego psychology as a replacement for the outdated catharsis theory, especially because it was Freud's last intrapsychic theory and, hence, the belief that it is Freud's true classical theory. But after discovering its inadequacy, instead of putting together one of their own, they shifted to the next best thing: interpersonal relationships.

Interpersonal relations are not a novelty; they are the most basic human psychical phenomenon. However, no one thought that they were something to think of, study, understand, and even make a profession of helping people in that regard until Freud discovered *that interpersonal relationships are reflections of intrapsychic conditions*. When the two theories of the intrapsychic collapsed, analysts turned to interpersonal relationships. Better, instead of looking for a real and more correct intrapsychic theory, analysts made a shortcut to interpersonal relationships. However, because they did not know what to look for or deal with in interpersonal relationships they fell back on the old, dependable idea of repression of the objectionable.

Whatever the response to my responses to the three queries, there is an issue to address: What happened to the two original issues Freud strove to address: the *Ucs.* in human phenomena and the structure of the human mind? All of Freud's endeavors would mean nothing now if we do not know, at least, what happened to the unconscious in our theories. Moreover, all our endeavors now, whatever kind of psychoanalyst we are, would mean nothing if we are not working toward a theory of the structure of the human mind.

Until those two stipulations are seriously considered, we should not accept a theory of psychoanalysis without the *Ucs.* being its center (Fayek, 2005) or accept relational psychologies as psychoanalytic substitutes for a solid and consistent intrapsychic theory of psychoanalysis.

FROM METAPSYCHOLOGY TO ITS PSYCHOLOGY

What is metapsychology without a psychology? The editor of the *Standard Edition* classified the four papers Freud dedicated to revise the core concepts of the catharsis theory as metapsychology papers. This classification, common among psychoanalysts, comes from confusing "metapsychology" with theory, with "scientifism," psychological with nonbiological, and representation with abstraction. Freud's definition of metapsychology was clear. He said: "I propose that when we have succeeded in describing a psychical process in its dynamic, topographic, and economic aspects we should speak of it as a *metapsychological* presentation (1915e, p. 181)." Accordingly, those papers are not metapsychological. They deal with the four phenomena (*Trieb*, or the originator of psychical life; repression; the unconscious; and regression). Those phenomena are not qualified for *psychological* investigations, let alone considering them metapsychological. More importantly, no psychoanalyst, pro or foe of metapsychology, ever came up with a fitting psychology for metapsychology. We have to look at this matter carefully because even *if those papers were considered by the psychoanalytic community as metapsychology, what psychology is behind those metapsychologies*?

Metapsychology without psychology is comparable to metaphysics without physics; it would be nothing more than unfounded beliefs or mythology. Many psychoanalysts came to the same conclusion and considered metapsychology myth or a fiction of sorts. Notwithstanding that fact, it is not possible for psychoanalysis, with its impressive and lasting impact on both psychotherapy and culture in the twentieth century, to be founded on merely faith and mythology. For metapsychology to remain essential to Freud's work until the end[2] and to maintain its important place in psychoanalysis, it must have had a psychology within it because only with a psychology behind it could it have kept its function as a theoretical framework. The question is what could that psychology be, and why was it missed in spite of the clear evidence that there must have been one?

When Freud wanted to find a term to describe his discoveries in the psyche and his formulations about the unconscious, he deliberately chose the term metapsychology and intentionally avoided using the term psychology (Freud, 1898, March 10). Freud realized from the beginning that it would be a contradiction of terms to call his formulation of the phenomena of the unconscious a "psychology." Psychology is the science of consciousness. However, in Brenner's opinion (1980), Freud "meant" by metapsychology the psychology of the unconscious processes. He then contradicted himself by saying, "He [Freud] called the theories he elaborated metapsychology, to distinguish them from psychological theories that maintained that what is not conscious is not mental" (ibid., pp. 301–302).

The difference between mere theoretical formulation in psychoanalysis and metapsychology is that metapsychology separates the psychodynamic functions from their subject matter, thus allowing further speculation on an abstract level. Separations between functions and subject matter does not make metapsychology an abstraction; they only become reference to the condition of the subject matter. When that difference is disregarded a complete confusion of functions and structures blurs the analyst's view of causes and effects. Freud as a physician aspired to build psychoanalysis on functional thinking. Functions are also the kind of reason that is derived from manifestations because they appear as insinuating the meanings of the observed. For instance, a slip of the tongue is semantically a function of a compromise between two preconscious signifiers; therefore the slip suggests the meaning of the compromise. But when we look for the signified in the slip we realize that it is a text and a complete sentence that embodies a signifier; the compromise reveals an intention to say something and refrain from saying something and to say something else instead. For the psychoanalyst, the intention should not be the noun or the content (hate, envy, love, etc.) but the organizing of the rhetoric of the slip. The reason for emphasizing this point is the tendency to regard meanings as causes, almost in total isolation of the subject who owns the antithetical intentions of the slip. Metapsychology does not deal with functions but only with structural features. The psychology of metapsychology should be of a subject matter that was a starting point of the whole of the psychoanalytic discovery and remained the core of that discovery. It must also be open to the three known metapsychologies, meaning that it could encompass economical, dynamic, and topographical features.

Those characteristics are convincingly present in Freud's concept of *affect*[3] since his *Project for a Scientific Psychology* and even before, though in a rudimentary form. It was a concept loaded with potentials. He started his *Project* with a brief explication of the functions and the dynamics of neural activity, and articulated a couple of principals that guided the development of his argument. He said in the first principal that the nervous system, as an inheritor of the responsiveness of protoplasm, is subject to states of excitation when it is stimulated. Its excitation manifests in a "quanta of energy" in the neural network that exerts pressure for freeing the system from it: discharge. Contrary to the belief that the concept of energy is a neurobiological concept, not a psychological one (see chapter 2), Freud used energy in the *Project* as a signifier of structural change in the neurons, not as a signified or a product of excitement.

Freud gave thought to the accumulation and discharge of the quota of excitation in the system and the associated sensation of pleasure and pain as results of that. In his major work on hysteria (1895d) he equated excitation, both before and after discharge, with an expression of tension relief. The term *quota of energy* changed to *quota of affect* and became a cornerstone of his burgeoning psychological explanations of psychical phenomena for a long time. This simple and very astute leap moved Freud from neurology proper to psychology, with no fanfare. His psychology was different from Wunt's (1878) and Brentano's (1874/1973) (psychologists at that time were interested in processes that create the psychical phenomena and not in the psychical phenomena themselves).

The leap to affect instead of dealing with neural energy (neural energy has no qualitative differential attributes) (Freud, 1915c, p. 123) moved the issue to dealing with its psychical corollary. He realized that affect is capable of transformation into different qualities. He noted that in indicating that "a quota of affect or sum of excitation, which possess all the characteristics of a quantity . . . , is capable of increase, diminution, displacement, and discharge" (1894, p. 60). Not only that, he distinguished three possible mechanisms of transformation: conversion (hysteria), displacement (obsession), and exchange of affect (anxiety and melancholia) (1894, May 21). If Freud's theory at that time was not about the transformations of the affective condition, it was at least loaded with the potentials of further forms of transformations.

In addition to the conception of the quota of energy Freud integrated into his budding psychological theory one more neural mechanism: the primary and secondary processes. He related the propensity of the quota of energy for total discharge to a primary reactivity, while a secondary function of the nervous system was to control that discharge and preserve a constant state of innervation. The two processes coexisted and worked, more or less, in dynamic opposition.

As he continued the study of hysteria his understanding of the process of the transformation of affect forced him to tackle the qualities of affect alongside the quantitative aspect: how the same quota of affect is capable of expressing pleasure with its varied derivatives and pain with all its attributes. In Green's opinion Freud obstinately wanted to keep the quantity factor separate from the quality factor in the quota of affect (Green, 2005). In my opinion the wish to keep the two conditions separate was Freud's later separation of the representation of the *Trieb* (thought) from its affective component, as I will mention later. However, it became obvious to Freud that a main principle in the *Project* indicated that quantity leads to quality in the form of affect of pleasure and pain. *Affect was identified as a content-less and form-less state that generates varied conditions depending on two factors: its intensity and discharge (primarily or secondarily*). Depending on the dynamics of the primary process and its secondary counterpart, the transformation would result in normal psychical phenomena or a psychopathological condition.

In psychopathology affect is transformed into misleading and mystifying forms and in warped chains of representations that make it difficult to identify. Freud's intuition was that a psychology of affect had to be researched first in regular psychical conditions, and he chose dreams. Dreams were always considered responses to "personal" causes, physical or metaphysical. His contribution was that the dream is a product of a state of affect or the function of representing a state of affect. As such, the dream could represent both an affect aroused by a psychological demand or a physiological one. In both cases *the representation or the dream will become a state of wishing, wishing the satisfaction of the affective demand.* It is important to underscore that the state of wishing in this formula was also content-less and form-less in the sense that the purpose of the dream is not conditional on the wish but on its fulfillment; the dream's function is fulfillment irrespective of what wishes it fulfills.

A first metapsychology came in *The Interpretation of Dreams* (1900a). It was the metapsychology of transforming affect into a wish and the way sleeping deals with satisfying that wish. Freud discovered that the mental processes in sleep use two mechanisms that are very analogous to the neurological mechanism of primary and secondary discharges of the quota of affect. Freud's leap from a state of affect to the state of wishing revealed a gap created in the mind between dealing with wishing in terms of the primary process (condensation or metaphor, and displacement or metonymy) and in terms of the secondary process (thinking). His previous simplistic conceptions of conscious and the unconscious underwent the first radical change, and he came up with the topographical model. This is exceptionally significant because Freud provided a *meta*psychology for the transformation of affect by which we can thus consider a psychical system that has different states without regarding their contents and could house affective contents according to their attributes: dynamic, economic, topographic. The state of wishing fit the topographic system that gives the psychical its qualification instead of the psychical designating the qualification of its state.

Freud's learning of the psychology of the wish in the study of dreams led to applying it to other psychological phenomena (parapraxes and jokes) with promising results. It also allowed him to appreciate the usefulness of the working of the primary and secondary processes in opening up the topic of sexuality in an unexpected way. *Three Assays on the Theory of Sexuality* (1905b) bear the imprint of the psychology of the wish as revised in the study of dreams: sexuality was no more a causative factor in hysteria, but sexual anomalies were. Freud came up with the new and intriguing concept of *Trieb* to deal with sexuality within his burgeoning psychological theory. The pressure of the endosomatic sensed as quanta of affect was called *Trieb*, denoting the pressure the endosomatic stimulus exerted on the mind. That pressure requires that it be represented (i.e., turns into a mental quality). Sexuality could be included in *Triebhaft* formation instead of considering it as pressure in its own right. The concept itself is intriguing because it allowed Freud to make a very central distinction in psychology between thought and feeling. (Academic psychology distinguishes cognitive function from emotional function in order to control the dependent and independent factors in experimentation). Freud did that, it seems, for another reason and not for the reason Green gave (1999a, p. 30). He did it to emphasize the difference between the representations of the *Trieb*, which are mental, and the affective residual, which is mostly feeling (*Gefühl*).[4]

The psychology of the *Trieb* forced Freud to consider the fate of the representation and the affective residual of the quota of affect that accompanies the state of wishing and the wish in the new metapsychology. This is when he revisited the three concepts, repression, *Trieb*, and the unconscious. He said, "For this other element of the psychical representative the term *quota of affect* has been generally adopted. It corresponds to the instinct in so far as the latter has become detached from the idea and finds expression, proportionate to its quantity, in processes which are sensed as affects [*Gefühl*]"(1915e, p.152). Moving from the quanta of affect to the state of wishing and then to the concept of *Trieb* enabled Freud to talk more about the transformation of the endosomatic stimuli instead of the stimuli themselves and to expand his horizons to formulate his discoveries in terms of psychical processes, whether in psychopathology or in other human phenomena. Freud was on the verge of a true theory of psychoanalysis founded on psychical processes instead of psychical entities. Psychical processes have economic aspects in terms of what happens to affect quantitatively. They also have topographic structures in terms of the participation of the three systems of *Cs.*, *Pcs.*, and *Ucs.* in deciding the dynamics of their final forms (i.e., they are amenable to metapsychological formulations).

Unexpectedly, for reasons discussed before (chapter 7), Freud turned to a psychology of the ego as the final theoretical formulation of psychoanalysis. Ego psychology, which was gradually taken by a great number of analysts as a favorable substitute for topographic metapsychology, was not meant to be a metapsychology.[5] It proved to be more of a problem than an answer. This is when Freud made a remarkable turnabout in his second theory of anxiety (1926d). He appeared as if he were dealing with the issue of *symptom formation*, or the problem of anxiety, when, in fact, he trounced the catharsis theory completely and advanced the psychology of metapsychology to a point where we could confidently elicit his theory of psychoanalysis.

In the early stages of the theory of catharsis the frustrated accumulated sexual excitation constituted the quanta of affect that manifested in the feeling of anxiety. With the theory advancing to the concept of *Trieb*, the representation of the endosomatic stimuli became containable by defense mechanisms, which would suppress it, while the affective component would be subjected to repression. Anxiety was regarded as the suppressed libido transformed into anxiety and became the product of repression in both cases, with a slight distinction: in one it was an affective state without substantial transformation and in the second it was a transformation that integrated symbolic notions in its final expression. This was the way Freud distinguished between hysterical anxiety and free floating anxiety. Freud reversed his description of anxiety completely when he said:

> I have in many occasions asserted that in repression the instinctual representative is distorted, displaced, and so on, while the libido [affect] belonging to the instinctual impulse is transformed into anxiety. . . . The description would be correct; and there does undoubtedly exist a correspondence of the kind asserted between the strength of the impulse that has to be repressed and the intensity of the resultant anxiety. But I have to admit that I thought I was giving more than a mere description. I believed that I had put my finger on a metapsychological process of direct transformation of libido into anxiety. I can now no longer maintain this view. And, indeed, I found it impossible at the time to explain how a transformation of that kind was carried out. (1926d, p. 109)

In my opinion the reversal of the relationship between repression and anxiety made Freud change his theory of anxiety from a function of repression to being the *predicate* for repression. I am founding this view on some basic postulates Freud made about anxiety within the place of anxiety in the psychology of the metapsychologies. He affirmed that anxiety could be an original reaction to satisfying a *Triebhaft* urge or an anticathexis to dissatisfying such an urge. Therefore, anxiety is not an affective entity but rather one of its vicissitudes that would be initiated by the particularity of the situation, that is, when it is not possible to discharge the tension of the affective component of the *Trieb*. In addition to that distinction Freud invoked his revision of repression to deal with two issues raised by anxiety as the precondition for repression. The part of the quanta of affect evolves into a thing representation, and the residual affective condition changes into feeling by virtue of primary repression. Primary repression, which creates a cleavage within that quantum, turns the feeling into something identifiable to the other (the caregiver) and vaguely to self. Once that happens, anxiety would be an advanced reaction to the failure of the message reaching the caregiver. *The most interesting and intriguing aspect in that process is the way it changes in content but not in nature or structure. It remains the same but changes to the phase of development; in the oral phase anxiety would be about losing the external support, while in the phallic phase it would be about losing identification with the parent of the same sex.* It is intriguing because we find the issues created by primary repression remain to be the most hidden and powerful and the ones that are the background of the phenomena of the aftereffect. I am highlighting this point because when we discuss aftereffect, as a psychical attribute of health or sickness, we will depend heavily on the nature of the link between the psychology of the metapsychology and metapsychology.

I end this section with a concluding statement about the psychology of metapsychology: *The unarticulated theory of psychoanalysis seems to be the psychology of the metapsychologies (i.e., a theory of what the psychology of the metapsychology is about).* This point of view requires us to deal first with entrenched misconceptions of major concepts in the catharsis theory, and to give those concepts their correct significations.

AFFECT (*AFFEKT*) AND FEELING (*GEFÜHL*) IN THE PSYCHOLOGY OF METAPSYCHOLOGY

In *Studies on Hysteria* Breuer and Freud summarized their main discovery by saying:

> *we found, to our great surprise, that each individual hysterical symptom immediately and permanently disappeared when we had succeeded in bringing clearly to light the memory of the event by which it was provoked and in arousing its accompanying affect, and when the patient had described that event in the greatest possible detail and had put the affect into words* [italics added]. Recollection without affect almost invariably produced no results. (1895d, p. 6)

In terms of a theory of pathology based on forgetting and recall, the affective component of "the repressed" was considered central in the process of cure. However, Freud detected that cure happens only when the *strangulated affect* came back in the "language" (not necessarily in the speech) of the patient, not just as an abreaction (i.e., came back as a feeling). Feeling was an affect that found the words or the symbols to identify its quality. The hypnotic phase of therapy soon came to an end because affective abreaction was useless if the patient did not experience it as a feeling; feeling is something to talk about.

In his two papers on the neuropsychoses of defense (1894a, 1896b) Freud makes a clear distinction between a *quanta of affect* and *memory traces*, which he considered to be representational of the former, thoughts, words, ideas, when feelings could be memory traces of an affective state. This distinction matched another distinction he made between stimulations stemming from the body itself (a state of need) and stimulations coming to the body through the senses, giving feelings a content. The first kind, before being processed through the system *Cs.*, is quantitative in nature (*quanta of affect*) and does not create memory traces. The sensory stimulation emerging from the external world has an intrinsic qualitative nature because it is processed through consciousness first and processed through ideation after; it leaves an aftereffect of memory traces. The two types overlap at the point where the endosomatic stimulus and the external stimulation link when it is still too difficult for the infant to distinguish between them. A hungry baby reacts to the smell of his mother's milk at first as if it is a bodily sensation. The main thrust of psychical development is to reach the distinction between affect as the *indication* of psychic energy (libido, the somatic, *Trieb,* and feeling) and as the *representation* of affect (thought, language, memory traces, relationships, and states of mind). This distinction was a critical point in a theory of psychoanalysis because it allowed understanding a basic structural difference between affect and feeling.

Affect originates in the state of excitation in the body. It brings the infant to the steps of awareness but not consciousness yet; affect is an *aconscious* state of mind. Green puts it well when he says: "Its proximity [affect] to the drive impulse made it a better pointer to drive activity" (1977, p. 139). In this meaning affect will not have access to consciousness before it is transformed into representation (mentation) and feeling (either pleasure or pain), and thus have access to consciousness. Representation does not become conscious immediately but has to undergo a secondary repression or repression proper. Freud's views on feelings were quite sophisticated. In that regard he says:

> We then come to speak, in a condensed and not entirely correct manner, of "unconscious feelings," keeping an analogy with unconscious ideas, which is not altogether justifiable. Actually the difference is that, whereas with *Ucs.* ideas connecting links must be created before they can be brought into *Cs.*, with *feelings* which are themselves transmitted directly this does not occur. Even when they [feelings] are attached to word presentation, their becoming

> conscious is not due to that circumstance, but they become so directly [italics added]. (Freud, 1923b, pp. 22–23)

There is no ambiguity that what Freud called feeling does not belong to the system *Ucs*. because it does not undergo the processes that the affects yield to in primary repression. Feelings are transformations of affect; they get modified but they do not transform into something other than feelings of pleasure and pain. The cleavage that Freud talked about as the predicate for repression is the separation and the gap within affect between representing it in a form of "mentation," and transforming its pleasure/pain aspect into urges or feelings. Once the cleavage between mental representation and feelings occurs, the link between them—also established by the primary process—becomes arbitrary, and each would take a separate course of evolving. Establishing this fundamental arbitrary link creates the seat of many foundational psychical conditions (psychosomatics, artistic penchants, intuitions, and psychoses too). Mental representations continuously generate representations of representations, and the links between them are as arbitrary as the initial one between the affect and its early representations (phallic fantasies, sexual desires, sexualizing or desexualizing interpersonal relationships, character formation and probably end up with sexual deviation). In the field of feeling we do not encounter arbitrariness outside ambivalence, reversal, negation, and apathy. Freud's insights about the separateness of thought and feeling and the arbitrary links between them address an important part of the basic dilemma of Western culture (see chapter 4): How does the transcending consciousness not change consciousness but leads to more transcendence? How can we know that we do not know and do not know that we know?

This Freudian insight has significant clinical applications too. Representation of affect, as it moves from thing presentation to word presentation, reaches for language to become meaningful to the other. The links between the presentations via things and then via words make those links as complex as their arbitrariness makes them difficult to trace. The quanta of affect—as considered in the literature—are *unbound energy*: free floating tension, in its way to binding to things and words, undergoes many distortions and disguises, while chains of presentation are forming distortions and disguises happen unconsciously. Considering all that, we should look at free association as the only means we have to get—as close as possible—to the disguised bound affect. Listing to a patient free associating entails expecting it to get better (more free) with time, coming closer to the origin of the transformed affect when appropriate interpretations are applied, and revealing the entwinement of the primary and secondary processes in those disguises, with more familiarity with the process. What made Freud discard the theory of the "strangulated" feeling so early in his career was because he became aware that there is no specific affect associated, in an intrinsic way, with any particular presentation. Symptoms revealed the arbitrary and contingent links between affects and their representations; therefore, those representations had to be perceived as arbitrary also. He even distinguished between hysteria and the obsessions by noticing that in hysteria affect is converted into physical symptoms, while the obsessions are displaced and hence relate to the wrong subject in the symptom. He said in that regard, "[T]he unconscious speaks more than one dialect [but speaks the same language]" (1913j, p. 177).

Contemporary psychoanalyses neglect the significant difference between affect and feeling, and treat them as synonyms. Neglecting that difference is associated with, if not caused by, neglecting the difference between the *Ucs.* and the *Pcs*. Pulver (1971) disputed the need or importance of distinguishing feeling from affect by saying, "Since unconscious in the descriptive sense includes preconscious, let us begin with some evidence of preconscious affect" (p. 350). Freud dealt with affect and feeling in terms of their conscious/preconscious and unconscious states and made clear that feeling could be preconscious but affect could not. Missing this point made Pulver go further to say, "[U]nconscious affect consists of situations in which the individual shows physiological, ideational and motor behaviour usually *associated* [italics added] with a central *feeling state* [italics added]" (1971, p. 351).

The implications of not differentiating feeling from affect created subtle but serious clinical confusions. Arlow (1977) talked about affect and its absence in the analytic situation as a significant clinical issue. Obviously, what they meant by affect in that context was feeling because affect has to be there in some sort of representation, of which feeling is only one. As such, when feelings are absent in analysis, it would mean that they must have found another representation for themselves (unfailingly *the absent affect would be found in the transference relationship*). In those cases we should, for example, consider the total repression of feelings equal in its defensiveness to its conversion into a hysterical paralysis. Limentani says,

> The success and failure of an analysis could in fact be said to rest on the degree of affective changes which take place during its course. . . . A feeling is an affective *presentation* [italics added], is an *internal* [italics added] rather than an overt activity, yet it is seldom out of touch with the external situation. (1977, pp. 172–174)

Though Limentani did not intend, in his paper, to deal with the psychology of affect separately from the phenomena of feelings, he made it clear that what we should aim to change in psychoanalysis is affect, and not feelings. In a theory of feelings, the success or failure of psychoanalysis will be measured by the *quantity* of changes in feelings more than by the *quality* of change. The root of those confusions is a common belief so that Freud "found it very useful to separate the feeling tone—or affect as it came to be called—from its concomitant or associated ideational content" (Arlow, 1977, p. 157). The separation Arlow and Brenner talked about is not something useful that Freud resorted to; it is *the discovery itself*, not just a preferred and useful measure but the way things are.

The English school of object relations had two reasons to prefer dealing with feelings instead of the concept of affect. The first is that the concept of fantasy has replaced the unconscious as the basis for relating to the other; therefore affect had to give its intrapsychic position to feelings, which become the criterion for the relationship with the object. The second reason is that feelings were considered the quality of the unconscious fantasy, and have taken a prominent place in transference and countertransference. The ideas of "projective identification" (Heiman, 1950; Klein, 1952; Ogden, 1986), the "container and the contained" (Bion, 1962), and the "holding environment" (Winnicott, 1955) are based on some sort of "feeling someone else's feeling." Feelings in that context are fixed reactions to situations, not representation of affect, which could be reactivated as is in another situation (in the transference). This conception of the relation with the object would rely on the phenomenon of feeling and would not have a place for a concept of affect, which is not contingent on the external situation but on intrapsychic dynamics (Green, 1977).

A psychology of affect distinct from a psychology of feelings might still be unclear to some. But it becomes clear if we try to answer this question: How could we understand an affective state or feeling as a defense (Arlow, 1977) or as a response to a "good" or a "bad" psychoanalysis (Limentani, 1977)? Only after analyzing feelings as compromise formations (exactly as we analyze dreams, symptoms, and parapraxes) could we recognize a defense or a transference reaction, and not before that. The same applies to analyzing feelings as responses to objects. It is possible to understand the relationship with the object as feeling for "good" or "bad" objects only if we think "simplistically" that "the object" transforms a quantum of affect into a relationship.

The two terms, if not distinguished from each other, will eliminate the chance to uncover the psychology of the metapsychologies and will allow some to justify eliminating metapsychology from psychoanalysis, and deprive it of its foundation.

AFFECT AND DRIVE (*TRIEB*)

Freud's discovery of the separateness of affect and its representation opened the way for two major formulations in the area of psychoneurosis. The *first* was that psychological symptoms (starting with hysteria) could be explained in terms of a psychopathological process, analogous to the physiopathological processes that produce physical symptoms. For the first time, a psychological symptom was to be understood in itself (metapsychologically) and was not to be explained as the reaction to an external cause. The *second* formulation was that such a process is a manifestation of a "force" *that impels the mind* to activity, which could go in different directions based on the absence of the essential contingency between that force and its manifestation. The manifestation of that force, or its representation as used in this context, was a quantum of affect. In that sense, the study of affect leads directly to the concept of *Trieb* since *Trieb* is a manifestation of affective pressure on the mind to act.

The concept of *Trieb* has been fiercely attacked as the trend to separate from classical analysis got stronger, ensued by dropping the concept of metapsychology. Doing away with those two components of the theory resulted in giving up the idea of "psychopathological processes." The way the concept of *Trieb* was dropped from present-day psychoanalysis deserves a closer look because it highlights the way the new psychologies have emerged in psychoanalysis. It was first translated by instinct, changing it from the initiator of mentation to an originator of behavior. This translation did not "sit well" with the French who used *pulsion*, which did not sit well with the English. Drive was suggested, and psychoanalysis became a "drive psychology." I could not trace the term *drive psychology*[6] to any specific source in psychoanalysis. Freud's text does not have a concept or a word that could translate correctly to the colloquial *drive*, which has a totally different meaning in the English language (it is a transitive verb and rarely used as an adjective or a noun). The *economic point of view*, as one of the three classical metapsychologies, is too sophisticated to be the basis for a simplistic drive psychology. The possible origin of the term could be in Hartmann's introduction of the term *instinctual drives* (Hartmann, 1948), possibly thinking that by adding the term *drive* to instinct it will be distinguished from *Instinkt* (German). The synonymy of the two terms permitted the dropping of one, *Trieb*, and keeping drive. Hartmann's endeavor allowed a semantic mistake to take hold of the Freudian doctrine, leading to the exact opposite of what he intended for the term *Trieb* to contribute to psychoanalysis. *Drive psychology* is presently a term that stands for everything that is trite and renounced in psychoanalysis.

Trieb is a peculiar concept in psychoanalysis. It is an insignificant concept to most analysts, including some of Freud's contemporaries. The most ardently orthodox analyst could disregard that concept completely without any obvious signs of deviation from orthodoxy appearing in his work. However, for some reason Freud considered the theory of *Trieb* as "the most *important* [italics added] part but at the same time the least complete of the psychoanalytic theory (1905d [1924, fn. 2, p. 168])." Every time Freud came to a new understanding of his clinical material that required modifications in the theory he went back to the concept of *Trieb* and modified it to tally the new modifications. The best example is the period between the introduction of narcissism (1914c) and the concept of repetition compulsion (1920g). During that time he paid attention to the vicissitudes of the instincts (1915c) and came to grips with the significance of the aggressive component in melancholia (1917e), and suddenly he replaced the concept of fixation with repetition compulsion. As a result, the theory of *Trieb* had to change to fit in the new theory of life and death. What is of special import in this regard is that the concept of *Trieb* did not instigate change, though it changed with the amelioration of theoretical understanding; and when it was subjected to change it was only to its content, but it stayed the measure of the pressure on the mind to mentalize. *It is not feasible for a concept of that nature to create a psychology on its own, but it is essential to a psychology of metapsychology.*

Replacement of *Trieb* with another initiator of mental representation fails in dealing with the intrapsychic and would only be good for the corollaries of the intrapsychic. Peskin for instance says, "However, in elucidating the psychology of human motivation, it is only *a psychological concept of drives* [italics added] which captures the innately endowed, self-enhancing, motivational push compatible with evolutionary theory while at the same time being consonant with the intrapsychic dynamics of psychoanalytic observation" (1997, p. 397). There are no psychological concepts of drive in psychology, but motivation has a place. However, it is noticeable that when we use drive as the initiator of a response, we fall into the trap of giving it the same name we give the behavior it initiates. Naming the drive after the behavior it initiates turns the intransitive verb into an adjective and changes the intrapsychic process of representation into a relational condition.

It is not possible to talk about a psychopathological process in terms of interpersonal relationships, yet it is possible to talk about interpersonal relationships in terms of a psychopathological process. For instance, we cannot understand the psychodynamics of an obsessive symptom in light of the relationship between the obsessional and his spouse, or even all his mother figures put together. But we can understand the relationship between him and them in light of the psychopathological process that structures his obsession. The basic ideas of the arbitrary link between affect and thought; the aim and the object of behavior; and the manifest and the latent, which are the essence of the intrapsychic and its psychopathology, are not recognizable in any psychopathological interpersonal relationships. Contemporary analysts talk of the totality of psychoanalysis as a process but do not talk of psychopathology per se; they describe pathological relationships but do not explain them.

As metapsychology remained without a defined psychology, it became an easy target for criticism, and a strong trend to eliminate it prevailed (Holder, 1970; Schafer, 1976). By eliminating metapsychology, psychoanalysis lost its "structuring" concepts and terminology. There was no replacement suggested, and the alternatives did not prove to be practical (Schafer's action language for instance). Gradually there was no obstacle for new psychologies to be created: the psychologies of the ego (Hartmann), the self (Kohut), the object (Klein and others), and the subject (Lacan). What was once heated debates in psychoanalysis changed to be schools of psychoanalysis; what was once one psychoanalysis changed to be many (Wallerstein, 1988). Since those psychologies got rid of metapsychology and did not have their own replacement, the preference of one to the other was haphazard. We are presently less clear about which psychoanalysis we do practice (Cesio, 1995).

Psychology versus metapsychology is the dichotomy that kept the Freudian doctrine internally consistent. Without a metapsychology in the new psychologies, other dichotomies, irrelevant to psychoanalysis, emerged. First, there was the dichotomy of the natural sciences versus the humanistic (Fairbairn, 1952; Guntrip, 1971). Then came the dichotomy of the clinical versus the metapsychological or theoretical (G. Klein, 1976). The third dichotomy was the biological versus the psychological (the Neu-Freudians). Waelder (1962) tried to contain this seemingly chaotic situation by suggesting a hierarchical system of classification for those dichotomies. Meissner (1981) also suggested a dichotomy of meaning (hermeneutics) versus structure (metapsychology), indicating the need for both. The latest dichotomy (Renik, 1998a) is between positivism (objectivity) and hermeneutics (subjectivity or intersubjectivity). Once again, we find ourselves in a confusing and riddled field of suggested alternatives to the basic dichotomy of psychology versus metapsychology. The problem does not seem to have an end because the definitions of some of the terminologies used in those dichotomies are not exact or not coming from their original sources; therefore they are sometimes incorrect, especially terms such as *hermeneutics* (see Bouchard, 1995; Renik, 1998b).

The plea to return to Freud and his text is a plea to put the "progress" that was made in the last half century into perspective. It is a plea to contain whatever is truly psychoanalytic in that progress in a clear frame of reference, to avoid what seems now to look like strifes with quasi-psychoanalytic issues.

Chapter Nine

Eliciting the Theory of Psychoanalysis from the Freudian Text

A Change of Orientation

Freud's other theory of psychoanalysis is implicit in his text, and identifying it as a replacement for the catharsis theory has to be done by separating it from two accumulations: an accumulation distortion of its basic premises either intentionally or merely for hanging on to the catharsis theory. The other accumulation is the criticism of the flaws in cathartic theory, which the other theory corrected indirectly and unnoticeably. I will begin dealing with those two obstacles by delineating some of the features of the true theory and then move to extracting the theory itself. Extracting the body of the theory has to meet certain criteria, which requires the analyst to reorient himself to a theory that is not based on repressions.

THE FIRST FEATURE

The concept of *Trieb* is a concept of polarity not plurality, and the two main polarities of sex/self-preservation and life/death were not meant to explain behavior but rather to depict conflict. Missing this fact led Compton and other psychoanalysts to deny that *Trieb* is an originator of the psychical processes. Thus he rendered psychical life to meaninglessness: it had neither the motivations that the catharsis theory was offering nor a substitute for its core propositions. Compton (1981a, b, c, d) deemed a mental activity instigated by somatic excitation to be in Freud's terms merely an instinctual reaction (Compton, 1983a, fn., p. 381). He said the following:

> [to] understand the theory of drives [*Trieb*] . . . , it is necessary to understand [its] constraints. They consist of Freud's excitation theories, transposed from a neurological to a psychological context, his early ideas on sexuality and the topographical model of the mind. The problems of excitation theories and Freud's early ideas on sexuality are part of the general problems of mind-body relationship. (1981a, p. 192)

Compton added to that accumulation that Freud's shift from the neurological to the psychological is to blamed for initiating a dichotomy of body and mind, when in fact it was *clearly* uncovering the naissance of the psychical from the neurological (biological). The body-mind dichotomy is an integral part of the catharsis theory, where bodily urges were given adjectival qualities. Freud was inclined to do that sometimes. When *Trieb* was replaced with drive to avoid those "pitfalls" the situation got even worse. But Compton decided to remove *Trieb* from that argumentation and found himself inadvertently talking about drives as they were used in academic psychology until the 1940s, to the extent that he considered it necessary to count their numbers. He said:

> Our concept of "instinctual drives" determines what phenomena we will try to explain by "drive" constructs. A problem of drive constructs is that they can readily explain too much: a different drive can—and has been—postulated as an explanation for every conceivable type of behaviour. Circumscription of the number of drives then becomes essential if the concept is to be useful or even meaningful. (1983a, pp. 378–379)

The first feature of psychoanalysis is that it is a psychology of the condition that brings out the psychical from its somatic-affective origin (i.e., it is a theory that does not deal with any originator of behavior but with the originator who has the qualifications to produce a psychical process). It is a psychology of the transformations that end up with the formation of the human phenomena; but because of lack of interest or maybe failure in finding the psychology of metapsychology, this feature was not just missed but was considered a weakness in the Freudian doctrine. To give this feature its proper value in the theory I will show how missing it was the effect of the catharsis theory.

THE SECOND FEATURE

The three metapsychologies were suitable for dealing abstractly with the psychology of affect and its transformations. The theory of the transformation of affect would have a significant gap and a fundamental lack without metapsychology. The basis of metapsychology is abstract and not concrete allusions to functions. Yet when Freud came up with a psychology of the ego in a new psychology it was counted as metapsychology; it was even suggested to displace the original three. A serious mix-up resulted from this ill-advised development. Compton says, "The relation of the id to the other psychic structures and to reality must describe the confines of the position of drives in personality, because in Freud's work id subsumed the earlier concept of the unconscious (*Ucs.*) and instinctual drives" (1983b, p. 404). This is a grave misconstruing of the meaning of *Trieb*, as well as of *id*, because Freud clearly stated, "I am in fact of the opinion that the *antithesis* of conscious and unconscious is not applicable to instincts. An instinct can never become an object of consciousness—only the idea that represents the instinct can" (1915e, p. 177). Compton's suggestion that id could subsume both the systemic *Ucs.* and the *Trieb* could be considered only if three misconceptions are established first: *Trieb* becomes drive, drive becomes *Ucs.*, and *Ucs.* becomes a property of only the id and is not shared by the ego and superego. We know that nothing of that concurs with ego psychology or even with Freud's theory of catharsis.

The second feature of the theory of psychoanalysis is not acknowledged by ego psychologists for more than what I underlined above. They had difficulty with the concept of psychical energy and preferred using concepts of more modern genre such as the communication theory and cybernetic theories. The reasons given were the link between *Trieb* (instinctual energy) and the economic point of view, claiming that the energy concept is a product of the rejected concept of *Trieb*. The concept of energy (psychical) was there in Freud's writing for more than two decades prior to introducing the concept of *Trieb*. It remained in his theory as a metapsychology until the revision of the pleasure/reality principle in 1920. He maintained the metapsychology of psychic energy because it kept his early views coherent in terms of later views. Laplanche and Pontalis's articles on affect and economics put it succinctly when they say:

> Instinct expresses itself in terms of affect and in terms of ideas (*Vorstellungen*). . . . Affect is the *qualitative* expression of the quantity of instinctual energy and its fluctuation. . . . Freud only invokes an energy, therefore, as an underpinning for transformations which numerous factors of an empirical nature seem to indicate. (1967/1973, p. 214)

Since the case is about the emergence of the concept of *Trieb* from the quanta of affect and the economic metapsychology from *Trieb*, it follows that ego psychology's rejection of *Trieb* dictated the rejection of several other issues in the catharsis theory. However, it did not change analysts' orientation to accept that an originator has to be behind the transformations that permeate psychical life and that we would need a new theory anyway to replace the catharsis theory. The replacement theory has to be about the originator of the process of transformation, putting the accent on the transformation and not the originator.

THE THIRD FEATURE

In *The Interpretation of Dreams* (1900) Freud used the model of the hungry baby to topographically represent the mind and to describe the process by which the psychic apparatus is instigated to come into being by the pressure of a biological need (hunger). Freud used the details of that model to deal with the objects of the *Trieb*, the early representation of its object, and a variety of other aspects pertaining to that situation, which we see later developed into significant theoretical insights. Though he went back to that example only once, eleven years later, in his paper on the Formulations on the Two Principles of Mental Functioning Formulations (1911b), this model became, as Rappaport put it (1951), "the conceptual model of psychoanalysis," and as Safouan (1983) saw it, as Freud's "epithet of his metapsychologies."

That model has far-reaching implications on the issue of metapsychology and psychoanalysis itself. I opted to discuss only one of its implications, that which has an impact on the phenomenon of *fantasy*, and how it is dealt with in both classical theory and the object relations theories.

The model of the hungry baby came five years before introducing the concept of *Trieb*. It was used simply to show the point of departure from the biological need to the emergence of the cleavage between the two psychical systems of *Ucs.* and *Cs*. Originally, it was not a model for the concept of *Trieb* but was intended to be a differentiation that creates psychical events. In other words, Freud used that model to supplement his model of the mind in its very elementary starting point of a helpless, hungry baby who is unaware (aconscious) of what hit her or from where.

The paper on the two principles (1911a) was more on the emergence of a principle from within another principle, and not on two dichotomous principles or on their opposition. It dealt with the manner by which the process of "attention" starts and how that leads to the formation of memory, thinking, and fantasies. The reality principle was perceived as a product of the pleasure principle and not as its antagonist. It also emphasized that "psychic reality" is a transformation that springs from the pleasure principle and therefore would relate to the systems *Cs.* and *Ucs.* This is in contrast to an autonomously independent "material reality," which is cognitive and relates to the perceptual-sensory systems. It is important to highlight this point for two reasons: (a) The main trend in psychoanalysis is to put psychic reality in contradistinction to physical reality (external), and it is considered the distorting factor in proper cognition of another the other reality (subjectivity). (b) Freud used to treat *fantasies as one of the products of the unconscious processes but not as its quality or its corollary.* He says, "[F]antasies possess *psychical* as contrasted with material reality [for] in the real world of the neurosis it is psychical reality which is the decisive kind" (1916–1917, p. 360). This is obviously not the object relationists' position on fantasies (Hayman, 1994; Isaacs, 1948). In other words, the actual conflict in a person's life is not between the pleasure and reality principles but between psychical and physiological realities, where fantasies, which are stunted psychical realities, could interfere with the resolution of such conflict.

Object relations theorists see the matter differently. In that regard Spillius says, "Basically Klein's view, as expressed by Isaacs, is that unconscious fantasies are 'the primary content of unconscious mental processes,' the mental corollary, the psychic representative of instincts. Fantasies are the equivalent of what Freud meant by the 'instinctual representative' or the 'psychic representative of an instinctual drive'" (1992, p. 5).

It is inevitable for the Kleinians to consider fantasies to be the content of the unconscious instead of the *Trieb* because *Trieb* is content-less; therefore it could not be projected or introjected, or *contain and be contained.* In Freud's theory of *Trieb*, fantasies would be representations of the instinct but not the content of the *Ucs.*

In the object relations theory, relationships with the object are representations of fantasies. This difference reveals a cardinal and more basic difference, though very subtle: when a Freudian analyzes a fantasy as a representation, she would be looking for unconscious mechanisms that structured the fantasy. On the other hand the analyst with object relations proclivity looks for the object relation within that fantasy.

Another reason for object relations theorists to overlook the third feature of psychoanalysis is because of the changes they made to the concept of the subject. They turned the subject into an "object," reifying him and transforming Freud's libido theory into object relations theories. Compton says, "Given [the] formal statement of libido theory, with its emphasis on objects integral to the basic concept and in contrast to the de-emphasis of objects in the general drive theory, it is not surprising that the libido theory has become the basis for subsequent 'object-relations' theories" (1981c, p. 350). Freud meant by *object* the object of the *Trieb*, not the subject. In the Freudian sense the relationship with the object is not a function of the ego but a function of directing a libidinal quantum of the affect to an object, a formative process of the ego. In other words, an object relation in classical analysis is not a relationship between a subject (ego) and an object (he); it is a relationship between a *Trieb* and its object. *Freud does not have a theory of object relations but has a theory of relating to objects.* Better, Freud's views on relating to other subjects (persons) are based on their intrapsychic origin.

THE FOURTH FEATURE

The fourth feature is derived from retrieving the correct signification of those distorted concepts and underlining that psychoanalysis is a theory of the transformation of the psychical more than a theory of the psychical. Transformations are the series and continual production of representations of originary sources of the psychical.

Free associating is mainly verbal and avers to the analyst the psychical conditions of the patient. Better, the verbal associations are representations of the psychical conditions of the patient. To differentiate between what the patient says and what he talks about is the nucleus of psychoanalytic work and the focal point in the theory of psychoanalysis. Psychoanalysis is the theory of interpreting what is averred verbally as an expression of something else nonverbal, based on the assumption that there is a gap between those two things. Moreover, it is a theory of what has happened before the child realized that talking could represent his affective condition and the many basic and significant representations that have been created before the verbal sphere was initiated.

Freud's concept of presentation comes from Brentano's work (1874/1973), which was influenced by German philosophy in general. Brentano was looking for the mental process that distinguishes the *physical* world from the *psychological* world. He found that process in what scholastics called "inexistentia" (i.e., "existing-in" or "existence-in"). The way an object is present in the mind is existence-in, or inexistentia, since *an object is merely an object-of-the-mind,* which means that the actual objects are only references to those mental phenomena and then in turn are functions of objects that exist. In other words, the object's "inexistentia" is the condition of its mentation; an idea is what is mental in a representation and the replacement of its existence. It should not escape us that Freud took the idea of "the object inexistentia is in the mind" and examined what the mind could and could not do outside its boundaries. Brentano considered psychology to be the study of the different ways by which the mind deals with objects.

He distinguished three stages of dealing with objects in the mind: presenting it by an idea, judging the idea, and then loving/hating it in its state as an idea.[1] *Presentation*, in the Freudian sense, is the act that processes the perceptual into the mental, giving up the *object* but having it in the mind as an idea (an idea is an archetype, a form, or "pure reason" in German philosophy). However, we should not forget that Freud talked about two states or stages of presentation: thing-presentation (*Dingvorstellung)* and word-presentation (*Wortvorstellung*). Thing-presentation (signifier) is eventually and inevitably replaced by word-presentation, a representation of a presentation (a signifier of a signifier). The point is that a representation is a signifier transformed into another signifier in the process of signification. This is a reminder of the transcendence of consciousness that creates another transcendence (chapter 4). The chains of representing the representation submit to the rules of the primary process. The term *Vorstellung* then has the very specific meaning of transforming the affective into a mental quality. In fact that presentation, in Freud's usage of the term, is the emergence of what is mental from a state of sensation or feeling. *There is no representation that is not, somehow, mental.*

The model of the hungry baby shows a new aspect of that process. When the "need" for food or a sense of hunger impinges on the infant's mind, he sucks his thumb, hallucinating the sensation of the breast. The act of sucking the thumb starts the process of *presentation.* The thumb (part of the body) is the first object-of-the-mind that signifies the real thing (the breast). The thumb is the first "thing that represents" and is the prototype of representations. Hallucination, therefore, is a function of presentation (i.e., a manifestation of *an absence*). The lack of actual satisfaction of hunger by hallucinating satisfaction will be followed by the "thing" being judged as unreal and not as the thing itself. The breast is then *rediscovered.* As Freud said, "Instead of it [hallucinating satisfaction], the physical apparatus had to decide to form a conception of the real circumstances in the external world, and to endeavour to make a real alteration in them" (1911b, p. 219). The representation of the thing is the initiator of its repression because the mental could be repressed but the object itself could not. The breast is not the original object of orality. The representation is repressed in order to give its place to the breast as a representation of a presentation. The breast's absence is the originary source of the chain of signification because it is the lack that is not a manifestation of a true lack but of a presence that has to be rediscovered. As Boesky says, if the object "[is] disconnected from drives . . . we are dealing with a totally different theoretic model" (1983, p. 567). *All representations, the whole psychical life of the person, emanates from a sense of lack, which suggests a false absence. Only then is it possible for word representation to take hold.*

Contemporary psychoanalyses have a different concept and understanding of the term representation. Boesky says, "[T]he term mental representation has come to mean too many things. The representational language of individual authors, who seem to be using the same terms, actually differs considerably in meaning from one author to another" (1983, p. 564). The specific meaning Freud gave to the process of representation has undergone radical changes, however gradual and subtle. It is possible to trace those changes to a major misunderstanding of Freud's concept of *reality testing.* As was mentioned previously, reality testing, within the original meaning of the term *Vorstellung*, is the second stage of mentation, which comes after the thing-presentation is established. In that stage *the mental process is directed to test the reality of the presentation, not to test external reality.* It is the stage when the *thing* that stood to represent the somatic need (the thumb) is judged to be the false object of the *Trieb.* The real object is rediscovered and is recognized as the object of the *Trieb*. Reality in those terms is the reality of the representation (i.e., the psychic reality).

Misunderstanding Freud's concept of reality testing and positioning it as the antithesis to the pleasure principle resulted in three interrelated and compounded distortions of the concept of representation:

- Putting "material" reality in diagonal opposition to what is psychological introduced a dichotomy between internal versus external and moved psychoanalysis, inadvertently, from an intrapsychic theory to a theory of relations: the relationships between the internal and the external. In this way treatment would concentrate on correcting misperceptions of the external world.
- By dividing the field into inner and outer, another dichotomy naturally resulted: that of *self* versus *object*. This new dichotomy located the object in the external world, and thus its representation was decided by the work of the primary process; but like any perceived object it would be construed as a reproduction and not as a representation.
- The representation of the object-in-the-world opened the door for all sorts of confusion, opinions, and theories of what representation is, in addition to what is represented. Contemporary psychoanalyses consider that realities (objects) are external and have a separate material existence. The psychical agency (the ego!) is supposed to internalize the object and make it part of the inner world, an internal object. This point of view is in complete opposition to Freud's concept of presentation, which is an intrapsychic process that makes the representation have an existence-in. This drastic deviation from the original concept of presentation changed the theory in different ways: First it added the adjectival prefix "mental" to the term *representation* (as if there are other types of representation). A second change is the disappearance of the dichotomy of *thing* and *word* representation, replacing them with the dichotomous poles of self-representation and object representation, or whole representation and part representation.

The notion that external reality is internalized and thus becomes mental in nature meant that the analyst has to refer representation to one of several psychological processes that differentiate what is "mental" from what is internalized. Those processes belong to the field of academic psychology, such as thinking, imagination, perception, memory, identification (identifying), and abstraction (see Friedman, 1995). The situation got more complicated because, when analysts added "mental" to representing the endosomatic need, it was no longer a psychoanalytic issue. What the internal world is in those theories was nothing more than the reproductions of the external world

(Beres & Joseph 1970; Jacobson, 1983; Novey, 1958; Sandler & Rosenblatt, 1962).

It is important to note that the disappearance of the dynamics of the intrapsychic from psychoanalysis was justified by the elimination of the endosomatic aspect of psychical life, the reversing of the concept of representing the endosomatic to introjecting the external object, the dismissal of metapsychology, and most of all *ignoring that the concept of affect is neither a concept of drives nor of feelings but a concept of the arbitrary and contingent link between the endosomatic stimulus and its presentation.*

The second source of confusion is the division of self versus object as fields of representation. Sterba (cited in Novey, 1958) defined mental as a unity of ideas, memories with their affective (emotional) component, and related that definition to self and objects as material for representation. This was the first time the concepts of self-representation and object representation were introduced. The tendency to replace this dichotomy for the dichotomy of thing and word looked more appealing to the new analysts, especially with the developing interest in interpersonal relationships and the receding interest in the *Ucs.* But this shift embodied an important problem from the developmental point of view. Since the newly born cannot perceive the breast as early as her oral need emerges, any idea, memory, or feeling associated with sucking the thumb comes before considering the breast as the original object. The thumb is the first object of the need. We have to then ask—What does the thumb lead to: a representation of the breast or of the self? If the answer is that sucking the thumb leads to discovering, in the world, the object of the need, then the emergence of object representation (the breast) is meant to replace the thumb, which is an object too. Therefore the dichotomy of object-self does not follow. But if the answer is that the thumb would lead to self-representation first, we have to assume that the infant has the ability to recognize the thumb as his and him from the beginning, which is not feasible. Another problem would still remain: How does the "object" representation come about?

THE FIFTH FEATURE

The concept of *Ucs.* is central to the theory of psychoanalysis because it is an originary system that constructs psychical phenomena. Therefore it is not something we rid the patient of but a system to make him familiar with. Contemporary "psychoanalyses," which are mainly object relations, do not have a concept of unconscious, nor is it considered necessary for the kind of work the psychoanalysts do. Their clinical orientation is to explore the patient's net of relationships to familiarize the patient with his "unhealthy" ways of relating. It is not surprising that they have no theory of relational pathologies nor a related source of those pathologies.

The *Ucs.* is the framework of the process of representation, which happens without the involvement of any function of the mind. In fact it creates the mind. The unconscious process that instigates the representation is *aconscious*, meaning it is a product of a primary repression and not of repression proper; therefore it could be said that representation in an indirect way provides the material that would become preconscious.

The aconscious is a structure that determines how the psychical will use the primary process to have access to consciousness. To be noted in this regard is the domination of the primary process in the formation of the human mind for a relatively long and important time, between birth and the *awareness* of word presentation. Although the infant is born in a world of language, words remain things among the other things that represent his wishes. It takes a while for him (gradually but not before age three) to start grasping that words exist in a system of communication. Then, and only then, the grip of the primary process on forming mentation weakens, and the secondary process begins its entwinement with it and makes it adapt to its rules. The domination of the primary process never disappears but becomes disguised.

RESTATING THE NORMAL AND ABNORMAL

What distinguishes the theory of psychoanalysis from any other theory is that all other theories are about psychical aspects, elements, attributes, entities, and so on that are *states* of the person's condition. The theory of psychoanalysis is a theory of the human condition in itself, *the person as his own indication and state*, because the aconscious representation of his endosomatic stimulus and the transformations it goes through are all his making, though unconsciously done. Yet they are constituents of the speaking *he*. Politzer said something similar regarding the "real" Freudian theory of psychoanalysis (1928):

> *Consciousness*, such as we now consider it, is something other than a form of experience: it is essentially an act of recognition, of responsibility, even of identification—in short, this aspect of individual actions by which their connection to the "I" becomes evident and their recognition effective.
> If Freud had directed his developments in that direction, he would have noticed that this *dynamics* of the representations, censorship, repression, and resistance assume relates to the very knowledge that the subject can have of his own behaviour, and so the limitations of consciousness would have meant only the negation of the omniscience of the subject vis-à-vis himself, negation that the psychoanalytic method already implies. Under those conditions Freud would not have needed to conceive, on the one hand, a world of unconscious

entities and, on the other hand, to make consciousness an organ of perception" (p. 78).

The emergence of consciousness from aconsciousness and the obvious intertwinement of the person's sense of being and her consciousness put the theory of psychoanalysis in a class of its own. No other theory—even the catharsis theory—has a conception of consciousness or of the sense of being, let alone their intertwinement. The special advantage of this approach is the comprehensiveness of the theory of psychoanalysis regarding the human phenomena in all its conditions: health and sickness, creativity and destructiveness, individual and group, and so on. Hence, it is better to start by eliciting the theory of psychoanalysis of the natural and regular in the human condition, which was in fact Freud's starting point in discovering the theory.

As mentioned previously, Freud had a second wind in his discoveries between 1914 and 1920 (chapter 5). In that period he revised four important concepts and changed identification from being a function of psychoneurosis to being a formative process of the sense of being. At the time identification acquired its new meaning, narcissism appeared in the Freudian text in almost the same capacity (i.e., not as a pathological condition but as an originary condition). Both changes happened in a subtle—if not a very subtle—way that even Freud did not pay the needed attention to, although he coined the hyphenated term *narcissistic-identification* (1917e). A theory of the normal psychical functions was ready to be articulated as part of a comprehensive theory of the psychic. The problem was in the concept of *fixation*.

Fixation was an old, basic concept in Freud's early conception of symptom formation (before the change of meaning of identification). In his theory of *Trieb* (1905b), fixation was considered an attachment of the libido to a particular instinctual object or aim. Although Freud invoked that concept in different theoretical contexts, it was used to explain neuroses without having an explanation. The first attempt at addressing that issue and giving an idea of its origin was in his paper on repression (1915d, p. 148).

The progress and elaboration of a system of psychosexual development (particularly by Abraham) shifted the emphasis in fixation from the *Triebhaft* object or aim to the totality of the developmental stage, comprising both the instinctual object and the instinctual aim of that psychosexual stage. Fixation was no longer on an oral object or on the oral aim but of the oral stage as a nonconflictual state. Fixation on the stage as a whole mean that the object and the aim of the *Trieb* will get a representation that is free from conflict or contradictions. This condition creates successful, nonpathological fixations. When fixation is on a totality of the psychosexual stage, it produces stable, predictable *characters.* Character establishes stable, predictable object relations, which are prototypical of that stage. This shift was supposed to free the concept from being descriptive and from merely pertaining to the dynamics of development and its arrest, making it a formative process of the person. However, Freud, until then, connected fixation to pathological conditions because he did not have a clear notion of normality. He stated that, "People never abandon a libidinal position, not even, indeed, when a substitute is already beckoning to them" (Freud, 1917e, p. 244). This characteristic controverts the basic premise that the working of the primary process should make it easy to replace and interchange the aims and objects of fixation. Fixation, as a case for psychopathology, needed explaining in light of also being the case for health. Freud in his usual intuitive mind noticed a difference between fixation and the act of repetition. While fixation is stability and predictability, repetition was something else and needed to be differentiated from fixation.

A few years after the major revisions to the catharsis theory, Freud came up with the concept of repetition compulsion (1920g). It was "more or less" the pathological form of fixation. His prototype of the compulsion to repeat was traumatic neurosis and fate neurosis. Freud was clearly searching for the power behind the insistence and persistence of something painful having a hold on the patient. This was his first step toward the concept of death as a pole in a new *Triebhaft* duet, which was more of a metapsychological explanation than anything else. But what is the psychological theory of the metapsychology of the death *Trieb*?

Freud was interested from his early years in finding a systematic distinction between the psychoneuroses and psychoses (1898). He started with a distinction between psychoneuroses and actual neuroses, passing by anxiety neurosis and neurasthenia, and finally coming to a distinction between narcissistic neurosis (psychosis) and transference neurosis (1924e). This last distinction was based on the degree of transference the patient displayed in analyses (a shadow of the libidinal theory), a rather peculiar criterion for a major differential diagnosis, as he intended it to be. However, transference neuroses were characterized by investing a good part of the libido in the analyst, thus allowing previous relationships, mainly with the parents, to be explored in the analysis. Narcissistic neuroses, on the other hand, were characterized by either serious withdrawal of libido in relationships and main investment of the libido in the self with almost no symptoms, or by a major inversion of the libido, where what was left of the psychical life was affectless.

We can safely say that Freud looked for a clinical event to distinguish between the two major groups of psychopathology and thought that transference was such an event. As it stands, he considered the *potential to repeat* the original pathological scene a sign of less pathology, which most analysts generally accept. In transference neuroses there is something to *repeat* in the transference, which with the help of the analyst, the patient can manage. Transference suggests that there is an uncomfortable gap between the *me* and the *I*, which allows the *I* to relate to the analyst. Such failure in attaining a stable identity does not completely affect the integrity of the *I*.

In narcissistic neuroses, the psychopathology is not *part* of the person's life or a manifestation of his unstable identity; it *is* the person's identity. In terms of the link or gap between the *me* and the *I*, one of the two components of the person's sense of being is absent. The missing component is replaced with a morbid sense of otherness. It is very intriguing that Freud characterized the psychoses as narcissistic, while he characterized the neuroses as transferential. *We should keep that in mind because we will soon find out that the link between fixation and the compulsion to repeat parallels the link between identification and narcissism.*

Fixation is a manifestation of a well-structured dynamic relationship between the *me* and the *I, a successful identification and a stable sense of being*. Depending on the predominance of the psychosexual stage of fixation the person would have attained a libidinal type (Freud, 1931a).[2]

The compulsion to repeat is a phenomenon of psychical failure: failure to have a point of fixation that becomes a character formation. Freud conceded the inadequacy of removing repression and making the unconscious resistance conscious to instigate a cure. He said, "The new impulse [instinctual repressible impulse] will run its course under an automatic influence, or under the influence of the compulsion to repeat" (1926d, p. 153). He complemented this observation by saying, "It must be that after the ego's resistance has been removed the power of compulsion to repeat—attraction exerted by the unconscious prototype upon the repressed instinctual process—has still to be overcome" (1926d, p. 159). Repetition compulsion was absent in the various models Freud had before for the process of fixation, although the compulsion to repeat was the most obvious feature in the pathological meaning of fixation and was considered a main derivative.

The compulsion to repeat, from its inception as a *separate* concept in 1920, did not display any psychodynamic or conflictual qualities; it was almost an automatic or an autonomous phenomenon. The conflict between the clinically observable phenomenon of the compulsion to repeat and the theoretically sound and expedient concept of the pleasure principle[3] did not fit in the topographic opposition between the *Cs.* and *Ucs.* Freud hoped to find a solution by moving away from the descriptive qualities of repetition compulsion and giving it a dynamic status. He proposed a different polarity between the ego and the repressed (1920g, p. 19). It was an unusual polarity because his polarities were typically dialectical—between antitheses and not between any two different issues. The compulsion to repeat was rendered merely a product of the psychodynamics of conflict—a useless solution.

Repetition compulsion does not point the analyst to any source in development where it originates or begins. From infancy we repeat our experiences. Development is not a factor in establishing it and has no specificity in coloring it, that is, *all repetition compulsions are the same, no matter what is compulsively repeated*. It is, by all means, a structuring affair. The compulsion to repeat is responsible for producing/reproducing symptoms and acting out character flaws, causing pain in both cases, and in all that is clearly not ego syntonic. It does not reveal any specific aspects of the intrapsychic formation, although its effects color the interpersonal field in direct and noticeable, though often indefinable, ways. In addition, repetition compulsion is ineffectual in resolving the implicit conflict in psychopathology that gives the impression to be intended to solve. Possibly, its teleological aim is to emphasize failure, as it originates from failure of identification. It seems that the theory of psychoanalysis is suggesting that psychopathology is an upshot of normality in the sense that abnormality is not a condition(s) created by other intrapsychic dynamics but by some intrapsychic dynamics of health (i.e., *psychopathology is the antithesis of health as the thesis, not a disease that attacks health*. Healthy fixation is the norm, but when it fails, the compulsion to repeat takes its place. We do not encounter conflictual problems in fixation proper, though its failure results in endless repetition of the unresolved conflict.

NARCISSISM, IDENTIFICATION, AND THE OTHER

The core of the narcissistic drama is the dilemma of identity, that is, emerging from self- obscurity to self-recognition and recognition of the other and by the other. Sandler and Perlow said,

> With the development of Freud's interest in narcissism (1914c), an interest which led eventually to the formulation of the structural theory (1923b), the concept of identification gained in importance. No longer was it taken as a process whereby symptoms or dream elements were formed; identification came to be recognized as an important developmental process. (1988, p. 9)

This statement avers that the changes introduced to the concept of identification were instrumental in configuring the concept of narcissism and that they were both linked. Historically speaking, we should remind ourselves that Freud's works between 1912 and 1917 were all interconnected through, first, the collapse of the catharsis theory and, second, the need for forming *a new theory of psychoanalysis that was founded on new and different dualities, not on the dualities of the libido theory*. It is a period that has the characteristics of the period between 1900 and 1905, when the formation of the topographic theory was established and the catharsis theory took shape.

Freud's (1896a) initial interest in psychopathological phenomena, especially hysteria, led him early to pay attention to the phenomenon of identification. It was a central mechanism in symptom formation in hysterical conditions in which the patient assimilated an attribute of the other and lived it as if it defined him (1900a). Abraham (1913) and Ferenczi (1912/1980) were instrumental in widening the scope of identification by adding two other mechanisms: internalization and introjection. Their contributions detailed the different types of identifications generated in each stage of development. Still, the differentiations made among the three mechanisms of identification kept them within the scope of "defense mechanisms" and maintained them as constituents of psychopathology. These new insights into identification coincided with Freud's budding awareness that identification was a process that needed to be explained, not used to explain other phenomena. In *Totem and Taboo* (1912–1913), Freud talked about the process of incorporation as the foundation of identification. It meant that if an attribute of the other becomes meaningful "of something" to the subject, it would be incorporated in the *I*, depending on the stage of development, through one of the three mechanisms of assimilation, introjection, or internalization. Laplanche and Pontalis (1967/1973) said that identification thus changed from being "simply one psychical mechanism among others, [to become] the operation itself whereby the human subject is constituted" (p. 206).

Ricoeur (1970) remarked that

> every theory contains concepts that are employed but not reflected upon in the theory itself. The elimination of such concepts would bring about a state of total reflection or absolute knowledge, which is incompatible with the finitude of knowledge. Hence, it is no criticism of psychoanalysis to find in it operative [functional] concepts that, in order to be thematised, would require a conceptual framework different from that of its topography and economics. (p. 473)

Neither Freud nor Abraham or Ferenczi studied the three forms of identification as processes. They remained metapsychological concepts. Identification before it was thematized was used to explain symptoms and had to be thematized before it was dislodged from its status as a mechanism and located within the formative processes of the subject. It depended on the theorist's angle of perceiving the totality of the theory to decide the way he would use that process. Ricoeur (1970) concluded that "identification is simply the shadow, projected onto the plane of an economics of instincts, of a process of consciousness to consciousness, and that process has to be understood through another type of interpretation" (p. 483). In other words, identification remained a functional concept in psychoanalysis for a long time, useful but not understood.

The human infant has no means to search for and find the object of its own need, and wish. The caregiver does that for the infant, identifies the content of his wish and prescribes the means to reach it. The dilemma is that the wishing infant needs the other to *tell* him what he wishes, tell him what is supposed to identify him. His knowledge of himself has to go through another to be identified. Humans are "predestined" to be narcissistically alienated: Who am I supposed to be . . . Mom?

Identification has two meanings: a cognitive meaning and a psychodynamic one, depending on whether it is used transitively or intransitively. The infant, according to his abilities, could—transitively—identify the stimuli emanating from his physical environment; he could see and hear his mother without his mother's participation in those "things." Identification in that case is cognitive in nature because the sensory input from physical reality creates direct perceptions of the object. In the early phases of development, the infant gains "thing presentations" of the objects of his physical world, while the role of the other in this process is secondary. The mother might associate presenting the bottle to the infant with a word, but the word would still be just an auditory thing, similar to a visual or other sensory representation that the infant could have acquired or produced on his own.

On the other hand, when the stimulus emanates from the body, identification becomes a very different process. There are no specific sensory organs to perceive hunger, the discomfort of intestinal fullness, or even sexual arousal. Those sensations create states of quasi-consciousness (content-less consciousness), which put pressure on the infant's mind to act. Identifying those stimuli suggests direct identification of the infant himself. This process of identification moves the infant to the domain of the relation with the other, who will be the sole provider of the verbal representation of the endosomatic stimulus, the linguistic sign for that "thing" that puts the pressure on his mind. *The caregiver's response to the infant's expression of an endosomatic pressure identifies the infant to himself through identifying that pressure*: giving the bottle means he is hungry, rocking him to sleep means he is tired, and so on. This is a crucial step toward identifying the infant to herself, but it is just a step in his identification. At this step, the somatic thing (hunger) is given a signification not by associating it with a signifier, but by giving it a meaning through the act of responding to it. The meaning "You are hungry" introduces the infant to the world of language, the world of communication, and also the world of alienation. Contrary to a common misunderstanding, the first communication between the infant and the mother is not a demand but a rhetorical expression, addressing the other. This process is almost like answering an implicit question of "What am I?" and the mother's answer, "You are . . ."

Identifying oneself, intransitively, through the other's input is tantamount to acquiring a counterpart but not an identity. The mother identifies the infant to himself by giving him his counterpart (e.g., "You are . . ." becomes "I am who is told what he is." This happens at each stage of development. In other words, identifying oneself is always psychodynamic (indirect, intransitive) and never cognitive (direct), always reflective and never perceptive. It also alienates the *subject* permanently from the identity embedded in his reflection. The person's *I*-dentity is always a counterpart, his counterpart. However, although the origin of identification is a counterpart configured by the other and a prototype for any possible future identification, it does not stop the person from trying to free himself from the identity embedded in the counterpart—an endless, always incomplete, but necessary process.

The infant enters the world of consciousness equipped for survival with only his *Trieben* but without a sense of being or any knowledge of his existence. Gradually he will identify the mother cognitively and thereby become the only "thing" that exists for her. It does not take long for the infant to acquire the traces of a sense of being but only as a counterpart for that other thing, the mother. This is a first duality in the phenomenon of identification. The infant's gaze at his mother's face reveals his fascination with that thing. His mother's face is his existence and being; without it he loses his sense of being. When his mother smiles at him, he smiles back, reflectively. It takes several weeks for the infant to show ecstasy in looking at his mother's face and to smile spontaneously at her, and it takes him more time to do that with strangers without their smiling first at him. The pleasure that seems to come from the object of the *Trieb* is assimilated, and gradually a sense of being develops to become the nucleus of a sense of *me-ness*, the seat of the *I*.

Satisfying the infant's need causes a sense of pleasure or relief as bodily sensation or, as Freud said it, "[T]he first ego is the body ego" (Freud, 1923a, p. 25). This sensation forms the infant's own probable likely identity because its source, though internal, feels to the infant first as if it is external. The mother's level of ability, willingness, and transparency in relation to the infant's needs will configure the nature of his sense of being, his identity. It is an identification that starts as *informative* but gradually becomes *formative*. The identity of the newborn will be formed by and with those reflections. However, the psychodynamics of the relationship with the mother determines the type and level of differentiation between *her* and *him*, as well as the degree of the mother's acceptance (tolerance) of that differentiation, and will determine the future of the person's ability to have and keep an identity without another providing or boosting it up. The psychodynamics of the formative process of identification decides the birth of the duality of infant/mother. Identification will also be affected by the stage of development. For instance, the infant's relinquishing the mother's breast in the process of identification in the oral stage is different from giving up something that belongs to him, such as his feces in the anal stage. In the anal stage, giving up the feces identifies the mother as either a deserving or usurping, undeserving other. The sexual nature of the genital phase would also affect the framework of the child's gender identity.

This same psychodynamic situation confronts the infant with new dynamics of identification. In the first contact with the mother, when the issue is to identify the physiological need, the mother reflects back to the infant her attitude about that need. With the anaclisis of the psychical functions, the infant is transformed into a subject with a need for nourishment and a wish for love, which he expects to be simultaneously satisfied. The anaclisis of wishes and needs creates a new duality between the subject and himself, in which the *me* (who needs) gives birth to the *I* (who asks). The *I* is the person who emerges from within himself (the *me*) as another and enters the world of alienation from himself. The *I* becomes the counterpart of the *me*, which will gradually replace the mother who spoke for the *me* until then. Thus, a narcissistic instance is created, where love and hate will gradually become entrapped in the relationship between the *me* and its counterpart, the *I*, not between the subject and an external object as it is conceived in the object relational models. In other words *narcissism is not an interrelational issue; it is an intrapsychic issue. It is not located between a subject and an object, not between Narcissus and his admirers, but between a subject and his own image.* Narcissus's drama lies in the impasse that neither he nor Echo were able to pass or bypass. He could not identify himself to him, as he failed to identify himself to his image. (Fayek, 1981; see chapter 6).

When identification fails and becomes a stifled process due to the mother's inadequacies the infant who is the future neurotic will reveal a major inability to define his wishes. Defining the wish—the core of any identity—is the primary achievement in the development toward turning it into a desire—a relation with the other—and breaking away from the confining link between *me* and *I*. A desire is what identifies one to the other, that is, one's desire becomes a declaration of his existence to the other. More precisely, a desiring person wishes to be desired; therefore, it is in the hands of the other to change the state of wishing into a state of desiring by simply acknowledging the wish and turning it into a subject, a response, be it positive or negative. The picture gets clearer when we consider that the basis of the infant's emerging consciousness (awareness of the other) and moving from narcissism to a relation with the object is turning wishes into demands for love instead of a need for love. Narcissus loved his image but did nothing to make it love him. This is the point where we should examine the formation of identity and its role in structuring narcissism.

NARCISSISM AND THE LINK BETWEEN THE ME AND I

The changes to the concept of identification had another significant outcome in regard to narcissism and the gap within the subject. Henry Wallon (1946)[4] worked on the infant's perception and recognition of his image in the mirror and developed two concepts of identification: centripetal identification (identifying the other with the self) and centrifugal identification (identifying the self by the other). Lacan (1977a) developed those ideas (Lacan did not refer to his friend H. Wallon in his published paper) and called the period between six months and a year and a half the "mirror phase," in which the child recognizes the *other* in the mirror before recognizing himself as reflected in that mirror. He said, "We have only to understand the mirror stage as *an identification*, in the full sense that analysis gives to the term: namely, the transformation that takes place in the subject when he assumes an image whose predestination to this phase-effect is sufficiently indicated by the use, in analytic theory, of the ancient term *imago*" (pp. 98–99).

He extrapolated this notion to introduce the concepts of the double, the self as an object, the body image, the imaginary, and several other concepts that started an inspiring psychoanalytic movement in Paris. However, it goes without saying that the mirror phase—concretely speaking, as Lacan puts it—is not a psychoanalytic term. However, the infant recognizes himself in *whatever* and *whoever* reflects to him an image of himself, and we could talk psychoanalytically about a mirror phase in that sense and only as it is the structuring process of objectifying the subject to himself.

When the infant acquires an identity, or some sense of *me*-ness, a relationship could be initiated between the subject (me) and the object (him or her), with the object becoming the counterpart. As the *me* gains awareness of its wishes, the infant moves toward wishing that the other would wish to fulfill his wish. As a result, the subjective *I* emerges and takes the place of the silent (nonverbal) *me* in dealing with the other by articulating (verbalizing) that wish. The *me* has to be suppressed in favor of the *I*; therefore identification changes from "*me*-him" to "*me-I*," with all the risks of confusing the *me* and the him, and the *I-me* dualities. The individual, therefore, is a narcissistic duality that is by definition intrapsychic. The final outcome of identification will be decided by the dynamics of the three parties involved: the other, the *I*, and the *me*, where the narcissistic stance is established.

In the oral stage, there is little place for an *I* until the mother gradually stops being an oral object (weaning the infant) (i.e., stops being the dual object of nourishment and love, and stands for love only). By doing that, the duality of *her/me* is ensued by a reversal of that duality to *me/her*, and a relationship begins with the mother through this new duality. In anality the child discovers that he can derive pleasure from parts of himself, maybe with some help from the mother but not from the mother's body. He finds out that he can oppose his mother without the fear of losing her source of pleasure. It is a situation where the object of the *Trieb*, being part of the body, takes duality a step toward object love. A duality within the infant's own identity emerges, this time between the owner *me* (the source) and the owned, which is part of *me* (the feces) and which gradually becomes the counterpart. If the mother becomes preoccupied with toilet training and not with the toddler himself, who considers this activity to be his own affair, the child might not experience this potential autonomy and lose his identity to the counterpart (feces and its derivations) or submit to the mother's demand and wish and assume them as hers. The same confusion applies to the genital stage. If the parents—particularly the father—put emphasis on the child's genitalia rather than on its role in identifying his gender, the child could lose his gender identity to the penis (and its representative). Instead of gaining a masculine identity, he develops a variety of attitudes and feelings about his gender. In other words, the other's contribution to identification depends on that other's intransitive identification of the infant's *I*.

When the mother identifies the wish of the infant correctly, she gives him an *I* that matches what the *me* wants "approximately." The infant could emerge from that basic duality of infant/mother reflecting the other more than the *me*, because the mother (as Other) is always the primal source of identifying the wish and giving it a name, or a signification. There are many prospects for providing the infant with a false *I*, foiling an authentic identification. If the other misinterprets the real wish of the infant, the encounter creates a false *I* instead, because *the mother cannot change the wish but can only distort it.*

The relationship between the *I* and the *me, or the narcissistic stance*, raises three issues: (a) What relationship could exist between the *I* and the *me*, and which will become subordinate to the other? (b) Which will engage in the relationship with the other, who is freed by then from being the counterpart: the true self (*me*) or its counterpart (*I*)? (c) What place does the other occupy within the narcissistic duality?

The sense of *me*-ness, which precedes the sense of *I*-ness, is the core of identification or the speaking individual. When the *me* recedes to give the *I* the role of representing it, the relationship with the other will be through the *I*. But because *me* is the seat of any *I*, which always addresses the other, the *I* is supposed to represent the *me* accurately. Nonetheless, the gap in that duality is subject to all sorts of distortions and degrees of inexactitude.

If the *me* suppresses the *I* and takes over, as happens in immature narcissistic personalities, the relationship with the other will be limited by what only the *me* is capable of doing, wishing. The object has to become the speaker for a *me* that has no *I* to pronounce its wish. The other would be important only in his capacity as the counterpart and will not be libidinously charged, but the relationship would be. As an example, an exhibitionistic person is attracted to a nice-looking woman; the *me* would be silenced in order for the *I* to take that woman as the counterpart that would speak for him. The relationship with that woman becomes the important issue and not the woman herself, meaning that she could be replaced by another woman who could fulfill the same function for the exhibitionist *I*. The effort would be toward maintaining the relationship, not keeping the woman. But if there is an *I* delegated to relate to the woman by expressing genuine attraction, a relationship develops between the subject and an object that is *not* a counterpart of *I* but the desire of the *me.* The object would then be "libidinously" charged: the woman would be loved and not the relationship with her would be cherished.

The relationist schools ignore this point, which raises the questions: Does the object create the relationship, or does the relationship create the object? Is the analyst the initiator of the transference, or does the transference determine the perception of the analyst? Relationships with and between others and the *me* require the mediation of the *I*, but an *I* that is so flexible to mean just anything to the other. The person has to have a degree of fixedness required to make him the same or at least consistent. The link between the *me* and the *I* will not be, in that case, a narcissistic enclosure; the *I* will not be an echo of the other but the voice of the *me*. If a gap linking the *me* and the *I* is not established in the process of identification, a state of distorted narcissism will supplant it. As it stands now, narcissism is taken as the new unhealthy content of psychical phenomena and some aspects of the healthy too (Federn, 1952; Kohut, 1987). That change, important as it was in dethroning the old dicta of sexuality and the libido, was not radical or strong enough. Narcissism was still taken as a functional psychical phenomenon. When the relational theories eventually discarded the notion of the developmental stages and did away with the specificity of psychopathologies, narcissism lost its explicit role in identification and was considered, as such, a pathological condition. It was even used as a nosological entity of no specific quality, as in the "narcissistic personality disorder" syndrome, which gained importance in the 1970s. It extended the main premise of the catharsis theory, the rejectionable repressible condition.

The plea to return to Freud and his text is a plea to put the "progress" that was made in the last half century into perspective. It is a plea to contain whatever is truly psychoanalytic in that progress, in a clear frame of reference, to avoid what seems now to look like struggles with quasi-psychoanalytic issues.

Chapter Ten

The Psychoanalytic Mind

The Replacement for the Catharsis Theory

Theorizing, especially in the idiographic sciences, faces a challenging problem: an inevitable degree of substituting the subject matter of the theory with its representation or dealing with the phenomena of the subject instead of the subject as is. This substitution, if not done prudently, would turn out theories of *holograms* of the subject (i.e., virtual but not real subjects). Another danger affects the theorist himself. Theorizing about the representations of his subject matter could make the theorist slip into generating ideas instead of verities. Strangely, when the theorist gets to that point he seems to produce theories that are tightly knit but have no bearing. This is an integral feature (in degrees) in idiographic theories; therefore all theories need other than the theorist to notice whether they have remained close to the subject or shifted to the manifestations of the subject. Economists for instance anthropomorphize their subject matter and talk about the market and the dollar as persons, ascribing to them temperamental traits. In psychological and sometimes in social sciences the subject is represented by his attributes (needs, defensiveness, narcissism, etc.). Those attributes, if the theorist is not careful, gain a life of their own and form a hologram of the subject.

The tempting ease of writing holographic psychoanalytic theories is clear in Freud's ego psychology. It is a model of a holographic theory of the subject (person). The same happened when he wanted to come up with a definitive theory of treatment and its limitation. He came up with a holographic conception of the clinical practice of psychoanalysis.

In preparation for presenting the main propositions of the replacement theory I have to recall two ideas that need to be highlighted further: (a) Psychoanalysis deals with the noumenal, or the unknowable in itself, not with the phenomenal or the already known. The unknowable is unconscious by virtue of being wrapped in misleading representations. (b) The subject matter of psychoanalysis is the structural aspects of the psychological functions, as mentioned in chapter 6.

Two gaps in *the human condition* are involved in originating a rich psychical life. Those gaps present several basic dualities in the human psyche. The first is a duality of mental processes that deal differently with endosomatic stimuli and physical stimuli. The gap between the two processes and the continuous work to integrate them in one response is a stipulation for the psychoneurosis (absent in the rest of the animal kingdom). Humans are bound to be neurotics by the mere existence of two separate mental processes that deal with two different stimuli emanating from the body and the world. Each mental process, the primary process and the secondary process, creates conditions for major distortions and misrepresentations. This gap was instrumental in the discovery of psychoanalysis, and only when Freud turned to its normal state did he discover the nature of the abnormal. This point has major implications in our understanding of psychoanalytic treatment and its outcome.

The second unavoidable gap is within the state of identification: the duality of the *me* and emergence of the *I* from it. This gap proffers a wide range of possibilities in the development of psychical states and is the source of the variety of and variation in people's personalities and idiosyncrasies. It is also the seat of the observable deviation to psychoneurosis, and more so than the other gap because the deviations caused by it show in interpersonal relationships or neurotic symptoms. It is a theory that is very much about the real subject, his real state of varied conditions, and most of all a theory of what is human about him as a human. When explaining those variations by functional banalities, whereby external issues such as interrelations, family psychodynamics, social circumstances, and so on are used for filling the gap, the theory would not be psychoanalytical.

Pondering those few points makes us realize that psychoanalysis could not have emerged from a conception of the psyche as a product of repressed objectionable urges, or could have come from configuring the psyche as a function that has no structure, or structured as tripartite entities, which stand merely as *holograms* of the person. Espousing a theory of that nature changes the analyst's mind-set concerning approaching the material he would be working with, whether it is clinical or nonclinical. I will mention six of the connected and interconnected changes that characterize the psychoanalyst whose mind-set understands and pursues Freud's other theory.

FREE ASSOCIATION: FROM FEED TO WORD

Representing the endosomatic is the equivalent[1] of perceiving and cognizing external stimuli. External stimuli are responsible for building cognitive reality; the endosomatic on the other hand builds psychical reality (Fayek, 2002). However, there is a twist in that statement: the representations of the need, whether givens or self-produced, have to find their physical material in the external world. The first representations are given by the caregiver and later will be either "named" by the caregiver or will take their signifiers from the language the child is born into. Better, the state of hunger turns into a state of wishing (for food, as an example) but very subtly becomes a wish for the breast. Food alienates in a breast. For that reason we should say that psychical reality, the integration of the representations of the endosomatic, is a network of alienated substitutes of original needs. The change in the condition will also embrace the shift from thing presentations to word presentations. This shift enables the person to speak for himself, selecting the best ways to say what he wants and talk about his world by selecting what he thinks is his words from the language around him. There is more than one way to say something about one's self; language is one of them: fainting, blushing, silence to express psychical reality. Although the external world requires the best equivalence between signified and signifier, the choice will always be the province of the subject's own intention. The gap between the endosomatic and exosomatic stimulus is seldom if ever noticeable in our daily lives. The best example is in art. A talented painter, in picturing a scene in front of hims, produces a painting that blends his psychical conception of the scene in its cognitive perception by a talent that distinguishes him.

Freud's intuition about psychical life and the endosomatic might seem to clinical psychoanalysts an abstract idea. However, integrating that intuition with infantile sexuality *is* the applied aspect of the theory of psychoanalysis. Development and evolution toward maturity require the transformation of the vital needs, such as respiration, hydration, energy, sex, and replenishing the vital elements and energy (Kubie, 1948) into psychical representations. When this is done, the infant moves into a member of the human society. The fabric of the human society is a linguistic network that translates need into words; therefore *language* should be able to transform needs into communication. Since the endosomatic pressure of the various vital needs is the same, it is *the erogenic zones from which the pressure originates and which will decide the verbal expression of those needs.* In other words, each vital need is related to a vital organ in the body (hunger/mouth, sex/genitals); therefore its transformation would be related to the function of that organ (hunger, full, empty, not enough, or not satisfactory, etc). A psychical oral need, for instance, will appear in a person's speech, revealing his particular experiences that channeled the evolving chains of association pertaining to that need.

Moreover, fantasies and the structures of daydreams, depicted in metaphorical and metonymical qualities, reveal their origins in specific erogenic zones.

In clinical practice we need to relate psychodynamic diagnoses to stages in psychosexual development in order to understand and make understandable the meaning of patients' complaints. A diagnosis becomes the background for the psychopathology of each patient. Listening to patients will eventually bring to our attention that they talk about two things at the same time; simply said, they talk about conscious things, which reflect interpersonal issues, and they talk unconsciously about other things that uncover intrapsychic "complexes." The unconscious material comes from the unresolved intrapsychic erotogenic conflict at certain developmental stages. Advancement in psychoanalysis came from improving this elementary idea and not from complicated revisions of its basic premises. For instance Freud had suggested a diagnosis of "actual neurosis" (1894, 1896c). Actual neurosis was—in Freud's perception—a direct expression of the somatic need in the psyche, without elaborate transformations. In the mid-1900s better understanding of Freud's assumptions regarding direct transformation permitted identifying a group of patients who suffered physiological symptoms instigated by psychological pressures, displayed in shallowness of affect, and demonstrated pseudo-abstract understanding of human conditions. The symptoms of those patients revealed fixed links between the endosomatic pressure and its representation in symptoms, as in the case of peptic ulcers in patients who craved attention or love, or skin conditions in patients who longed for intimacy and closeness. Physiological symptoms were always related directly to an endosomatic stimulus because we are "the animal with language" and we live in a world of symbols. The concrete links between the physiological and the psychological always carried symbolic meaning, which was derived intrapsychically from the erotogenic zone that it emerged from. This category of patients was diagnosed as *psychosomatic*, a better diagnosis than actual neurosis.

Transformation of the endosomatic into psychical phenomena became (nine decades after Freud's intuition) a significant topic in neurosciences. Damasio (1999) explored the physiology of the brain, in dealing both with the external world and the body, and ended by saying:

> While your visual system changed dutifully at the mercy of the object it mapped, a number of regions in your brain whose job is to regulate the life process and which contain preset maps that represent varied aspects of your body did not change at all. . . . *The body remained the "object" all along and will remain so until death ensues* [my emphasis]. There are several reasons behind this asymmetry. First, the composition and general functions of the living body remain the same . . . across a lifetime. Second, the body changes that continuously do occur are small, in terms of their quantity. . . . I have come to conclude that the organism, as presented inside its own brain, is a

> likely biological forerunner for what eventually becomes the elusive sense of self. (pp. 21–22)

There is a large body of literature refuting the validity or viability of free association in psychoanalytic work. There is no doubt that free association as a request is difficult for the patient to fulfill; it is a questionable concept that makes it look like a doubtful method. It was an unfortunate term that Freud used to contrast it with the method of asking questions, which was the spine of his treatment method before. Nonetheless, all psychotherapists have to listen to the patient associating about his condition, whether we assume it to be the method of choice or not. Even the therapist who resorts to asking questions to get patients' material does not know beforehand what the answer will be. The intent of free association (as it should be explained to the patient) is *to encourage talking in order to know not to talk about what is already known*, as much as possible. When that is clarified at the beginning, we usually find a gradual change toward freeing the associations from the known to associating as a means to hear the subtly disguised unknowns: the subtleties of the *me*, the primary process, the *Ucs*. We need to revise the term *free association* if not because it is inaccurate then because we have to ask the patient to do something that could not be done. The classical analyst listens patiently to gradually get the thread of the patient's chains of representations; there is no other way to do that.

At the same time that Freud discovered the network of representations he discovered the nature of the connections and interconnections between the representations and the representations of representations. It would have been impossible to discover one without the other, and as the theory of psychoanalysis orientates us to the notion of representations it also provides us with the right tools to discern a representation from another.

THE PRIMARY PROCESS AND THE ANALYZABLE MATERIAL

When Freud used free association instead of hypnosis he realized that patients *resisted* recalling certain past events (sometimes even present ones). With the catharsis theory in mind he called that difficulty *defense mechanisms*. However, he got the intuition that getting to the right chain of presentations through free association was not always possible because of repression but most of the time, because of the arbitrariness of the links between those chains, arbitrariness that gives the analytic material the look of a riddle or a rebus of verbal images. This clear idea suggests a strong need to change the mind-set of the psychoanalyst toward what he listens to and what to do with the material (as will be discussed later). The analyst should not expect to discover or uncover something repressed but has to find the solution to the riddling associations. He should keep in mind that the patient is unconscious of the riddle in his material, of the way it got to that condition, and most of all that that riddle that has no function (defensive) or does not serves a purpose but rather is the outcome of an inevitable aconscious process.

The process of representation is systemically unconscious (*Ucs.*) because the primary process controls it. Until age six the infant has faint conceptions of sequence (time), abstraction (distinctions), specificity (object identity), replacement (symbols), and several other elements of thinking in the secondary processes (see Piaget's work on thinking in children ages three to six). Those are the constituents of the primary process as Freud indicated and were complemented by Blanco (1988). This guides the child's means of expression and sometimes his way of understanding adult expressions. Better to put it this way: The absence of rules of logic in early childhood creates a complex network of representations that entwine with the secondary process and remain to form our daily mentation in adulthood; and in some cases, those mental products are warped to become psychoneuroses.

Freud (1915d) said, "[T]he repressed does not cover everything that is unconscious. The unconscious has a wider compass: the repressed is part of the unconscious" (p. 166). He added that "we have grounds for modifying our inference about ourselves and saying that what is proved is not the existence of a second consciousness [unconsciousness] in us, but the existence of psychical acts which lack consciousness [aconsciousness]" (1915b, p. 170). This means that the psychoanalyst would find *within* the patients' associations all that was formed by the primary process and not repressed or defended against. This is a fundamental difference from the prevailing notion of defense mechanisms in the catharsis theory. It means that the act of *analysis is in fact an act of extricating the aconscious from the conscious and the preconscious, which is there, nonrepressed* in the patient's association but just woven into the fabric of the associations in a way that disguises it.

A second change in the mind-set of the psychoanalyst who espouses the theory of psychoanalysis is to consider that the conscious and the preconscious material that he gets in free associations are not always linked in a logical, understandable way. The link is influenced by the rules of the primary process, which are practically the absence of rules, and that link is systemically unconscious or the only thing that is unconscious.

Because the link between the conscious and the preconscious is the only focal point in the act of psychoanalysis, we have to examine the way of finding it first and then deal with what we find. The reason I underline this issue is its relation to the significant problem of meaning and cause in the theory of psychoanalysis. Although this is a theoretical problem, it plays a very important role in the application of the theory, especially clinically: Do we provide the patient with the causes or the meaning of his neurosis? Do we try to reach the meaning conveyed by *The Picture of Dorian Gray*, or do we want to reach what caused its events or even the reason Oscar Wilde wrote it?

TRANSFERENCE: THE SEARCH FOR MEANINGS AND CAUSES

Flugel (1953) defined the whole of the psychoanalytic process as the analysis of transference, based on the notion that psychoanalysis is geared toward recovering the genetic source of the neurosis, which is best revealed in transference. The implicit understanding of transference among analysts is that it is the analytic relationship generated by the act of analysis (Gill, 1979, 1982). This idea discounts that transference is the background of all relationships in and out of analysis. The reason is that any relationship has to acquire a meaning to become significant. People do not enter relationships with *clean slates* and postpone defining the new relationship until after examining it. At best, they transfer to it previous relationships until they find the specifics of this one. The difference is in the difference between the relationships. The analytic situation, when structured on the Freudian triple restrictions of neutrality, anonymity, and abstinence, allows the transference to repeat the basics of its genetic core, the parental relationship. Understanding the working of condensation and displacement is the analyst's only clue to what could be brought to the analysis from that relationship. Because the patient is oblivious of what he transfers, transference demands deciphering. Thus, transference is *the* subject of interpretation because there is nothing to explain transference, as the rest of the analytic material always averred within the transference.

Waelder identified transference as a special case of compulsion to repeat and said, "One cannot possibly talk about the handling of transference without talking also about interpretation; and one cannot talk about resistance either, without taking in consideration the interpretation of, and the use of interpretation against resistance" (1941–1942, p. 49). Ricoeur (1970) added about psychoanalysis that "the problem of interpretation is coextensive with the problem of meaning or representation. Hence, psychoanalysis is interpretative from beginning to end" (p. 66).

Interpretation has different meanings depending on the different contexts in which it is used. Interpreting from one language to another is not the same as interpreting a dream, or a painting, or a religious text. If a meaning of interpretation is borrowed from one field and used in another the work of interpretation loses its purpose; if we interpret a painting as if it were a dream, we end up with ridiculous results. Worse, if we stick to the literal meaning of the term instead of considering it a denotation, a denotation dictates the nature of the act of interpretation instead of the reverse.

The common understanding of the act of interpretation in psychoanalysis is influenced by the literal meaning of the word, which is to explicate something by something else (e.g., interpreting a dream by a wish). This meaning had an unfavorable effect on psychoanalysis: analysts resort to the theory as reference for giving meaning to what is to be interpreted. Interpretation in that sense, instead of being directed at the aconscious links between associations to expose them, *forges* the theoretical links as substitutes. It is unacceptable if the analyst believes that the psychoneurosis is a phenomenon of ignorance and cure comes from better knowledge, which are both wrong in any theory of psychotherapy. We need to use the term *interpretation* carefully so we do not let the literal meaning blind us to the fact that psychoanalytic material has its own meaning within it and it would not be derived from theory. Interpretation in psychoanalysis stems from analyzing the material to get to the meaning embedded in it and not using outside sources to interpret. It is also important to know that *interpretation in psychoanalysis is not what cures but reconstruction does.*

Nasio (1984) said, "If we want to sum up the analyst's comportment, we may say: silence is the norm, explanatory interventions are frequent, and interpretations are rare" (p. 403). I would add to this succinct statement a small point of elucidation. The patient's speech is almost in all cases an intricate system of explanations, which can be right or wrong. The analyst's silence is the way to prevent the patient's explanations from becoming statements of circumstance or fact, which could lead to interfering with the analytic work of interpretation later on. Therefore, silence is not a passive segment of analysis but rather an active part of interpretation. Laplanche and Pontalis said, "Interpretation is the heart of the Freudian doctrine and technique" (1967/1973, p. 227). Freud very early on used the metaphor of analysis as interpreting one psychical system to another (1896b), putting something of a system in the way the other system would understand. He was, intuitively, talking about interpreting what is aconscious to consciousness by putting it in the form that fits the system of consciousness; thus, the primary process could connect with the secondary process. In other words, the task of the analyst is to interpret the primary process as it appears within the "speech" of the secondary process to the language of the secondary process. Considering the illusive link between meaning and cause in psychoanalysis, interpretation becomes the psychoanalytic act par excellence because by giving the aconscious link its meaning it will replace the false and incorrect logical causes/effects explanation in consciousness. Yet Freud did not give a well-defined description of a psychoanalytic interpretation, and we have to find what could clarify what Freud left unclear.

Ricoeur (1970) considers the general theory of hermeneutics, or the theory of meaning, a theory of interpretation. He specified two types of interpretation, which happen to correspond to the theory and practice of psychoanalysis. The first is *interpretation as the restoration of meaning*, and the second is *interpretation as the demystification of an illusionment.*

The restoration of meaning in psychoanalysis comes from deducing from the material a lost meaning and restoring it. During development, and through a series of misrepresentations and obscure discourses by the speaker (the parents and later the analyst of the transference), the patient misreads and misunderstands the intentions of the other; consequently he would develop a distorted *me* in the form of an *I*, which is living a meaningless or a wrong existence. The parallel miscomprehension by the listener (the child that later becomes the patient) causes the meaning of the discourse to be lost and makes the *I* a bad representative of the *me*. Psychoneurosis conveys a state of lost meanings, misconstrued intentions, and the patient's futile efforts to replace the lost meaning. In talking about the past and going through the memories of childhood, and with the gradual lifting of infantile amnesia (not just of events but of early thinking flaws too), the analyst will have the chance to interpret the misconstrued events and restore their meaning. A an example, a talented writer had writer's block after learning about his brother's inoperable cancer. In his analysis, before getting to that point, he perceived his relation with his brother as a big concern for their mother. He felt that he had to hold him back so that his brother would not feel intellectually inferior. Restoring the wrong meaning his mother gave to his distinction interpreted the blockage as protecting his brother, as mother always did, from feeling unfortunate and lacking. The meaning of the neurosis, which is implied in the neurotic discourse, is restored through and by the genetic interpretation, which is meant to bring to light how the old discourse got lost in the first place.

The other source of material, or the other means to getting to the genetic origins of the neurosis, is transference. Transference is an illusion of a relationship but an illusion that has such a strong grip on the patient that she perceives her experience as real, even more real than the narrative of her childhood. To appreciate the illusion created in the relationship with the analyst by transference we should keep in mind two factors: (a) The only means to understanding a new experience is by invoking an old one that has some semblance to it or an old experience that could not be comprehended until a new and similar event links with it. This is the basic notion in the concept of aftereffect (see the section titled Aftereffect and the Analytic Mind in this chapter). Transference, in this way, is the only means to relate to the analyst, who should maintain Freud's recommendations to allow the past to pass to the present with as little distortion as possible. The interpretative stance the analyst takes regarding transference would gradually reveal its illusionary quality. Interpreting transference demystifies it and eventually prepares its genetic equivalent and source for reconstruction. Transference as material for interpretation discerns the past from the present and reveals which was in need for the other to gain a meaning. Transference interpretations, the demystification of its illusionment, is mainly inductive in nature; we induce from it what is aconsciously repeated.

The psychoanalytic act comprises those two types of interpretations: deductive to restore distorted meanings in the patient's narrative and inductive to induce from transference what would demystify illusions that could also be recognized in relationships other than the one with the analyst. The most specific thing about interpretation is the stipulation of refraining from engaging with the patient in a nontransferential manner, thus obstructing the aconscious from being dealt with. The noninterpretative relation with the patient would invite acting out the parental distorted relationship that ought to be changed.

The two types of interpretations are supposed to complement each other. This is done in two ways: the analytic relationship is a dialectical work between analyst and analysand, whereby the demystification of an illusion opens the way for genetic material to emerge that seeks restoration of its lost meaning. When allowing it to influence transference it creates a spiral progression from one act to the other. Strachey's (1934) germinal contribution to the concept of interpretation is closely related to this idea. The mutative interpretation moves from the restoration of meaning to the demystification of illusionment and further to the next duality.

However, this spiral of dialectical progression puts us face-to-face with the most important aspect of the psychoanalytic act: construction and reconstruction. Interpretation opens the way for the genetic source of the "complaint" to subtly inch in in the associations. The genetic source is the actual condition where the meaning of an event was lost or was distorted and a replacement illusion was initiated. It is where the chain of representation took a turn toward symptom formation or character disorder. The complementary relationship between the transference and the genetic material finds its dialectical synthesis in a process of putting together for the patient a new construction, a new narrative, or a new reconfiguration of events, to reconstruct what was analyzed. Freud said:

> I think that construction is by far the more appropriate description [of the psychoanalytic technique]. Interpretation applies to something that one does to some single element of the material, such as an association or a parapraxis. But it is construction when one lays before the subject of the analysis a piece of his early history that he has forgotten. (1937b, p. 261)

Although is not difficult to deduce from Freud's statement a clear link between interpretation and reconstruction we find ourselves asking the question: Is what we do in psychoanalysis a search for meaning or for cause? Laplanche (1992) elaborated this point by saying, "Interpretation . . . finds itself trapped in the unresolvable dualism of pure factuality on the one hand [the genetic] and creative imagination on the other: in the one case, it patiently reconstitutes facts which it hopes will prove to be the source of determinism, explaining the present by the past" (p. 441). The issue is not as puzzling as it might appear. The patient's problem is a text constructed and written by his neurosis in a way that does not enable him to read and comprehend. For example, a patient who *suffered* from a sense of lack of definition (identity confusion) mentioned in an early session a screen memory: a toddler trying helplessly to get up on the sofa where his mother was sitting. He did not help him to get beside her as he wanted. His older brother saw that and put him next to his mother. Many aspects of his sufferings with lack of identification were related to his helplessness to get his mother's attention or in her accepting him beside her. His transference depicted the same text in his relationship with the analyst. The screen memory was a text he was unable to read as a toddler, and it has largely remained the text of his adult life, which was written in the same vocabulary. Using the screen memory as the Rosetta Stone to read in it his dilemma permitted revealing the meaning of his suffering, which to him was the genetic cause.

It has to be underlined that the psychoanalytic interpretation is not the simple (or even the complex) act of attributing a set of associations (signifieds) to another set of associations (signifiers). It is not even a process of referring the present to a certain past. Technically, the Freudian analyst does not seek the content or the latent in the material but uses explanations as a step to reaching the aconscious structure that links within that material (make sense of it). The demystification of the transference is meant to give the genetic origin the chance to emerge from within it but not replace it. In that way both analyst and analysand work on restoring its meaning as it exists within the patient's speech. The patient begins analysis with the belief that his symptoms or complaints have a corresponding hidden system of causes that could explain them. Psychoanalytic interpretations reveal to the patient the falsity of that conviction and aim to show him that his present symptoms, though they have a past from which their meaning came, are products of a process that links the past with the present in a peculiar way that eludes him. By making that link conscious, we introduce the patient to the workings of the primary process, which disguises the meanings and the intent of the symptoms.

We could address now how interpretations and reconstruction work. There was—as there is still—a great deal of confusion among analysts of all veins about the influence of the analyst's theoretical orientation and his interpretative inclinations. The main belief is that analysts use theory in constructing their interpretations. The problem is not simply how we conceptualize or contextualize the material (Boesky, 1998); this is only one aspect of the psychoanalytic act of interpretation (Busch & Schmidt-Hellerou, 2004). A

Kleinian would see in the material the struggles of the depressive position, while an "intersubjectivist" would see something else. Dealing with contents could be explained according to the analyst's preference for special contents. The problem is that analysts are still locked into the catharsis model of psychopathology. They ignore the fact that we do not deal with the content of the conscious/preconscious system or the manifest and its latent. However, the analyst who adopts the psychoanalytic theory will stick to the systemic unconscious, which is content-less. He would deal with the unconscious structuring of contents, which become symptoms. The *Ucs.* only creates to the link within a chain of representations, whatever the representations are and contextualized; it is merely the link that needs to be interpreted. The screen memory mentioned previously was not interpreted; it was used to interpret his relationships.

But because the dynamic unconscious has become the "official" unconscious of the IPA and as plurality was established as a fact, we have to proceed to examine construction more extensively since it is where the application of the theory of psychoanalysis is vested, whether it is the clinical or nonclinical application.

THE PRIMAL AND THE PRIMARY IN RECONSTRUCTION

Confusing or ignoring the difference between the *Ucs.* and the *Pcs.*, on one hand, and between primary repression and repression proper, on the other, led analysts to minimize, if not dismiss, the difference between interpreting and explaining. Patients talk but use explanations as an integral part of their speech. They do that preconsciously. Their explanations are different from the ones the analyst sometimes uses. The patients' explanations are more rationalizations or repetitions of meanings given to their behavior by others. The explanations given by the analyst are supposedly reformulations of what the patient has already said in order to highlight some *preconscious* content in his statement. These reformulations still address material the patient is aware of, that is, the analyst reformulates the same external causes given by the patient but shows the patient in a gradual way that they are mostly justifications and rationalizations. The analyst does not attach causes to the patient's associations but merely connects dispersed contents from different associations, revealing the looseness of those connections. In this way, explanations free the psychical events from their bond to the *Cs./Pcs.* The patient in that case discovers that there must be an *Ucs.* meaning to the same material, sometimes by remembering its genetic source or through a noticeable shift in the transference.

Explanations always offer something of a conscious quality because the latent is nothing more than another hidden manifest. They deal with the vocabulary of the psychical phenomenon but are not its grammar (purpose and teleology). The result is framing the patient's associations within the secondary process without considering the incursion of the primary process on the preconscious. It is common in that case that the analyst would resort to his theoretical framework to formulate an explanation. This has happened more frequently in the 1970s and created the crisis and the deterioration of clinical practice. Deterioration came in the form of dealing with ego functions such as defense mechanisms and projective identification as explainable aspects of the analytic theory and considering relations and subjectivity as issues to correct. Analysis became an act of explaining what needs to be corrected. It was common to find analysts who advocate opening psychoanalysis to all methods of dealing with all sorts of material without specification or distinguishing psychoanalysis from other psychotherapies. Gabbard and Westen (2003) said, "We no longer practice in an era in which interpretation is viewed as the exclusive therapeutic arrow in the analyst's quiver [meaning there are other arrows]" (p. 823). This viewpoint missed that interpretation is not merely a method of practicing psychoanalysis or a separate act that is preferred to others; it is the only act that is natural and stems from the interpretable material. *We have no choice but to interpret a dream or just ignore it, just as we have no choice but to interpret metaphors and displacements to understand what is said.* Interpretation is the only act possible in dealing with psychical issues if the purpose of psychotherapy is to induce the meaning of phenomena. Moreover, meaning is the common principle and foundation of the Freudian doctrine's substantial contributions to understanding nonclinical phenomena (Delusions and Dreams in Jensen's *Gradiva* [1907a], The Uncanny [1919h], *Civilization and Its Discontents* [1930a], and *Moses and Monotheism* [1939]).

Interpretation, on the other hand, does not deal with the psychical act but with its intent (meaning). The intent of the psychical act is what it could have achieved if it were not obstructed by the neurotic structure. The intent of the psychical event is always entwined with the act itself (the manifest), and the patient does not notice that it is hidden (latent) in the event. Interpretation aims only at connecting the intent of the psychic event to the internal particulars of the patient's neurosis that are revealed in his associations. For that reason, *it could be said that interpretations do not follow any theoretical lines and do not lead to any theoretical verifications*. The theory of psychoanalysis is neither used to formulate a specific clinical direction nor as vocabulary in interpretation.

In the chapter on dream work (Freud, 1900a) and in his work on the transference phenomenon (1912b), as well as in his views on symptom formation (1916–1917), Freud showed that the final psychical product was a secondary elaboration of another psychical formation. Secondary elaboration, as such, was seen as an interpretation in its own right and part of the psychical event itself, and dealt with as a representation of a representation. In other words, secondary elaboration was considered an interpretation in the sense used in theater, where the director interprets the playwright's intent, but the actors interpret the director's interpretation of that intent in their actual performance. Crossing the barrier between the *Cs*. and the *Ucs*. in the Freudian theory—where the act of interpretation is required—comes when the purpose of the event emerges from within the explanations without the patient's awareness that something else than what he said revealed itself.

Explanation and interpretation are a duality within free association, where the same material could be explained and could be interpreted, depending on who is meant by the material. However, it is a duality that encompasses another more profound duality that is the very heart of the way we choose what to interpret and provides the criterion and timing of the interpretation. This duality is the duality of the primal and the primary in the entwinements we encounter in the patient's free associations.

The Primal (*Ur-*) and Its Interpretation

Freud used the adjective *primal* with sixteen entries, such as primal phantasies (*Urphantasien*), primal horde, and primal father. Primal denotes a primitive state that once existed but no longer exists in the same state. It creates a sequel of its own. The sequel state cannot be understood without deducing from it what was once its primal form. For instance, we would not be able to understand the relationship with the analyst without deducing from it its primal parental relationship, which is in itself a sequel to primal scenes. On a larger scale, Freud would not have been able to understand childhood sexual theories without deducing from them their origin in primal fantasies. *The primal is deductive in nature*.

Understanding the place of what is primal in Freudian psychoanalysis, consequently in interpretation, requires going back to one of Freud's most controversial dualities: the genetic versus the phylogenetic. The phylogenetic factor was referred to as a constitutional base, which is inherited as whole structures from generations back. Freud was unsettled about what aspects of that past influence the present and how. Moreover, the phylogenetic was not a needed concept to complement the genetic source of the neuroses, because Freud already formulated a good theory of *aftereffect* [deferred action] in symptom formation. Nevertheless, when his clinical experience introduced him to the concept of fantasy (1900a, 1905d, 1908a), he encountered what seemed to be general and commonly shared fantasies in children, an observation that showed an aspect of infantile sexuality that surpasses the functions of the aftereffect and maybe is its background. Those fantasies made him ask the question: "Whence comes the need for these phantasies and the material for them? . . . I am prepared with an answer, which I know will seem daring to you. I believe these primal phantasies, as I should like to call them, and no doubt a few others as well, are a phylogenetic endowment" (1916–1917, pp. 370–371).

On the surface, primal fantasies in Freud's thinking were a priori structures that imposed their attributes on the individual's experience. The primal, as deduced, was very much one of the structures of the intrapsychic and a constituent of its grammar. It is at least close in meaning to the systemic unconscious *Ucs*. The *Ucs.* based on the primary is not acquired after birth but is activated by birth. Therefore, if we reject the notional aspect that is integral in a concept of phylogeny (Laplanche, 1989), there is still a very important place for phylogeny in the concept of the primal because it relates to a primitive and primordial quality of the human mind. We can do away with the concept of phylogeny if we so wish, but we cannot do away with the concept of the primal; it is the concept that pertains to the structure of the unconscious and to its structuring powers. There are attributes of the *Ucs.* that are not acquired but could only be inherited; otherwise, we will miss most of the nonrepressed *Ucs*. We cannot ignore the oedipal structure in the triangulation of the family when we analyze the prototypes of interpersonal relationship (we could if we are not doing psychoanalysis).

Clinically, transference pertains to what is primal in analysis because it is an a priori phenomenon, inevitable in any analysis. The Freudian analyst does not consider transference a simple sequel taking the form of reliving the past, or as a presentment of the ego's inability to process the demands of the here and now, or as the distorted mirroring of an old self-object. It is a sequel to primal infantile phantasies, which facilitate understanding the parental relationship that has undergone several distortions. Hence, in practice, transference is the occasion where the analytic setting discloses its metonymical link with the distorted past. The analyst can deduce the setups that prompted distorting the primal and reveal most of that distortion. "If transference neurosis is displayed then it will be possible to understand the pathogenic memories and fantasies that are in the intrapsychic conflict" (Ellman, Grand, Silvan, & Ellman, 1998, p. 278). The criterion for interpretable transference material is the loss of the sense of time, character, function, or expectation of the analyst (i.e., when the patient regresses in the transference to a wishing state). Those moments usually show clinically by an inability to finding the correct words that are expressible within the common usage of language. It is a feature in the analysis that reveals to the patient the fallacy of the here and now. Freudian psychoanalysis aims not at establishing for the patient a criterion for reality but at introducing him to his subjectivity (his *me*-ness) as the only possible reality, and that happens through analysis of the transference as the sequel to genetic events. The subjectivity extracted from the transference shows the patient that he can still relate to the "other" (make the *I* speak) without his subjectivity or his intrapsychic distorting what is "not him" (i.e., he can live his subjectivity in nonneurotic ways).

The significance of interpreting the duality of the primal/sequel is that it reveals to the patient the effect of primary process on separating the *Cs.* from the *Pcs*. At that level of interpretation, what is revealed to the patient would be more of a functional quality because its aim is to demystify the transference.

The Primary (*Primärer*) and Its Interpretation

Freud used *primary* as an adjective for four phenomena: representation (primary process), narcissism, masochism, and identification.[2] I will concentrate on the primary process only because the other two are very clinically and psychopathologically specific and examining them would deviate from the main issue of this chapter.

Primary pertains to an origin that has not been transformed into something else, in spite of having generated multiple secondary forms of itself. It is something that still exists along with its secondary forms but disguised within the entwinement with them. Primary masochism, for instance, is noticed in acts and fantasies of sadism in which the subject and the object are the same. The disguise of the primary could be removed only by inducing it from its secondary forms or from within other material that hides it (in contrast to the primal that is deduced from the sequel that replaced it). For instance, in the case of Katharina, Freud (1895d) was able to uncover two missing memories that restored the meaning of her anxiety attacks by a process of inductive examination of her symptoms. Later, he had the same intuition in reading the working of the primary process in dreams through inducing them from the manifest dream content. In other words, the secondary is always infiltrated by the primary and carries it within its operations; therefore, a dialectical process of "translating" between the *Ucs*. and the *Pcs*. is almost continuous in our psychical lives.

The primary process has two attributes. First, in terms of the economics of psychical energy, the unbound energy cathects ideas by the loose means of metaphor (condensation), without the restrictions of logical causation. Second, a process creates arbitrary links between cause and effect and structure and function, and ignores the necessity of distinguishing between the whole and the part, or the similar and the dissimilar. The secondary process distinguishes between ideas and cathects them selectively according to logical causalities. However, symptoms, dreams, parapraxes, and even our daily events of life stipulate that they are products of both logical and illogical causalities. They always suggest that something primary is lurking in the background, waiting to be induced, without which it is impossible to understand those phenomena. Getting to the primary state from the patient's associations by inducing it from within the secondary states restores the disguised meaning—or better, restores the lost intent—of the psychical act. For instance, uncovering the act of doing/undoing in the obsessions will give the obsessional act its lost meaning. The lake of interest in restoration of meaning of the material mirrors the disappearance of the distinction between the *Ucs.* as a system and the dynamic unconscious.

The duality of primary/secondary is predominant in analysis because the primary persists and is there in every aspect of psychical life (while the primal gives its place to a sequel). The prevalence of the primary is more obvious when the material is not derived from the transference and the patient talks about events that he encountered or lived in his life as a neurotic patient. The neurotic aspect of those particular events is usually expressed through metaphors, similes, symbolic expressions, and, most of all, as events that dictated the way they should be expressed. For instance, a patient talks about his in-laws with irritation and says that he is crowded by their presence in his and his wife's life: "They are like a dark shadow hanging over our heads." When asked about the simile of shadow, he talked about their being everywhere in their life. He elaborates about feeling their bearing on his life even when they are not around, a notion of their effect on his sexual freedom with his wife. The criterion for what and when to interpret condensation is when the condensed expression gives way to some of the condensed thoughts behind it. The significance of interpreting the duality of the primary/secondary is to reveal the working of the primary process and the impact it has on the conscious ideas. Interpretation brings the unconscious to consciousness through clearing the vagueness of the conscious content and effecting structural changes in it.

Unfortunately, the duality of the primary/secondary process is one of the most misunderstood in psychoanalysis and hampers the work of the few analysts who still adhere to it. Accepting and rejecting this duality is influenced by separating the attributes of each, missing the specific *mentations* in each, and the distinctiveness of the mental operations generated by each. The separation was even associated with maturity and immaturity, where the primary was considered a primitive state that disappears with maturation. Freud is responsible for this unfortunate misunderstanding, to an extent, because he did not underscore clearly that the primary process is the mode of thinking in regard to the endosomatic stimuli, irrespective of when that happens. The absence of any measure of checking the responses, as it is possible with the perceptual foundation of thinking of the external world, dictates the predominance of the primary process. He did not emphasize enough that the secondary process is a product of the primary process as the representation of the endosomatic gets a form and "speaks" to the other. Better, the two processes are not set apart but are always entwined in the speech to the other. *There is no rhetoric that is not representational, and there is no representa-*

tion that is rhetorical. The attention to the primal and the primary in the patient's speech is the fabric of the work of reconstruction. Those two concepts facilitate noticing the distorted meaning that needs restoration and its mystifying impact on the patient's narrative.

PSYCHOPATHOLOGY WITHOUT REPRESSION OR DEFENSE MECHANISMS

Most of the writers about the Freudian doctrine and the crisis in psychoanalysis revert to an imaginary delineating line between the classical theory and the contemporary theories, which if crossed, the theory is no longer psychoanalytic. However, it seems, with the enlargement of the boundaries of psychoanalysis (see Ricoeur, 1970) the criterion of that line has become rather trivial. Eagle (2011) specified four Freudian fundamentals as the criteria for that line: constancy principle, isolation of mental contents, drive theory, and repression.[3] These criteria show that the catharsis theory, even after its demise, remained as the prototype of all the theories that remained behind the "delineating" line. The template of a theory of something unacceptable and that deserves repression to protect the ego from its negative effects endured in most of the contemporary schools of psychoanalysis. They changed only what is unacceptable and what is protected. Therefore, contemporary psychoanalytic theories could claim that they are still psychoanalytic, provided they embrace the template of the catharsis theory.

The prevailing notion of defense mechanism on one hand, and the misconception of the primary process on the other, shifted the attention from the process that creates the psychical phenomena to the outcome of that process. Defense mechanisms—if there are any—are constructs of the psychoneurosis, while the primary process is not a mental entity but the fabric of mentation. This is how Freud put it: "I looked upon psychical splitting *itself* [my emphasis] as an effect of a process of repelling which then I called defense and later repression" (1914b, p. 11). Freud and psychoanalysis as a whole faced major problems by adhering to the notion of repression. Despite considering the repressed the prototype of the unconscious and defending against it, Freud had to acknowledge that the concept of defense mechanism revealed an aspect of the unconscious that undermines it as the key to psychoanalytic "thought." Defense mechanism—as an issue—made him say, "We have come upon something [resistance] in the ego itself which is also unconscious, which behaves exactly like the repressed" (1923a, p. 17). He realized that the link he previously suggested between repression and the unconscious was instead between the *Ucs.* and defense. This was the clear admission that "defenses" *are* the neuroses and not products or causes of the neuroses. It is curious that Freud did not call on his previous insight about the vicissitudes of the *Trieb* to establish this new link. If he did, he would have also added his theory of symptom formation (1926) to what analysts do when they listen and of what they do to interpret. From the sequence and details of Freud's writings, it seems that repression was central in his theory of psychopathology only until he was no longer able to ignore that defenses are not causes but effects of psychopathology (1926).

In that sense, he had to account for the conscious defensive nature of symptoms: *symptoms are conscious and they elude the subject's understanding of himself, whether as a defense or just by the nature of their formation.*

Freud's unsettled views about repression were evident in *The Ego and the Id* (1923a). He admitted that the *Ucs.* is more than the repressed. Consequently, a third unconscious had to be postulated; otherwise the whole attribute of the unconscious would be unviable. It was nonsensical and paradoxical to say that something is the unconscious while acknowledging that it was not repressed. Freud, like most others, equated consciousness with cognition, which is not always the case. He went further to consider part of the ego as "undoubtedly" *Ucs.* but not latent like the *Pcs.* He justified presuming an unconscious part of the ego, which is not *Pcs.*, by stating that it could be activated without becoming part of cognition (1923a, p. 18). Once again, Freud did not find his way to solving the problem of repression and defense, in spite of having already discovered all the necessary elements for that solution.

If Freud raised some pertinent questions and answered them he would have discovered that he had discovered a very different theory of psychoanalysis than the one he advocated: If a defense mechanism, such as repression, is a function of the ego, how could it remain unconscious after being activated? If the unconscious in the ego could be activated and still remain nonrepressed, doesn't that bring us to the four vicissitudes depicted in the working of the *Trieb* (1915a)? In other words, Freud discovered that defense mechanisms could be assigned to the nonrepressed unconscious regardless of what agency was activating them. Nevertheless, Freud remained firm that the working of the primary process is unconscious though not repressed. It is active while we are asleep or awake, sick or healthy, joking or serious. *Freud did not need the concepts of repression and defense mechanism to deal with psychopathology because he already exposed the role of the primary process in structuring the system Ucs. and the symptoms.* This was enough to explain the formation of symptoms and the healthy state in the exact same terminology within the framework of metapsychology. The analyst needs to decipher the speech of the patient to hone in on what the primary process has discovered to make him feel that it is something "bad" and needs to be defended against.

Quite early in his career Freud defined repression as "a failure in translation [from one psychic system to another] that is what is known clinically as repression" (1896, December 6). Even though it is more likely that Freud used "translation" as a metaphor for crossing the barriers between two psychical systems, it was an auspicious metaphor. A few months later he added, "It is not sufficient to take into account the repression between preconscious and the conscious; we must also consider normal repression within the system unconscious itself. Very important, still very obscure" (1897a, pp. 250–253). Once again, he had the insight that "normal" repression is a condition within the unconscious—and that was years before he talked about primal repression and repression proper (1915b). He was insightful enough to notice that the mechanisms that keep the *Ucs.* separate from the *Cs./Pcs.* are different from the ones that keep the *Pcs.* separate from the *Cs.* He outlined that difference in dreams by showing that the censorship between the *Ucs.* and the *Pcs.* was lowered in the dream of "Autodidasker" (1900a, pp. 298–302) but not in the dream of the "burning child" (ibid., pp. 509–511). In the Autodidasker dream, the day's residues (*Pcs.*) had to be worked extensively by the primary process in order to connect with the unfulfilled *Ucs.* wish. On the other hand, the dream of the "burning child" exemplified the lowering of the censorship between the *Pcs.* and *Cs.*, where the conscious wish was fulfilled in a more direct way (1900, p. 542).

Freud's discovery that the working of the primary process and the structure of the systemic *Ucs.* distinguished between primary repression, the sequel of splitting affect and thought, and repression proper, which would deal with the representations of the split thought. Repression proper was adequate to dealing with infantile sexuality and taking the child through the latency period. But we have to go back to something Freud stated in regard to repression and fixation to put repression in its proper context. He said distinguishing primal repression from repression proper makes it clear that preventing the ideational representation of the *Trieb* from entering consciousness creates a point of fixation (1915d, p. 148).

The way Freud talked about repression, fixation, and the *primary* after 1915 was different from the way he did before. He was talking about psychopathology as a product of a process that distorts releasing the *Trieb* from the somatic and obstructing it from entering the realm of the sign, that is, to be present in the ideational field. Thus, the sign, not the *Trieb*, becomes the subject for repression proper. For instance, the increase of sensations in the infant's mouth have to be primarily repressed before the hunger sensations of sucking change to representation of oral frustration/satisfaction. Thereafter, the frustration/satisfaction attached to sucking becomes the target of repression proper; as he indicated, it is not the *Trieb* that gets repressed but its representation.

Repression is not a defense mechanism but the manifestation of a process that creates obscurities and disguises, and produces unfamiliar representations of the *Trieb* and the rest of the vicissitudes of the *Trieben*. In other words, repression, which was the indelible relic of the catharsis theory, proved to be nothing but the result of the working of the primary process—a process that is not activated to defend anything or as a function of any agency. *Repression (the unfortunate term) is the primary process in its action to represent the endosomatic in separation from its ideational form.*

The phenomenon of primal repression is not, in essence, the process of avoidance or keeping away. It is simply the process of translating the *Triebhaft* into metaphors, metonyms, and perceptive (images) equivalents of ideas, which could later become the core of the equivocal quality of language (Ricoeur, 1970). The outcome of that process is the emergence of the "sharp cleavage" between the conscious and unconscious, creating the two systems and producing a link between them that is determined by the known means of that process. A *Triebhaft* component locked in a conscious sign behaves as a nucleus that other ideas could attach to without the intervention of the secondary process (creating fixation). The analyst, therefore, searches the *Pcs.* for what could "explain" the *Cs.* When analysis changed from interpreting free association to a sensible and thoughtful explanation of the ego's flaws, the analyst's work changed from interpreting to the patient what he said to talking to him about what he did not say or meant but missed to say (i.e., showing him his projective identification, intersubjective distortions, or relational expectations). Contemporary schools ignore the *Ucs.* by bypassing repression in favor of dealing with the complexities of relating and correcting relational conceptions in the patients' minds (Cooper, 1998; Jacobs, 1999; Mitchell, 1998; Renik, 1998b; Storolow & Atwood, 1997, 1992).

AFTER-EFFECT AND THE ANALYTIC MIND

What is the usefulness of the core principles of psychoanalysis to the clinical analyst? This question could be put in a more challenging way: Do we practicing analysts have to keep the core principles in mind when we practice? The answer depends on what the analyst considers his main objective in practice. If the analyst deals with relationships, intersubjective interactions, separation/individuation, and so on, he does not need the core principles of psychoanalysis. All he needs is an outline of the optimum condition of the phenomena he considers the seat of psychopathology to guide the patient to reach and adopt that optimum. If the analyst deals with "things psychological"—psychical structures that decide the rest of the patients' psychological life—he would need firm knowledge of three basic issues: what the "things psychological" are, when and how they become psychological things, and what changing them means.

The core principles of psychoanalysis pertain to those three basic issues. Freud's intuitive idea that psychical life emerges from contentless, formless states of excitation, which arise from the autoerotic zones of the body, is basic to an analyst. If not, what else is going to help him make sense of what the patient complains of? It will help him listen to the patient's associations as expressions of chains of representations, which have to have originated somewhere. Because representations are formed unconsciously, the analyst has to decipher the working of the primary process and differentiate between the primary and primal in the material. Without this second step the patient's associations and transference will be incomprehensible, absolutely subject to theoretical formulations and not to interpretation. The third step of the basic issues shows that the only acceptable psychoanalytic act is interpretation. *The core principles are not things to keep in mind; they are our psychoanalytical mind.*

A psychoanalytic mind is what differentiates the analyst from the nonanalyst and the good from the not so good analyst. Freud had a unique psychoanalytic mind (we should remember that he did not have any model with which to measure and compare his mind, while we have thousands). His matchless intuitions attest to that uniqueness. I chose two of them to confirm the specificity of the psychoanalytic mind: the phenomena of aftereffect and psychical determinism.

In the *Project*, Freud (1950) said, "We invariably find that a memory is repressed which has only become a trauma by deferred action [aftereffect]" (p. 156). We can safely say that he noticed very early in his endeavors that a content of psychical matters is an *aftereffect*, an inherent feature of psychical events. A new first event, such as a childlike sexual seduction, is merely an event and is meaningless to the child. The repetition of that event gives it its meaning, an aftereffect. One year after that insight, he added to it, "The trauma of childhood operates in a different fashion as though they were fresh expressions; but they do that unconsciously" (1896b, fn. 2b, pp. 166–167). How did he discover that what he was dealing with was not the original event but a representation of a previous event? Adding the notion of the unconscious to aftereffect indicates—almost directly—that he already grasped the workings of the primary process.

He had that clinical insight long before he talked in a clear manner—in *The Interpretation of Dreams*—of content-less wishes looking for content. Unfortunately, the aftereffect phenomenon was used by analysts in a limited way to explain trauma, though it is in the fabric of psychical life and maturation, with some bumps here and there when experiences become traumatic. Freud's analytic thinking was preparing his mind for further intuitions that would not have been possible if he did not think of psychical life as a two-step event. The intuition about the aftereffect was very close to the fundamental notion of primary repression and repression proper, in which the latter targets the representation and not the primary event.

The capacity of the human mind to bridge two separate events by metaphors or metonymies is expressed in deferring a meaning of an event until another like it comes about. We have to ask: If the aftereffect is the fabric of our lives and a product of the primary process, does our psychological lives mean anything? How does psychological life maintain meaning if it derives its meaning from aftereffect, if not all the time, then in most cases? Freud became aware that if his theories were to survive, they had to address the place of the unconscious in our daily lives and not only in the psychoneuroses.

Once again, Freud's psychoanalytic mind sensed the problem, addressed it, and posed a question that he left without an answer. Nonetheless, the answer could still be found in his text. The problem is as follows: Is there logic behind the seemingly illogical, unmotivated psychical events such as misspellings, slips of the tongue, and choices of numbers? Could the unconscious explain psychical events that look incomprehensible, though they are not pathological? He dedicated two whole works to that subject (1901b, 1905c) and wrote several papers on the psychological foundation of certain unexplainable events (1907i, 1910, 1910c, 1919b). His work in this area was interesting, and successful, but brought out the issue of determinism in psychical phenomena. He showed that the content of psychical events was not haphazardly chosen, and, if we work *retrogressively*, we find the "reason" behind those parapraxes and they become logical (1901b, p. 214). However, it is not the same when we work *progressively.* Why can we understand the logic of a parapraxis only after the fact and not predict it before the fact? (1916–1917). He gave the psychoanalytic hint to the answer, though he did not give a complete one.

Discovering the motivation behind the parapraxis reveals the chain of mental events that led to it, so analyzing a parapraxis uncovers the dynamic unconscious or the *Pcs*. It is possible to find logical links within the dynamics of the duality of primal and its sequel but not between the primal and the primary (the *Ucs*.). In other words we can go only so far in understanding determinism if we stay at the level of the *Cs./Pcs.* Beyond that, we need the psychoanalytic doctrine with its core principles. The issue of psychical determinism complements the issue of aftereffect by emphasizing that that duality is part of the material the psychoanalyst works with. However, it is structurally determined and not functionally created.

CONCLUDING REMARK

The six main propositions of the classical theory are internally consistent, logically interrelated, and unique in illuminating the issue of human duality, which for all reasons and purposes is the initiator of psychoanalysis as the extension of *German Idealist Metaphysics*. They all came to Freud the way intuitions come to gifted thinkers, not the way deductions are reached by scientists. They also interweaved into the fabric of Western civilization and are no more novel ideas. Even the adversaries of the Freudian doctrine are incapable of disregarding it in their suggested "better" theories.

The theory of psychoanalysis with its core propositions is distinguished by its comprehensiveness and has one grammar that permeates the entirety of the human phenomena, with its varied intrastructural attributes. When this fact disappears from our scope of reasoning, we fall back into functional thinking, as Freud did several times while his theory was evolving. This is the reason he left us a two-track theory: a purely structural track, for which I highlighted its core propositions, and another that is functional, stemming from the concept of catharsis. Although he tried a few times to expand his functional conception to encompass nonclinical phenomena, he was successful only in making his effort look like applied psychoanalysis.

Contemporary schools tried but did not succeed in demising the catharsis theory or replacing it with their own fictional formulations. However, it would be difficult for them—judging from the way they construct their theories—to do the same with Freud's other theory of psychoanalysis. There are two reasons for that: the replacement of the functional concepts with other functional ones does not change a theory in any radical way; it would only be a cosmetic change. Second, Freud's functional concepts had their structural foundation, while the new schools have functional concepts that lack the corroboration and validation of structural principles. Psychoanalysis is cluttered with theories, quasi-theories, and pseudo-theories of all kinds. It is very difficult for the new generation to learn psychoanalysis with so many useless distractions. Another reason for that clutter is Freud's flair with language and his ability to give ordinary words deeper and wider connotations. Some contemporary analysts envisaged that it is legitimate to do that, with no reservations. So they went on creating terminologies of their own in a reckless manner. Those trends have to be scrutinized to clear the field from the clutter of false theories and meaningless terminologies. This is a task for the IPA if there is a serious intention to save psychoanalysis from oblivion and to give the new generation of analysts a chance to make educated choices.

Some analysts still have the ambition to compose the "one theory" that will replace the Freudian doctrine. However, in psychoanalysis, *the name of the father happened to be the father's name: Sigmund Freud.*

Notes

1. WHAT IS PSYCHOANALYTICAL IN PSYCHOANALYSIS?

1. The 101st Annual Meeting of the American Psychoanalytic Association: Chicago, June 2012. Discussion group #24.

2. In spite of the qualitative differences in the literature between classical writings in the past and present, the present classical literature is still psychoanalytical and maintains the trademark of the Freudian doctrine. It is different from the writings of the contemporary schools. Present-day analysts are struggling with fundamental conceptions in classical analysis (the catharsis theory), which are problematic but believe they have to hold on to them so as not to stray away from psychoanalysis. Contemporary psychoanalyses, on the other hand, rejected those conceptions outright and strayed completely away from psychoanalysis. Nonetheless, they usurped the name unjustly. Although "modern classical psychoanalysis" appears less psychoanalytical it has attributes worthy of attention because if we should want to keep psychoanalysis distinct we could find in it what we need to identify our field anew.

3. If the training syllabus in an institute is limited to studying *The Interpretation of Dreams*, the *Three Essays on the Theory of Sexuality*, the paper "On Narcissism," the three metapsychology papers, and *Inhibition, Symptoms and Anxiety*, the candidate would get the basis of psychoanalytic thinking.

4. *Trieb* was translated first to *instinct*, which Strachey admitted was an incorrect translation, and was later translated to *drive*, which is an even worse translation. To avoid the wrong denotations of the wrong translations, I am using *Trieben* in this book in its original German. Thus, *Trieben* is the plural and *Triebhaft* is the adjective form. I will explain the reason for that in later chapters.

2. THE ROAD TO THE CRISIS OF PSYCHOANALYSIS

1. My statement is supported by serious published material coming from the international organization and from different regional societies and institutes. I am not documenting my statement relying on the familiarity with those publications and on the lack of any publication that would refute and disapprove of it (see *The American Psychoanalyst*, 2002–2007).

2. It is an oxymoron to call the divergent contemporary schools of analysis orthodox sects, because orthodoxy is the presumption of the only right way. Sects could develop only by

deviating from orthodoxy. The fearful and trembling analysts who belonged to the orthodox doctrine were so because they were aware of their poor adherence to the three principles of practicing analysis: anonymity, abstinence, and neutrality. Those three principals were the most rebelled against and the least understood by contemporary analysts (Fayek, 2011).

3. In this book, I am using the German *Trieb* (instinct), *Trieben* (instincts), and *Triebhaft* (instinctual) to avoid the two imprecise translations of *instinct* and *drive*. The concept of *Trieb* pertains to the process that leads to mental representation and has no behavioral connotation. Missing this fact resulted in calling the Freudian doctrine a "drive psychology"; it is a grave mistake because Freud's presumed theory of the originators of behavior was limited to two duets: sex/self-preservation and life/death. We can hardly call those two duets drives, if at all consider them outside their symbolic forms.

4. Sandler and Rosenblatt (1962) defined object relationship as "essentially an intrapsychic role relationship, depicted via mental representations, and forming an intrinsic part of [a] wish. After a certain point in development, we cannot speak of a wish which does not have an ideational content; and this ideational content is, for the purpose of our work as psychoanalysts, very often centered about the representation of oneself in interaction with the object" (p. 133).

5. The intrapsychic is the clinical test of a psychoanalyst's ability. It shows his sensitivity to recognize it separate from, or through the details of, interpersonal relationships and to make a proper diagnosis of it, tolerate its ambiguities, deal with the demands it puts on him, and endeavor to change it, all that through acts of interpretations without any explanations.

6. Relationships are explainable but not interpretable because to interpret we have to bring out a link between the cause and its effect, a link that is not apparent in the relationship as is. That link is always intrapsychic in nature and thus unconscious.

7. Compton (1981a), in an extensive review of the concept of *Trieb* (to him it was instinct), concluded that "instinct [is] . . . a hypothetical force which is held responsible for certain kinds of behaviour called instinctual behaviour" (p. 205). There is nothing in metapsychology that even hints at a psychology of that sort (drive psychology), not even naming any behavior as a manifestation of a particular driving inclination in the two pairs of *Trieben. Trieb* had no content and was always depicted in a polarity and in a plurality. Holder (1970) clearly showed that Freud mentioned *Instinkt* on five occasions in his writing as a fixed behavioral pattern. He related that only to animals but used *Trieb* about human behavior only. *Trieb* is without any *behavioral* manifestation and is manifested only in representing the endosomatic stimulus.

8. There is no clinical theory of medical practice, no theory of practice in architecture, civil engineering, or even law. The practice of a profession is inherent in its core principles, as free association and interpretation are the inherent mode of psychoanalytic practice (Freud, 1912e, 1913c, 1914g).

9. Wallerstein's ambition to verify psychoanalysis in the tradition of the experimental model (1996) is impossible to fulfill. The experimental model is founded on determining the "independent" variables in a phenomenon in order to verify a "dependent" variable. It also requires the means to quantify the correlational relations between the two types of variables. Neither the analyst nor the experimental scientist could at any point isolate and quantify psychical variables to submit them to experimentation in that model. I think of dreams as an example of that impossibility.

3. THE PUZZLING FREUDIAN DOCTRINE

1. I am quoting Edelson from his introduction because he summarized his ideas in the introduction better than any of my efforts to summarize his thoughts from the book.

2. Grunbaum supports this view based on Freud's abandonment of the *Project for a Scientific Psychology*, which was intended to be used as a purely neurological model to build a theory of psychology. This is true, but Grunbaum did not notice that the abandonment was for another reason, seldom if ever mentioned, which relates to the discovery of the theory of psychoanalysis in a most significant way. Freud said in the *Project*: "[E]very psychological theory, apart from what it achieves from the point of view of natural science, must fulfill yet

another major requirement. It should explain to us what are we aware of, in the most puzzling fashion, through our 'consciousness' and, since this consciousness knows nothing of what we have so far been assuming—quantities and neurones—it should explain this lack of knowledge to us as well" (1950, pp. 307–308). Freud abandoned configuring a psychology based on a neurological model when he realized that consciousness is not enough for building a psychological theory. However, he did not present that point portending the existence of an unconscious but suggesting that there is another aspect of consciousness that needs to be discovered (see chapter 4 for the roots of that idea in Western culture).

3. However flawed and erroneous of Freud to seek causation in psychical phenomena, it should not deprive him of a major advent at explaining the psychoneuroses in a very distinct manner. Before the catharsis theory, psychoneurosis referred to physical, physiological, medical, and rarely to societal causes. The causes were external to and identified separately from the pathological condition. Freud's causation of the psychoneurosis was from within the neuroses themselves (i.e., psychological). Causation in his catharsis theory was intrinsic to the condition (e.g., sexual frustration). This shift required a major change in understanding the pathological condition (e.g., although, at one time, coitus interruptus was part of the psychical condition, it had to be repressed to reemerge as a cause in creating the condition).

4. Politzer is a left-wing French philosopher. As did his compatriots in the early years of the twentieth century, he recognized the significance of the Freudian doctrine even before it was firmly established as a clinical specialty. Although Politzer in 1928 came up with his critique of psychology (psychoanalysis) ten years before Freud's last works were published, I did not find anything in Freud's literature between 1928 and 1939 that refuted Politzer's distinctions (i.e., his views about metapsychology or his critique of psychoanalysis as a psychology founded on metapsychology). Distinguishing the human drama that analysis has put in focus, whether in sickness or health, stands until now as the most valuable in the discovery of psychoanalysis, although rarely did clinical analysts ever show that side of the story in their case histories.

5. The conflictual nature of the existence of things (theses) is the Hegelian basis of dialectics. A thesis begets an antithesis (the counterpart subject or object), which is defined by it (a slave begets a master and not anything else). The conflict is a result of each of the antagonists becoming aware, or we become aware, that its existence is conditional on the existence of the other. Such conflict ushers in a synthesis that is a higher level of existence of the conflicting elements. Not every conflict or encounter between two subjects is dialectical, only unless the antithesis is clearly a product of the thesis that stands as its counterpart.

6. Einstein described the moment he came to his first theory of relativity: "I was sitting in the patent office in Bern when all of a sudden a thought occurred to me; if a person falls freely, he won't feel his own weight. . . . I was startled. This simple thought made a deep impression on me. It impelled me toward a theory of gravitation" (cited in Calaprice, 1996, p. 242). Freud describes something very similar that happened to him when he came to the idea that dreams are wish fulfillment (Jones, 1954).

4. A CULTURAL IMPASSE AND THE FREUDIAN SOLUTION

1. The essence of theories is their laws. A law in a theory is merely a mode of presentation and thus says nothing about a concrete reality or a particular "thing." The laws of gravity apply to the phenomenon of attraction between bodies in motion regardless of what those bodies are. Laws introduce new terms to the language of science or introduce new ways of using old terms (sexual attraction, human gravitation toward equality). Better, theoretical laws change the comprehension of the internal structure or grammar of reality, allowing spoken language to reveal the internal construct of what is manifest. It is not possible to reject a grammatical system, such as the system of kilo weights, but it is possible to prefer another system of weights (see Elder, 1994). Accordingly, formative theories have the capabilities of replacing other theories but are not replaceable by any other theory. No theory could replace the theory of

evolution, which replaced a number of theories of creation, without falling short of what it said about the origin of humans.

2. Most of the material in the next two sections of this chapter is derived from Edwards, 1996; Reese, 1999; and Wiener, 1968.

3. In a post-Cartesian movement, the relationship between the thinking matter (mind) and the extending matter (brain) evolved into what later was called "attributive dualism." This theory proposed that even if brain and mind are inseparable, they should be considered two distinct attributes: psychological and physical.

4. There is a subtle but fundamental difference between this suggestion and Freud's theory of dreams. Leibniz considered dreams—which are manifestations of consciousness—events suitable for the unconscious to use. Freud's theory refers to the event of dreaming as the activity of the unconscious in its attempt to express itself. Therefore it is an unconscious event that uses consciousness.

5. It has to be mentioned that duality in idealistic metaphysics was not identified (even after Kant) as an attribute of the issue of the argument or as inherent in the nature of precepts but only as a convenient approach to arguing issues, accordingly reflecting a quality of the mind. Descartes's duality was the opening of the door to analyzing the individual after his long slumber in unity or as a singularity.

6. Fichte's conception of the *I* was indirectly assimilated into Freud's concept of narcissism. Regretfully, the *I* in ego psychology was seriously distorted and came to be represented as an object of sorts (see chapters 6 and 7); thus the concept of narcissism was badly conceived in the 1960s and 1970s by analysts such as Kohut and Kernberg.

7. Schelling took the opposite position from Kant's view of where duality existed. Schelling was of the opinion that duality is a quality inherent in nature because nature effectuated and expressed itself according to the law of "polarities," or as pairs of opposite, though complementary, forces.

8. Freud's thinking manifests three features of German idealistic metaphysics. The first is the theme of duality in every aspect of his formulations. Second, he named his psychological endeavors "metapsychology" because he intended—even then—to go beyond empirical psychology, which was founded on positivistic findings. The third feature was the place the process of mental representation occupied in the theory of psychoanalysis and the way representation created ideas (see Fichte's and Schopenhauer's representations of the unconscious). In addition to representation, the concept of the *Ich* as the antithesis of identity played a role in Freud's best and worst theoretical configurations.

9. The philosophical movement in England in the seventeenth century and after was quite different from its counterpart on the Continent. It was interested in natural philosophy and empirical knowledge, not in idealistic metaphysics. Therefore it is difficult to say categorically whether idealism or empiricism has had more influence on modern thought in the nineteenth century.

5. DREAMS AND THE PSYCHOLOGY OF THE WISH

1. This relationship is well depicted in the myth of Narcissus and Oscar Wilde's *The Picture of Dorian Gray*.

2. Freud repeated this same idea, slightly differently, when he said: "Psycho-analysis cannot be accused of having applied to normal cases findings arrived at from pathological material. The evidence in the latter and the former was reached independently and shows that normal processes and what inscribed as pathological one follow the same rules" (1913j. p. 166).

3. Freud said in the same letter: "The fact that dreams are hypermnesic and have access to material from childhood has become one of the corner-stones of our teaching." We should keep in mind that wishes from the "prehistoric period of life" have to be more than just preverbal. They also very close to the endosomatic type of stimulation.

4. *The Interpretation of Dreams* was translated to Arabic in 1959. In that version *wish* was translated by the Arabic word for *desire*. At that time I did notice the possible difference

between wish fulfillment and satisfaction of desire. However, I wondered then how the dream could fulfill a dreamer's desire or how the dreamer could experience its satisfaction if the dreamer does not know what desire the dream meant to identify. I did not get an answer to this question from my mentor, who did the translating. I will try to give that answer in this chapter as I make the distinction between wish and desire. Freud used *Wunsch* (wish) and not *Begierde* (desire) to identify what gets fulfilled in dreams. A wish is a passive state that does not contain the means for actual fulfillment; therefore, it does not go beyond creating a fantasy, a day-dream, or a night dream. It has no identifiable prospect of its fulfillment (e.g., I wish I had told him (but I didn't) or I wish I could tell him (but I can't). A wish is a muted statement, and the wisher is not intended to declare it. Desire, on the other hand, is a state that has the means to actual satisfaction because it comprises its objective, which is the deliberate "act" of satisfying it (I want her to notice me or reciprocate my admiration). Moreover, it has a definable objective of what is expected if it were enacted; it has a defined statement that could be transmitted to the object of desiring. Another subtle difference is that we could be unconscious or preconscious of a wish but always conscious of a desire. This distinction is essential in understanding Freud's intuition that a dream needs the day residues to form a manifest for its content. Freud's secret "megalomania" about his budding discoveries, hopeful successes, and a future of a legend was a wish that could not be expressed. Otto's remarks activated that wish and gave it a theater of the medical scene of patient and ignorant physicians, who also condemn Otto, his foe. Freud made a similar distinction in the *Project* by separating affect from motive.

5. In regard to dreams as the guardians of sleep, Freud (1920g) said,

> It would seem that the function of dreams, which consists in setting aside any motives that might interrupt sleep, fulfilling the wishes of disturbing impulses, is not their original function. It would not be possible for them to perform that function until the whole mental life had accepted the dominance of the pleasure principle. If there is a "beyond the pleasure principle," it is only consistent to grant that there was a time before the purpose of dreams was the fulfillment of wishes. . . . May not the dreams which, with a view to the psychical binding of traumatic impressions, obey the compulsion to repeat, may not such dreams occur outside analysis as well? And the reply can be a decided affirmative. (pp. 32–33)

Freud admitted in this statement that wish fulfillment is not the drive behind dreams and that a functional explanation of dreams is erroneous. Dreams do not protect sleep, but sleep is the precondition for dreaming.

6. The *Ucs.* has a major role in dream formation besides providing the motivating force for the fulfillment of the wish. The working of the primary process, which is unconscious, is responsible for the formation of the manifest dream and its pictorial quality. If wishes are fulfilled in dreams it is not because they are unconscious motives but because they are managed by the unconscious primary process, which has no means to express anything other than to state a fact.

7. Freud later added a footnote to the effect that "a dream expresses a wish of the second agency," meaning that some dreams could be the fulfillment of the wish to censor another wish (1930a, p. 146).

8. The real psychoanalytic endeavor is to bring out the meaning of the psychical phenomenon, not its cause or motive. The motive, whatever it was, is external to the formation of the psychical phenomenon (Otto's remark was external to Freud's wish for glory). The dream, like any other psychical formation, is an entity that embodies its own reason and is not a product of an exterior force. Motives (Freud's megalomaniac ambition), although subjective in source, are also external to the psychical phenomenon because they always seek an external objective (Elder, 1994, pp. 62–68).

9. Neurophysiology supports the notion of two categories of consciousness: primary and secondary, or consciousness and awareness of consciousness. Primary consciousness is regarded as "mental life I" and a higher order of consciousness as "mental life II." This distinction does not preclude that those two categories coexist, overlap, and feed each other. There are

reasons to believe that events in mental life II are never divorced completely from the happenings in mental life I (Edelman & Tononi, 2000, p. 205).

10. In chapter 6 of the book on dreams there is what seems to be the opposite of this notion but not definitive about the existence of the two types of unconscious.

6. THE STRUCTURAL CORE OF THE FREUDIAN DOCTRINE

1. Freud has a very significant letter, written in September 21, 1897, about realizing the impact on him and his theory of discovering this fact.

2. In 1898b, Freud noted the significance of the *aftereffect* factor (delayed reaction) in relating childhood sexuality to adult sexuality, where it acquires its traumatic impact, thus creating the neuroses. This was a pure intuition because there is no clinical or theoretical experience that could have led to it. It appeared at that time as an innocuously insignificant idea. But, as we will see later, it is a central idea in the process behind the content-less wish finding its object and *Trieb* gaining a content.

3. It is very peculiar that in *The Interpretation of Dreams* Freud did not show in any of the tens of dreams he interpreted the existence of an infantile wish reinforcing the wish of the day residue. However, when we go to the Irma dream, for instance, we cannot miss that the size and the extent of the megalomanic wish to overrule all the physicians in the dream was not clear in the day residues but must have gotten its impetus from an additional source, infantile in its omnipotent power. The notion that a childhood wish is needed for an adult dream to form, and as we know now in the neuroses too, was the precursor of the concept of the *aftereffect.*

4. The difference between unconscious and a-conscious is very central in the revision of the concept of unconscious, although Freud did not suggest it. The prefix *un-reverses* and cancels an action, causing it to no longer be. Hence, unconscious is a reversal of consciousness and being aware. The prefix *a*—as in *a*morphous, *a*sexual, and *a*pathy—*negates* the quality of the subject mentioned and renders it without qualifications. This is the distinction between the preconscious, which is repressed consciousness, and the a-conscious, which was never conscious. Freud's *Ucs.* is aconscious because, as we will see later, it never enters consciousness.

5. The myth goes like this: When Narcissus was born, his mother, Leiriope, asked Teiresias the seer whether her newborn child would live long. He replied, "If he never knows himself." Narcissus grew to be a very beautiful youth who was adored by many lovers of both sexes. Among those who loved him in vain was the nymph Echo. She had previously been doomed by the goddess Hera to forcefully repeat the words spoken to her by others. Hence, Echo was unable to initiate a conversation with Narcissus, and her love for him was mute and wasted. She was not recognized and vanished in her wasted voice. A young man whom Narcissus had spurned, as he spurned many other admirers, put a curse on him to love unrequitedly. Nemesis, the goddess of retribution, arranged it so that Narcissus would see his reflection on the surface of a pond. He fell in love with his image and laid beside the water unable to tear himself away from his image. He faded away and was transformed into a flower beside the pond. Teiresias's prophecy was thus fulfilled (Tripp, 1970). Narcissism was a loss in the other, or a loss of the other, in his-self. He existed only in his image, even to himself.

6. This distinction was not in focus when the culture of the subject puzzled about the subjective and the objective nature of the person (see chapter 4).

7. EGO PSYCHOLOGY AND THE SECOND THEORY OF ANXIETY

1. Spruiell (1981) points out that in translation, *Das Ich* became ego. The *Ich* in German stands for an experiential sense of self and not an experiential sense of the one (ego). However, in Anglo-Saxon psychoanalysis, both self and ego have become abstract concepts, and the reflexive meaning of *I* disappeared from psychoanalysis when the two meanings were com-

bined. *I*, the pronoun of the first person, does not constitute on its own a subject for a psychology. At best, it would be considered a reflection of the speaking person, his or her personality. The Anglo Saxon's approach and findings were descriptive of types of personality and their manifestations and functions. The only psychologist who came close to a psychodynamic structure of personality was Raymond Cattell (1957).

In psychoanalysis, the ego is the agent of negation (Freud, 1925). It is peculiar that ego psychologists did not notice that their psychology was, by definition, a psychology of negation. Yet that psychology fits well with Hartmann's valued contributions, such as neurosis versus adaptation, ego versus self, and conflict-free ego versus conflictual ego. The metapsychological points of view also suited ego psychology well because metapsychology was used in talking about the agency of the ego as a psychoanalytic entity (see chapter 6) rather than in terms of the structural nature of the topography of the system's *Cs./Ucs.*

2. Although Freud studied and was influenced by Brentano (philosopher/psychologist) he did not claim that he was qualified to use psychoanalysis as a basis for psychological theorizations. However, his amateurish attempts at that point show where he felt that academic psychology could enrich psychoanalysis.

3. If there was a better time for that work to appear, it should have been at the time the libido theory was collapsing and the first theory of anxiety was defunct.

8. THE PSYCHOLOGY OF METAPSYCHOLOGY

1. I have to repeat that the problems of ego psychology are not my idiosyncratic point of view but rather the final verdict given by "most" contemporary analysts of all walks.

2. Freud says, "Without metapsychological speculation and theorizing I had almost said 'phantasysing'—we shall not get another step forward" (1937a, p. 225). He added in a footnote, "It is impossible to define health except in metapsychological terms" (1937a, p. 226). Freud was clearly of the opinion that metapsychology has an irreplaceable function in his theory, even if it looked like a *witch* of a thought.

3. Green's thesis on the subject of affect (1999) is most extensive and comprehensive. He acknowledges the significance of the mutual meaning of that term, in both the German and French languages, where it could get confused with the connotations of feelings and motives. He also implied that Freud sometimes used more than one word to denote the *meaning* of affect. To avoid summarizing his elaborate exposition of this problem and to remain true to the denotation of the term, I am taking a different direction: I will stipulate the initial *denotation* of *affect* in Freud's text and trace his usage of that denotation in other related words (e.g., pleasure/pain, wish, *Trieb*, and anxiety. What concerns me about affect is not how it progressed to connote feelings and emotions but how it progressed to be denoted by other terms in the Freudian text, and thus was the implicit psychology of his metapsychology.

4. Linguistically, *affect* is a mental state, intention, desire, mood, or feeling (p. 210), while *feeling* is "[a] . . . physical sensation or perception through the senses of touch or the other general sensibility of the body (*The Oxford Dictionary*, p. 806)." This distinction is between a state that transforms into conditions and a condition that could be created by other resources. Thus affect is a subject matter of psychology, while feeling is a psychological condition.

5. Hartmann (1950) aspired to use the structural point of view as a stepping-stone toward a psychology of adaptation, a psychology of psychotherapy, and a developmental psychology. He suggested several areas of interest to be researched that mostly pertain to classical psychology. His disciples went further to suggest that psychoanalysis (ego psychology) could constitute a general psychology (see Loewenstein, Newman, Schur, & Solnit, 1966). This notion demonstrates a grave misconception of psychology as a science and of psychoanalysis as a psychological theory of a different subject. Psychology is the study of human functions that are separable from the subject of the study (the person), such as intelligence, perception, learning, and imagination. The individual unit is not the subject of psychological investigations, although the individual unit could become the subject for psychological investigation if it is a unit in an experimental group. The notion of a psychology of the ego (the person) or the *Ich* (the *I*) is not

workable as a theory of psychology because the *I* is inseparable from the subject of the study, such as memory or perception, unless the ego is considered the person-ality. Personality was, and still is, extensively and better studied in psychology than in any psychoanalysis, not just because it could be turned into a human function but because it is very different in nature from subjects such as affect, repression, or *Trieb.*

6. The only drive theory in psychology is McDougall's *hormic* psychology of the 1920s.

9. ELICITING THE THEORY OF PSYCHOANALYSIS FROM THE FREUDIAN TEXT

1. Note the exact resemblance of this sequence to the sequence in Freud's paper, Formulations on the Two Principles of Mental Functioning, as Safouan (1983) has illustrated.

2. It is easier to accept Freud's characterization of personality types in libidinal terms than to assign them to the three phases of development. Nonetheless, the descriptions of the erotic, obsessional, and narcissistic types corresponds to the oral, anal, and phallic phases in psychosexual development, and the character formations that fixation on those phases could produce.

3. Freud's efforts to reconcile the contradiction between the two concepts in *Beyond the Pleasure Principle* deserve attention because they are useful in responding to the critics of metapsychology. The unsatisfactory explanations of the compulsion to repeat in economic or dynamic terms were taken as limitations of metapsychology. Yet, when the limited understanding of the link between fixation and the compulsion to repeat was explored further, it was possible to put that link into a metapsychological perspective. The problem was not with metapsychology but with proper understanding of what was to be talked about metapsychologically.

4. Henri Wallon was a philosopher and prominent child psychologist (1879–1962). He developed a school of psychology and child psychology, in particular, that had a very strong impression on the academic as well as the intellectual circles in France, especially that he was also an active political figure. Due to that, he was a friend of J. Lacan. A great number of his followers (Laplanche, Didier, and possibly Lagache) joined the psychoanalytic movement, and his impact on their conceptions of Freud's endeavor was very evident in the way French psychoanalysis enriched the Freudian doctrine over the years.

10. THE PSYCHOANALYTIC MIND

1. I use the term *alienation*, influenced by its origin in Karl Marx and the changes that were introduced to it in the existential philosophical movement, to explicate the process of representation. Marx use it to mean the way the workers were indoctrinated to alienate their efforts in their wages and their sense of value in their class affiliation. Hence, exploiting them was possible by manipulating the representation of their realities and not by reality itself. The existentialists used alienation to connote inauthenticity. The endosomatic is alienated in its representative, which depending on the help the infant gets from the caregiver, could become inauthenticated.

2. Freud used the adjective *primary* differently with identification. By primary identification he meant a primitive type of identification (assimilation) that is replaced with different, more advanced identifications, as dictated by the advancement from one erogenic zone to the next. However, the primitive type remains operative behind all its successors. Therefore, as a process that is unique in being a formative process and one that does not have one secondary replacement but more than one, it is preferable to distinguish it from the other three phenomena.

3. The four fundamentals specified are vapid. The constancy principle is part of the concept of homeostasis, which Freud invoked indirectly in his elaboration of the death *Trieb*. It is not fundamental in the theory of psychoanalysis but a fundamental principal in the phenomenon of transformation. The isolation of mental contents is very wrong because under the influence of the primary process those contents get mixed in with processes of condensations and displacement all the time. I proved that Freud's theory is not a theory of drives (see chapters 6 and 8); besides, any theory that deals with any living entity—from amoebas to humans—has to have a concept of an originator of self-preservation. The dynamic unconscious was canonized by the IPA due to a failure to understand the meaning of the systemic unconscious *Ucs*.

References

Abraham, K. (1913/1953). The first pregenital phase of the libido. In *Selected papers of Karl Abraham*. New York: Basic Books.

The American Psychoanalyst (2002). *Quarterly Magazine of the American Psychoanalytic Association.*

The American Psychoanalyst (2003). *Quarterly Magazine of the American Psychoanalytic Association.*

The American Psychoanalyst (2004). *Quarterly Magazine of the American Psychoanalytic Association.*

The American Psychoanalyst (2005). *Quarterly Magazine of the American Psychoanalytic Association.*

The American Psychoanalyst (2006). *Quarterly Magazine of the American Psychoanalytic Association.*

The American Psychoanalyst (2007). *Quarterly Magazine of the American Psychoanalytic Association.*

Andreas-Salome, L. (1962). The dual orientation of narcissism. *The Psychoanalytic Quarterly, 31, 1–30.*

Arlow, J.(1977): Affects and the psychoanalytic situation. *International. J. Psycho-analysis*, 58. 157-170.

Arlow, J., & Brenner, C. (1964). *Psychoanalytic Concepts and the Structural Theory*. New York: International University Press.

Aron, L. (1990). One person and two person psychologies and the method of psychoanalysis. *Psychoanalytic Psychology*, 7,475–785.

Balint, M. (1968). *The Basic Fault*. London: Tavistock.

Beres, D. (1965). Structure and Function in psycho-analysis, *International. J. Psycho-analysis., 46, 53-62.*

Beres, D., Joseph E., (1970): The concept of mental representation in psychoanalysis,. *International. J. Psycho-analysis,* 51, 1-8

Bion, W.(1962): *Learning from Experience.* London: Marsfield.

Blanco, M. I. (1975). *The Unconscious as Infinite Sets: An essay in Bilogic*. London: Duckworth.

Blanco, M. I. (1988). *Thinking, Feeling, and Being* (A Tavistock Professional Book). London and New York: Routledge.

Blass, R. (2002). *The Meaning of the Dream in Psychoanalysis*. New York: State University of New York Press.

Boesky, D. (1983). The problem of mental representation in self and object theory, *Psychoanalytic Quarterly*, 52, 564–83.

Boesky, D. (1998). Clinical evidence and multiple models. *Journal of the American Psychoanalytic Association*, 46, 1013–1020.

Bornstein, R. (2001). The impending death of psychoanalysis. *Psychoanalytic Psychology*, 18, 3–20.

Bouvet, M. (1967). *La relation d'objet*. Paris: Payot.

Bouchard, M-A. (1995): The specificity of hermeneutics in psychoanalysis: leaps on the path from construction to recollection, *International. J. Psycho-analysis,*76, 233-256.

Bowlby, J. (1981). Psychoanalysis as a naturel science. *International Review of Psychoanalysis*, 8, 243–256.

Brenner, C. (1980). Metapsychology and the psychoanalytic theory. *The Psychoanalytic Quarterly*, 49, 189–214.

Brenner, C. (1981). Defense and defense mechanisms. *The Psychoanalytic Quarterly*, 50, 557–569.

Brenner, C. (1982). *The mind in conflict*. New York: International University Presses.

Brentano, F. (1874). Psychology from an Empirical Standpoint , transl. by A.C. Rancurello, D.B. Terrell, and L. McAlister, London: Routledge, 1973. (2nd ed., intr. by Peter Simons, 1995).

Busch, F., & Schmidt-Hellerou, C. (2004). Reflections on clinical judgment formation. Journal *of the American Psychoanalytic Association, 52, 689–707.*

Calaprice, A. (1996). *The Quotable Einstein*. Princeton: Princeton University Press.

Calaprice, A. (2000). *The expanded quotable Einstein by Albert Einstein*. Princeton: Princeton University Press.

Cassirer, E. (1953). *An Essay on Man*. New York: Anchor.

Cattell, R.B. (1957). *Personality and motivation: Structure and measurements*. London: Harrap & Co.

Cesio, F. (1995). The crises of psychoanalysis: an overview Report to the House of Delegates' Committee on "The Actual Crisis of Psychoanalysis: Challenges and Perspectives*." International Psychoanalytic Association Publication,*2-7.

Chertok, L., & de Saussure, R. (1979). *The Therapeutic Revolution: From Mesmer to Freud*. New York: Brunner/Mazel.

Compton, A. (1981a). On the psychoanalytic theory of instinctual drives. The *Psychoanalytic Quarterly*, 50, 190–218.

Compton, A. (1981b). On the psychoanalytic theory of instinctual drives. The *Psychoanalytic Quarterly*, 50, 219–237.

Compton, A. (1981c). On the psychoanalytic theory of instinctual drives. The *Psychoanalytic Quarterly*, 50, 345–362.

Compton, A. (1981d). On the psychoanalytic theory of instinctual drives. The *Psychoanalytic Quarterly*, 50, 363–392.

Compton, A. (1983b): The current status of the psychoanalytic theory of instinctual drives, *Psychoanalytic Quarterly*, 52.

Compton, A. (1983b): The current status of the psychoanalytic theory of instinctual drives, *Psychoanalytic Quarterly, 52*, 402–426.

Cooper, S. H. (1998). Analyst subjectivity, analyst disclosure, and the aim of psychoanalysis. *Psychoanalytic Quarterly*, 67, 379–407.

Damasio, A. R. (1994). *Descartes' error: Emotion, Reason, and the Human brain*. New York: Avon Books.

Damasio, A. R. (1999). *The Feeling of what Happens* (A Harvest Book). San Diego, New York, and London: Harcourt.

Damasio, A. R. (2003). *Looking for Spinoza: Joy, Sorrow and the Feeling brain* (A Harvest Book). New York: Harcourt.

Descartes, R. (1999). *Discourse on Method and Related Writings*. (D. Clarke, Trans.). London: Penguin Books. (Original work published 1637).

Eagle, M.N. (2011). Systematic empirical research versus Clinical Case Studies: A valid antagonism, *Journal of the American Psychoanalytic Association*, 59, 791–817.

Edelman, G., & Tononi, G. (2000). *A Universe of Consciousness: How Matter Becomes Imagination*. New York: Basic Books.

Edelson, M. (1988). *Psychoanalysis: A theory in a Crisis*. Chicago: Chicago University Press.
Edwards, P. (Ed.). (1996). *The Encyclopedia of Philosophy*. New York: Macmillan Publishing Co. & The Free Press.
Eisold, K. (1994). The intolerance of diversity in psychoanalytic institutes. *Th e International Journal of Psychoanalysis*, 75, 785–800.
Eisold, K. (2007). The erosion of our profession. *Psychoanalytic Psychology*, 24, 1–9.
Eizirik, C. L. (1995). Report to the House of Delegates' Committee on "The actual Crisis of Psychoanalysis: Challenges and Perspectives." *International Psychoanalytic Association Publication,* 1–2.
Elder, C. (1994). *The Grammar of the Unconscious: A Conceptual Foundation of Psychoanalysis*. Pennsylvania: Pennsylvania University Press.
Ellman, S. J., & Moskowitz, M. B. (1980). An examination of some recent criticism of psychoanalytic "metapsychology." *The Psychoanalytic Quarterly*, 49, 631–662.
Ellman, C. S., Grand, S., Silvan, M., & Ellman, S. J. (Eds.). (1998).*The Modern Freudians: Contemporary Psychoanalytic Technique.* Northvale, NJ: Jason Aronson.
Evens, A., Haghighi, M., Johnson, S., Ocana, K., & Th ompson, G. (1998). Another always thinks in me. In Deleuze & Guattari(270–280). *Minneapolis: University of Minnesota Press.*
Fairbairn, W.R.D. (1952): *The Psychoanalytic Study of the Personality,* London, Routledge& Kegan Paul.
Fairbairn, W. R. D. (1954). *An Object-Relations Theory of Personality*. New York: Basic Books.
Fayek,A. (1980). From interpretation to the death instinct, *International. J. Psycho-analysis,* 7,447-457.
Fayek, A. (1981). Narcissism and the death instinct. *The International J. Psycho-analysis*, 62, 309–321.
Fayek, A. (2000). Affekt: die psychologie der metapsychologien (Affect: the psychology of metapsychology). *Zeitschrift fur Psychoanalytische Theorie und Praxis*, 4, 491–520.
Fayek, A. (2002). Psychic reality and mental representation. *Psychoanalytic Psychology*, 19, 475–500.
Fayek, A. (2005). The centrality of the system Ucs. in *Psychoanalysis.Psychoanalytic Psychology,* 22, 524–543.
Fayek, A. (2009). *The Crisis in Psychoanalysis: in Search for a lost Doctrine,* Huston, Texas, Bridgeway Books.
Fayek, A. (2011). *The Clinical Application of the Theory of Psychoanalysis*, London, Karnac.
Flugel, J. (1953). The death instinct, homeostasis, and allied concepts. *The International J. Psycho-analysis*, 34, 43–73.
Federn, P. (1952). *Ego psychology and the Psychoses*. New York: Basic Books.
Ferenczi, S. (1912/1980). On the definition of introjection. In *The final contribution to the problems of psychoanalysis*. H. Balint (eh.), M. Mosbacher (trans), 316–318. New York: Brunner/Mazel.
Foucault, M. (1970). *The Order of Things: An Archeology of Individual Sciences*. London: Tavistock Publications.
Friedman, L. (1995): Psychic reality in psychoanalytic theory, *International. J. Psycho-analysis,* 76. 25-28.
Freud, A. (1936). The Ego and the Mechanisms of Defence. Ne York: International Universities Press
Freud. S. (1894). Letter May 21, 1894. *The complete letters of Sigmund Freud to Wilhelm Fliess*, 1887–1904. (J. M Masson, Ed. & Trans.). Cambridge, MA & London: The Belknap Press of Harvard University Press.
Freud, S. (1894a). The neuropsychosis of defense. *Standard Edition*, 3, 41–61. London: The Hogarth Press and the Institute of Psycho-Analysis.
Freud, S. (1895). Letter October 20, 1895. *The complete letters of Sigmund Freud to Wilhelm Fliess,* 1887–1904. (J. M Masson, Ed. & Trans.). Cambridge, MA & London: The Belknap Press of Harvard University Press.
Freud, S. (1895d). *Studies on Hysteria* (Breuer, J., & Freud, S.). *Standard Edition*, 2. London: The Hogarth Press and the Institute of Psycho-Analysis.

Freud, S. (1896). Letter February 13, *The complete letters of Sigmund Freud to Wilhelm Fliess, 1887–1904*. (J. M Masson, Ed. & Trans.). Cambridge, MA & London: The Belknap Press of Harvard University Press.

Freud, S. (1896). Letter April 16, *The complete letters of Sigmund Freud to Wilhelm Fliess, 1887–1904*. (J. M Masson, Ed. & Trans.). Cambridge, MA & London: The Belknap Press of Harvard University Press.

Freud, S. (1896). Letter December 6, *The complete letters of Sigmund Freud to Wilhelm Fliess, 1887–1904*. (J. M Masson, Ed. & Trans.). Cambridge, MA & London: The Belknap Press of Harvard University Press.

Freud, S. (1896a). Heredity and the aetiology of the neuroses. *Standard Edition*, 3, 141–156. London: The Hogarth Press and the Institute of Psycho-Analysis.

Freud, S. (1896b). Further remarks on the neuropsychosis of defense. *Standard Edition*, 3, 157–186. London: The Hogarth Press and the Institute of Psycho-Analysis.

Freud, S. (1896c). The aetiology of hysteria. *Standard Edition*, 3, 187–222. London: The Hogarth Press and the Institute of Psycho-Analysis.

Freud, S. (1897a). Draft M, May 25, *The complete letters of Sigmund Freud to Wilhelm Fliess, 1887–1904*. (J. M Masson, Ed. & Trans.). Cambridge, MA & London: The Belknap Press of Harvard University Press.

Freud, S. (1897). Letter September 21, *The complete letters of Sigmund Freud to Wilhelm Fliess*, 1887–1904. (J. M Masson, Ed. & Trans.). Cambridge, MA & London: The Belknap Press of Harvard University Press.

Freud, S. (1898). Letter March 10, *The complete letters of Sigmund Freud to Wilhelm Fliess, 1887–1904*. (J. M Masson, Ed. & Trans.). Cambridge, MA & London: The Belknap Press of Harvard University Press.

Freud, S. (1898a). Sexuality in the aetiology of the neuroses. *Standard Edition*, 3, 259–286. London: The Hogarth Press and the Institute of Psycho-Analysis.

Freud, S. (1899). Letter January 3–4, *The complete letters of Sigmund Freud to Wilhelm Fliess, 1887–1904*. (J. M Masson, Ed. & Trans.). Cambridge, MA & London: The Belknap Press of Harvard University Press.

Freud, S. (1900a). *The Interpretation of Dreams*. *Standard Edition*, 4–5. London: The Hogarth Press and the Institute of Psycho-Analysis.

Freud, S. (1901b). *The Psychopathology of Everyday Life*. *Standard Edition*, 6. London: The Hogarth Press and the Institute of Psycho-Analysis.

Freud, S. (1905c). *Jokes and Their Relations to the Unconscious*. *Standard Edition*, 8. London: The Hogarth Press and the Institute of Psycho-Analysis.

Freud, S. (1905d). *Three Essays on the Theory of Sexuality*. *Standard Edition*, 7. London: The Hogarth Press and the Institute of Psycho-Analysis.

Freud, S. (1907a). Delusions and dreams in Jensen's Gradiva. *Standard Edition*, 9, 1–93. London: The Hogarth Press and the Institute of Psycho-Analysis.

Freud, S. (1908a). Hysterical phantasies and their relation to bisexuality. *Standard Edition*, 9, 155–166. London: The Hogarth Press and the Institute of Psycho-Analysis.

Freud, S. (1909b). Analysis of a phobia in a five-year-old boy. *Standard Edition*, 10, 1–147. London: The Hogarth Press and the Institute of Psycho-Analysis.

Freud, S. (1910c). Leonardo da Vinci and a memory of his childhood. *Standard Edition*, 11, 59–138. London: The Hogarth Press and the Institute of Psycho-Analysis.

Freud ,S. (1910e). The antithetical meaning of primal words, *Standard Edition*, 11, 153-162. London: The Hogarth Press and the Institute of Psycho-Analysis.

Freud ,S. (1910h). A special type of choice of object made by men. *Standard Edition*, 11, 163-176. London: The Hogarth Press and the Institute of Psycho-Analysis.

Freud, S. (1910i). The psychoanalytic view of psychogenic disturbance of vision. *Standard Edition*, 11, 209–218. London: The Hogarth Press and the Institute of Psycho-Analysis.

Freud, S. (1911b): Formulations on the two principles of mental functioning, *Standard Edition*, 12.,216-226, London: The Hogarth Press and the Institute of Psycho-Analysis.

Freud, S. (1911e). The handling of dreams in psychoanalysis, *Standard Edition*, 12, 89–96. London: The Hogarth Press and the Institute of Psycho-Analysis.

Freud, S. (1912b). The dynamics of transferences. Standard Edition, 12, 97-108. London: The Hogarth Press and the Institute of Psycho-Analysis.

Freud, S. (1912d). On the universal tendency to debasement in the sphere of love. Standard Edition, 11, 177-190. London: The Hogarth Press and the Institute of Psycho-Analysis

Freud, S. (1912e). Recommendations to physicians practicing psycho-analysis. *Standard Edition*, 12, 109–120. London: The Hogarth Press and the Institute of Psycho-Analysis.

Freud, S. (1912g). A note on the unconscious in psychoanalysis. *Standard Edition*, 12, 255–266. London: The Hogarth Press and the Institute of Psycho-Analysis.

Freud, S. (1912–1913). The Totem and Taboo. *Standard Edition*, London: The Hogarth Press and the Institute of Psycho-Analysis.

Freud, S. (1913c). On beginning of treatments (further recommendation on the technique of psychoanalysis I). *Standard Edition*, 12, 121–144. London: The Hogarth Press and the Institute of Psycho-Analysis.

Freud, S. (1913j). The claims of psycho-analysis to scientific interest, Standard *Edition*, 13, 163-190. London: The Hogarth Press and the Institute of Psycho-Analysis.

Freud, S. (1914c). On narcissism: An introduction. *Standard Edition*, 14, 67–104.

London: The Hogarth Press and the Institute of Psycho-Analysis.

Freud, S. (1914d). On the history of the paycho-analytic movement, 14, 1-65, London: The Hogarth Press and the Institute of Psycho-Analysis

Freud, S. (1914g). Remembering, repeating and working-through (further recommendations on the technique of psycho-analysis II). *Standard Edition*, 12, 145–156. London: The Hogarth Press and the Institute of Psycho-Analysis.

Freud, S. (1915c). Instincts and their vicissitude. *Standard Edition*, 14, 109–140. London: The Hogarth Press and the Institute of Psycho-Analysis.

Freud, S. (1915d). Repression. *Standard Edition*, 14, 141–158. London: The Hogarth Press and the Institute of Psycho-Analysis.

Freud, S. (1915e). The unconscious. *Standard Edition*, 14,159–204. London: The Hogarth Press and the Institute of Psycho-Analysis.

Freud, S. (1916–1917). Introductory Lectures on Psychoanalysis. *Standard Edition*, 15–16. London: The Hogarth Press and the Institute of Psycho-Analysis.

Freud, S. (1917d). A metapsychological supplement to the theory of dreams, *Standard Edition*. 14,219–236. London: The Hogarth Press and the Institute of Psycho-Analysis.

Freud, S. (1917e). Mourning and melancholia. *Standard Edition*, 14, 237–258. London: The Hogarth Press and the Institute of Psycho-Analysis.

Freud, S. (1918a). The taboo of virginity. *Standard Edition*, 11, 191-208. London: The Hogarth Press and the Institute of Psycho-Analysis.

Freud, S. (1918b). From the history of an infantile neurosis. *Standard Edition*, 17, 1–122. London: The Hogarth Press and the Institute of Psycho-Analysis.

Freud, S. (1919e). A child is being beaten. *Standard Edition*, 17, 145-156. London: The Hogarth Press and the Institute of Psycho-Analysis

Freud, S. (1919h). The uncanny. *Standard Edition*, 17, 217–252. London: The Hogarth Press and the Institute of Psycho-Analysis.

Freud, S. (1920a). The psychogenesis of a case of female homosexuality. *Standard Edition*, 18, 145-172. London: The Hogarth Press and the Institute of Psycho-Analysis.

Freud, S. (1920g). Beyond the Pleasure Principle. *Standard Edition*, 18, 1–64. London: The Hogarth Press and the Institute of Psycho-Analysis.

Freud, S. (1921c). Grays psychology and the analysis of the ego. *Standard Edition, 18*, 65–144. London: The Hogarth Press and the Institute of Psychoanalysis.

Freud, S. (1923a). Two encyclopedia articles. *Standard Edition*, 18, 235–262. London: The Hogarth Press and the Institute of Psycho-Analysis.

Freud, S. (1923b). The Ego and the Id. *Standard Edition*, 19, 1–58. London: The Hogarth Press and the Institute of Psycho-Analysis.

Freud, S. (1924e). The loss of reality in neurosis and psychosis. *Standard Edition*, 19, 183–190. London: The Hogarth Press and the Institute of Psycho-Analysis.

Freud, S. (1925h). Negation. *Standard Edition*, 19, 235–240. London: The Hogarth Press and the Institute of Psycho-Analysis.

Freud, S. (1926d). Inhibitions, Symptoms, and Anxiety. *Standard Edition*, 20, 75–176. London: The Hogarth Press and the Institute of Psycho-Analysis.

Freud, S. (1927c). The Future of an Illusion. *Standard Edition*, 21, 1–56. London: The Hogarth Press and the Institute of Psycho-Analysis.

Freud, S. (1930a). Civilization and its Discontents. *Standard Edition*, 21, 57–146. London: The Hogarth Press and the Institute of Psycho-Analysis.

Freud, S. (1931a). Libidinal types. *Standard Edition*, 21,215–220. London: The Hogarth Press and the Institute of Psycho-Analysis.

Freud, S. (1933a). New Introductory Lectures on Psychoanalysis (lectures XXIX–XXXV). *Standard Edition*, 22. London:The Hogarth Press and the Institute of Psycho-Analysis.

Freud, S. (1937c). Analysis terminable and interminable. *Standard Edition*, 23, 209–254. London: The Hogarth Press and the Institute of Psycho-Analysis.

Freud, S. (1937d). Construction in psychoanalysis. *Standard Edition*, 23, 255–270. London: The Hogarth Press and the Institute of Psycho-Analysis.

Freud, S. (1939a). Moses and Monotheism: Three Essays. *Standard Edition*, 23, 1–139). London: The Hogarth Press and the Institute of Psycho-Analysis.

Freud, S. (1940a). *An Outline of Psycho-Analysis, Standard Edition, 23*, 139–207. London: The Hogarth Press and the Institute of Psycho-Analysis.

Freud, S. (1940e). Splitting of the ego in the process of defense. *Standard Edition*, 23, 271–279. London: The Hogarth Press and the Institute of Psycho-Analysis.

Freud, S. (1950). Project for a scientific psychology, *Standard Edition.*,1, 295-397. London: The Hogarth Press and the Institute of Psycho-Analysis.

Gabbard, G., & Westen, D. (2003). Rethinking therapeutic action. *The International J. of Psycho-analysis*, 4, 823–842.

Gedo, J. (1999). *The Evolution of Psychoanalysis: Contemporary theory and Practice*. New York: Other Press.

Gill, M. (1979). "Topography and systems in psychoanalysis." *Psychological Issues, Monograph 10*. New York: International Universities Press.

Gill, M. (1982). *Analysis of Transference*. New York: International Universities Press.

Goldberg, A. (Ed.). (1978). *The Psychology of the self: A casebook*. New York: International Universities Press.

Goldberg, A. (1998). Self psychology since Kohut. *The Psychoanalytic Quart*erly, 57, 240–255.

Green, A. (1977): Conceptions of affect, *The International J. of Psycho-analysis*, 58, 129- 157.

Green, A. (1998). The primordial mind and the work of the negative. *The International J. of Psycho-analysis*, 79, 649–664.

Green, A. (1999c). *The fabric of Affect in the Psychoanalytic Discourse,* A. Sheridan (Trans.). London and New York, Routledge.

Green, A. (1999b): On discriminating and not discriminating between affect and representation, *The International J. of Psycho-analysis.,* 80, 227–316.

Green, A. (2000). The intrapsychic and intersubjectivity in psychoanalysis. *The Psychoanalytic Quarterly*, 69, 1–40.

Green, A. (2005). The illusion of common grounds and mythical pluralism. *International J. of Psycho-analysis*, 68, 627–632.

Green, A. (2005), *Key Ideas for a Contemporary Psychoanalysis*, Tr. A.Weller, Routledge, London & New York.

Greenberg, J. (2001). The analyst's participation: A new look. *The International J. of Psycho-analysis*, 49, 135–170.

Greenspan, S. (1977). The oedipal-pre-oedipal dilemma: A reformulation according to object relation theory. *The International Review of Psycho-analysis*, 4, 381–392.

Grunbaum, A. (1984). *The foundation of psychoanalysis*. Berkeley: University of California Press.

Grunberger, B. (1979). *Narcissism: Psychoanalytic Essays*. (J. Diaminti & M. Oliner, Trans.). New York: International Universities Press. (Original work published 1971).

Guntrip, H. (1967). The concept of psychodynamic science. *The International J. of Psycho-analysis*, 48, 32–43.

Guntrip, H. (1971): *Psychoanalytic theory, object relations and the self,* New York, Basic Books.
Hanly, C. (1995). On facts and ideas in psychoanalysis. *International J. of Psycho-analysis*, 67, 901–908.
Hartman, H. (1948): Comments on the psychoanalytic theory of instinctual drives, in *Essays on Ego Psychology, Selected Problems in Psychoanalytic Theory*. New York, I.U.P.
Hartmann, H. (1950). Psychoanalysis and developmental psychology. In *The psychoanalytic study of the child* (5, pp. 7–17). New York: International Universities Press.
Hartmann, H. (1964). *Essays on ego psychology: Selected problems in psychoanalytic theory.* New York: International Universities Press.
Hayman, A.(1994): Some remarks about the "controversial discussions". *The International J. of Psycho-analysis*.75, 343–358.
Heiman, P. (1950): On counter-transference, *The International J. of Psycho-analysis,*31, 81–84.
Hegel, G.. (1845): *Hegel's Philosophy of the Mind*, Oxford, Oxford University Press, (1971).
Holder, A. (1970). Instinct and drive. In H. Garma (Ed.), *Basic Psychoanalytic Concepts on the Theory of Instincts (Vol. III)*. London: The Hampstead Clinic Psychoanalytic Library.
Holt, R. (1965a). A review of some of Freud's biological assumptions and their influence on his theories. In N. S. Greenfield & W. C. Lewis (Eds.), *Psychoanalysis and Current Biological Thought* (93–124). Madison: University of Wisconsin Press.
Holt, R. (1965b). Ego anatomy re-evaluated. *The International J. of Psychoanalysis*, 47, 151–167.
Holt, R. (1976). Drive or wish: A reconsideration of the psychoanalytic theory of motivation. In M. Gill & P. Holzman (Eds.), *Psychology versus metapsychology: Psychoanalytical essays in memory of G. Klein (159–197). Psychological Issues, Monograph 36. New York:* International Universities Press.
Holt, R. (1981). The death and transfiguration of metapsychology. The International Review of Psychoanalysis, 8, 129–143.
Holt, R. (2002). Quantitative research on primary process. *Journal of the American Psychoanalytic Association*, 50, 457–482.
Home, J. (1966). The concept of mind. *The International J. of Psychoanalysis*, 47, 42–49. International Psychoanalysis (December 2003*). News magazine of the International Psychoanalytic Association.*
Issacs, S. (1948). The nature and function of phantasy, in *The International Journal of Psychoanalysis, 29,* 73-97.
Jacobs, T. (1999). On the question of self disclosure by the analyst; Error or advance in technique? *The Psychoanalytic Quarterly*, 68, 159–183.
Jacobs, T. (2001). On the unconscious communications and covert enactments: Some reflections on their role in the analytic situation, Psychoanalytic Inquiry, 21, 4-23
Jacobson, J.(1983 b): The structural theory and the representational world: Developmental and Biological Considerations, *Psychoanalytic. Quarterly,* 52, 514-542.
Jones, E. (1954). *Sigmund Freud: Life and work (Vol. 1)*. London: Hogarth Press.
Jones, E. (1957). *Sigmund Freud: Life and work (Vol. 3)*. London: Hogarth Press.
Kanzer, M. (1981). Freud's 'analytic pact': The standard therapeutic alliance. Journal of the American Psychoanalytic Association, 29(1).
Kernberg, O. (2006). The coming changes in psychoanalytic education: Part 1. *Journal of the American Psychoanalytic Association*, 87, 1649–1674.
Klein, G. (1976): *Psychoanalytic theory: An Exploration of essentials,* New York, I.U.P.
Klein, M. (1952). *The origin of transference. The International Journal of Psychoanalysis, 33,* 433–438.
Kohut, H. (1987). *Analysis of the Self: An Approach to the psychoanalytic Treatment of narcissistic Disorders*, Illinois: Chicago University Press.
Kubie, L. (1948).Instincts and Homeostasis. *Psychosomatic Medicine*, 10:8-15.
Kuhn, T. S. (1977). *The essential tension: Selected studies in scientific tradition and change.* Chicago: Chicago University Press.

Lacan, J. (1977a). The mirror stage as formative of the functional, 1–7. *Ecrties: A Selection*, A. Sheridan (Trans.). New York: Norton.

Lacan, J. (1977b). The function and field of speech and language in psychoanalysis, 30–113. *Erites: A Selection*, A. Sheridan (Trans.). New York: Norton.

Laplanche, J. (1976). *Life and death in psychoanalysis*. (J. Mehlman,Trans). Baltimore: The Johns Hopkins University Press. Original work published 1970).

Laplanche, J. (1989). *New foundations for psychoanalysis*. (D.Macey, Trans.). Oxford: blackwell. (Original work published1987).

Laplanche, J. (1992). Interpretation between determinism and hermeneutics. A restatement of the problem. *The International J. of Psycho-analysis*, 73, 429–446.

Laplanche, J. (1997). The theory of seduction and the problem of the other. *International J. of Psycho-analysis*, 79, 653–666.

Laplanche, J., & Pontalis, J-B. (1973). *The language of psychoanalysis*. (D. Nicholson-Smith, Trans.). New York: Norton. (Original work published 1967).

Lévi-Strauss, C. (1955). The structural study of the myth. *Journal of American Folklore*, 68, 113–144.

Lévi-Strauss, C. (1966). *Anthropologie structural*. Paris: Press Uninversitaire de Paris.

Lévi-Strauss, C. (1973). *Tristes tropiques*. Atheneum.

Lichtenberg, J. (1989). Psychoanalysis and motivation. Hillsdale, NJ: Analytic Press.

Limentani, A. (1977): Affects in the psychoanalytic situation, *The International J. of Psychoanalysis,* 58, 171-182.

Loewenstein, R., Newman, L., Schur, M., & Solnit, A. (Eds.). (1966). *Psychoanalysis as a general psychology: Essays in honor of Heinz Hartmann*. New York: The International Universities Press.

Mackay, N. (1981). Melanie Klein's metapsychology: Phenomenological and mechanistic perspectives. *The International J. of Psychoanalysis*, 62, 177–186.

Makari, G. (2008). *Revolution in Mind: The Creation of Psychoanalysis*.New York, Harper Collins Publishers.

Malinowski, B. (1955). *Sex and Repression in Savage Society*. New York: Meridian Books.

Mead, M. (1955). *Cultural Patterns and Technical Change*. Denver: Mentor Books.

Mead, M. (1961). *Cooperation and Competition Among Primitive Peoples*. Boston: Beacon Press.

Mehlman, J. (1976). Introduction, in *Life and death in psychoanalysis*. (J. Mehlman,Trans). Baltimore: The Johns Hopkins University Press.(Original work published 1970).

Meissner, W. W. (1979a). Critique of concepts and therapy in the action language approach to psychoanalysis. *The International J. of Psycho-analysis*, 60, 291–310.

Meissner, W. W. (1979b). Methodological critique of the action language in psychoanalysis. *Journal of the American Psychoanalytic Association*, 27, 79–105.

Meissner, W. W. (1981). Metapsychology—who needs it? *Journal of the American Psychoanalytic Association*, 29, 921–938.

Meissner, W.W. (1989). A Note on Psychoanalytic Facts, *Psychoanalytic Inquiry*, 9, 193-219.

Meissner, W. W. (1998). Neutrality, abstinence, and the therapeutic alliance. *Journal of the American Psychoanalytic Association*, 46, 1089–1128.

Meltzer, R. (1978). *The Kleinian development part 1: Freud's clinical development*. Perthshire: Clunie Press.

Mitchell. S.A. (1983). Discussions, Contemporary *Psychoanalysis*. 19, 171-176

Mitchell, S. A. (1998). The analyst's knowledge and authority. *The Psychoanalytic Quarterly*, 67, 1–31.

Nagel, T. (1994). Freud and his permanent revolution. *New York Review of Books*, 41, 34–38.

Nasio, J-D. (1984). The unconscious, the transference, and the psychoanalyst's interpretation: A Lacanian view. *The Psychoanalytic Inquiry*, 4, 401–411.

Nemiah, P. (1965). The development of the concept of intrapsychic conflict in Freud's writing. *The International J. of Psycho-analysis*, 46, 367–371.

Novey, S.(1958): The meaning of the concept of mental representation of the object, *Psychoanalytic Quarterly,* 27, 57-79.

Ogden, T.(1986): *The matrix of the mind: Object Relations and the Psychoanalytic Dialogue*, New Jersey, London: Jason Aronson.

Orenstein, P. (1995). Critical reflections on a comparative analysis of a self psychology and intersubjectivity theory. In A.Goldberg (Ed.), *The impact of New Ideas: Progress in Self Psychology* (11, pp. 37–54). Hillsdale, NJ/London:Analytic Press. *Oxford English Dictionary* (1933): Oxford University Press.

Peskin, M. (1997). Drive theory revisited. *The Psychoanalytic Quarterly*, 56, pp. 377–402. PDM (2008): The psychodynamic Diagnostic Manual.

Pine, F. (1990). *Drive, ego, object, self.* New York: Basic Books.

Politzer, G. (1994). *Critique of the foundation of psychology*. (A. Appry, Trans.). Pittsburgh: Duguene University Press.(Original work published 1928).

Primbram, K. H. (1998). A century of progress? In R. M. Bilder & F. F. LeFevrer (Eds.), *Neuroscience of the mind on the centennial of Freud's project for a scientifi c psychology*. New York: Academy of Science.

Primbram, K. H., & Gill, M. (1976). *Freud's 'project' re-assessed.* New York: Basic Books.

Pulver, S.(1971): Can affects be unconscious, *The International J. of Psycho-analysis,* 52, 347-354.

Rabin, R. M. (1995). The liberating effect on the analyst of the paradigm shift in psychoanalysis. *Psychoanalytic Psychology*, 12, 467–482.

Rangell, L. (2002). Th e analytic theory and its vicissitudes.Journal of the American Psychoanalytic. Association, 50,1109–1138.

Rangell, L. (2004). *My life in theory*. New York: Other.

Rangell, L. (2006). An analysis of the course of psychoanalysis: The case for a unitary theory. *Psychoanalytic Psychology*, 23,217–238.

Rapaport, D. (1951). The conceptual model of psychoanalysis. In Knight & Friedman (Eds.), *Psychoanalytic Psychiatry and Psychology, Clinical and Theoretical Paper*. New York: International Universities Press.

Rapaport, D., & Gill, M. (1959). The points of view and assumptions of metapsychology. *The International Journal of Psychoanalysis*, 40, 153–162.

Reese, W. (1999). *Dictionary of philosophy and religion: Eastern and Western thought*. Amherst, NY: Humanity Books.

Renik, O. (1996). The perils of neutrality. *Psychoanalytic Quarterly*, 65, 495–517.

Renik, O.(1998 a): The analyst's subjectivity and the analyst's objectivity, *Journal of the American Psychoanalytic Association,* 79, No.3.

Renik, O. (1998b).Getting real in analysis, *Psychoanalytic Quarterly*, 67, 566–593.

Ricoeur, P. (1970). *Freud and philosophy: An essay on interpretation*. (D. Savage, Trans.). New Haven: Yale University Press.

Robinson, P. (1993). *Freud and His Critics*. Berkeley,University of California Press.

Roudinesco, E. (2002). *Why Psychoanalysis?* (R. Bowlby, Trans.).New York: Colombia University Press. (Original work published 1999).

Rosenblatt, A., & Thickstun, J. (1977). Modern psychoanalytic concepts in a general psychology, *Psychological Issues, Monograph 42/43*. New York: International Universities Press.

Rubinstein, B. (1997). Psychoanalysis and the philosophy of science, In R. Holt (Ed.), *Psychological Issues, Monograph 62/63*.Madison, CT: International Universities Press.

Safouan, M.(1983)*: Pleasure and being*, London, MacMillan Press.

Sandler, J. (1992). Reflections on developments in the theory of psychoanalytic technique. *The International J. of Psycho-analysis*,73, 189–198.

Sandler, J., & Rosenblatt, B. (1962). The concept of representational world. In *The Psychoanalytic Study of the Child,* 17,128–145.

Sandler, J., & Perlow, M. (1988). Internalization and externalization. In J. Sandler (Ed.), *Projection, Identification and Projective Identification*. Great Britain: Karnac Books.

Sandler, J.(1987): The concept of projective identification, in *Projection, Identification, Projective Identification,* ed. J.Sandler, Madison, CT: I.U.P.

Sanville, J. (1995).The crises of psychoanalysis: an overview Report to the House of Delegates' Committee on "The Actual Crisis of Psychoanalysis: Challenges and Perspectives*.*" *International Psychoanalytic Association Publication,*12-17.

Schafer, R. (1975). Psychoanalysis without psychodynamics. *The International J, of Psycho-analysis*, 56, 41–56.
Schafer, R.(1976): *A new language for psychoanalysis,* New Haven, Yale University Press.
Simons, R. (1981). Panel, Contemporary problems of psychoanalysis. *Journal of the American Psychoanalytic Association*, 22, 643–657.
Spillius, E.B.(1992): On the concept of phantasy, Paper presented to C.P.S.Montreal.
Spruiell, V. (1981). The self and the ego. *The Psychoanalytic Quarterly*, 50, 319–344.
Stepansky, P.E. (2009). *Psychoanalysis at the Margins*, New York, Other Press professional.
Storolow, R., & Atwood, G. (1992). The three realms of the unconscious. In S. Mitchell & L. Aron (Eds.), *Relational Psychoanalysis*. Hillside, NJ: Analytic Press.
Storolow, R., & Atwood, G. (1997). Reconstructing the myth of the neutral analyst: An alternate intersubjective system theory. *Psychoanalytic Quarterly*, 431–449.
Strachey, J. (1934). The nature of the therapeutic action of psychoanalysis. *The International J. of Psycho-analysis*, 15, 127–186.
Summers, F. (2008). Theoretical insularity and the crisis of psychoanalysis. *Psychoanalytic Psychology*, 25, 413–424
Swanson, D. (1977). A critique of psychic energy as an explanatory concept. *Journal of the American Psychoanalytic Association*, 25, 603–633.
Thomson, M. G. (1996a). Freud's conception of neutrality. *Contemporary Psychoanalysis*, 32, 25–42.
Thomson, M. G. (1996b). The rule of neutrality. *Psychoanalysis and Contemporary Th ought*, 19, 57–84.
Tripp, E. (1970). *The Meridian Handbook of Classical Mythology*. New York: New American Library.
Waelder, R. (1941–1942). "On psychoanalytic technique: Five lectures". In Guttman, S., & Guttman, I., with the assistance of I. K.Guttman (1987). *Psychoanalytic Quarterly*, 46,1–68.
Wallerstein, R. (1986). *Forty Two Lives in Treatment*. New York: Guilford.
Wallerstein, R. (1988). One psychoanalysis or many? *The International J. of Psycho-analysis, 69, 5–21.*
Wallerstein, R. (1990). Psychoanalysis: The common grounds. *The International J. of Psycho-analysis*, 71, 3–20.
Wallerstein, R. (1996). Psychoanalysis as a science: A response to the new challenges. *Psychoanalytic Quarterly*, 55, 414–451.
Wallerstein, R. (1998). The new American psychoanalysis: Commentary. *Journal of the American Psychoanalytic Association*, 46, 1021–1044.
Wallerstein, R. (2002). The growth and transformation of American ego psychology. *Journal of the American Psychoanalytic Association*, 50, 135–169.
Wallerstein, R. (2005). Will psychoanalytic pluralism be an enduring state of our discipline? *The International J. of Psycho-analysis*, 86, 623–626.
Wallerstein, R. (2007).Reply, *Psychoanlytic Psycholology.*, 24, 515-517.
Wallon, H. (1946). The Influence of the other in the formation of the awareness of the self. *Egyptian Journal of psychology.* 2:1-39.
Willock, B. (2007). Comparative-Integrative psychoanalysis: A Relational Perspective for the Descipline's Second Century. New York, Rotledge.
Winnicott, D.(1955): Clinical *varieties* of transference. in *Collected Papers: Through Paediatrics to Psychoanalysis*.New York, Basic Books(1958). Unwin. (Original work published 1876).
Wiener, P. (Ed.). (1968). *Dictionary of the history of ideas: Studies in selected pivotal ideas.* New York: Charles Scribner's Sons.
Wisdom, J. (1984). What is left of the psychoanalytic theory. *The International Review of Psycho-analysis*, 11, 313–326.
Wittgenstein, L. (1982/1948–49). *The last writings on the philosophyof psychology (Vol. 1)*, (G. H. von Wright & H. Nyman, Eds.; C. G. Luckhart & M. A. E. Aue, Trans.). Chicago:University of Chicago Press. (Original work published 1982).
Wundt, W. (1878). *An introduction to psychology*. (R. Pintner, Trans.). London: Allen & Unwin.

Index

About the Author

Ahmed Fayek, PhD, is a clinical psychologist by profession and a trained/training psychoanalyst. He was trained before the proliferation of the contemporary schools of psychoanalysis and knew psychoanalysis as it was known for six decades before its crisis started. He also witnessed the dissatisfaction with it over the past five decades. He thinks that the revolt against the classical theory was unavoidable and in a way justified because of some serious flaws in its catharsis core. However, he is not at all convinced that the contemporary movement has offered anything of value to replace the Freudian doctrine. He believes that the Freudian doctrine comprises another solid theory of psychoanalysis that needs to be formulated better. He is the author of several books including *The Clinical Application of the Theory of Psychoanalysis.*

www.ingramcontent.com/pod-product-compliance
Ingram Content Group UK Ltd.
Pitfield, Milton Keynes, MK11 3LW, UK
UKHW040910190926
475560UK00008B/78

9 780765 709578